Cyberpunk
· · · · · · · · · · · · · ·
and the
· · · · · · · · ·
Future
· · · · · · · · ·
of
· · ·
Narrative
· · · · · · · · · · · ·

Fiction
2000

Edited by

George Slusser

and

Tom Shippey

THE UNIVERSITY OF GEORGIA PRESS   Athens and London

Designed by Mary Mendell
Set in Melior by Tseng Information Systems, Inc.
Printed and bound by Thomson-Shore, Inc.
The paper in this book meets the guidelines for
permanence and durability of the Committee on
Production Guidelines for Book Longevity of the
Council on Library Resources.

Printed in the United States of America

96 95 94 93 92   C   5 4 3 2 1
96 95 94 93 92   P   5 4 3 2 1

Library of Congress Cataloging in Publication Data
Fiction 2000 : cyberpunk and the future of narrative / edited by
George Slusser and Tom Shippey.
p.   cm.
Includes bibliographical references and index.
ISBN 0-8203-1425-0 (alk. paper). — ISBN 0-8203-1449-8
(pbk. : alk. paper)
1. Science fiction—History and criticism.   2. Fiction—20th
century—History and criticism.   I. Slusser, George Edgar.
II. Shippey, T. A.
PN3433.6.F53   1992
809.3'8762—dc20   91-40087
CIP
British Library Cataloging in Publication Data available

"Newness, *Neuromancer*, and the End of Narrative," by
John Huntington, was first published, in different form, in
Fictional Space: Essays on Contemporary Science Fiction,
edited by Tom Shippey (Oxford, Eng.: Blackwell, 1991)

Contents

Contents

Fiction
2000

Introduc-

tion:

Fiction

as

Informa-

tion

. . . .

George Slusser

Fiction 2000. This seems, in light of the essays gathered here, less a millennial than an inaugural date. For it is the date that marks fiction's entry into its own brave new world— the world of information. But if fiction at this threshold is taking leave of two thousand years of mimetic tradition, what is going to replace that relation between story and reality we call imitation? Story telling is entering the future of the electronic den, a wraparound world of images and signals and data. All our present boundaries fall, and observer and observed become part of a same network, bid now to "interface" instead of merely to interact. But with these changes the boundaries between illusion and reality also fall. If they do, what role will fiction, something whose very name places it under the old mimetic dispensation, be able to play?

In the 1950s, halfway through this millennial century, Ray Bradbury still looked on this electronic den with horror, and in *Fahrenheit 451* saw second, third, and even fourth "walls" closing in on his characters, intruding lives of images on their lives, literally erasing the reading experience by making it physically impossible to close the book. Today, however, on the eve of Telesis, we have begun to consider these electronic walls differently. They are no longer contractions but rather extensions of experience. We are increasingly comfortable with interactive television and telecommunications. Soap opera time obviates mimesis by going one better; that is, by becoming a literal physical extension of our world, a window for a real-time hour into another room, an extended space that moves to our temporal rhythms yet is patently electronic in nature. Video games have become performative theater in which we are both audience and actors, indeed we must learn to move effortlessly between these stances if we are to function at all. Twenty-four-hour news channels offer us—with their alternation of slow events like the Iran-contra hearings and fast-paced news clips—what no novel can: ongoing dramas in which we literally can no longer distinguish object from image. Indeed, for all but the few who fought in it, the Gulf

War was just another CNN production. Sitcoms and MTV accelerate the pace of dramatic "action" until tragedy and comedy blur in a welter of images and sounds. And events like the Gulf War or Tian'anmen Square, beamed simultaneously into all our homes, have made concepts like *global village*, which in the old binary system of walls and divisions retained the force of a paradox or oxymoron, into tensionless commonplaces.

At stake here is nothing less than the old Platonic idea of mimesis, and its dominant allegory of the cave. The situation here is directional viewing: the observer chained with face to the wall of flickering shadows; or by extension the reader in his chair, focused on the fictional world of his book. This polarization of light source and image, or of reader and text, supports further Platonic concepts that until today have dominated our idea of how fiction works, such as *conversion*, the figurative turning around that redirects our gaze beyond the reading experience. And *education*, in the sense of *leading* the reader out from the appearance world of "plot" and "character," and toward the "reality" they can now be said to symbolize.

The new electronic den that has replaced this cave, however, is both permeable and multidirectional. It is a genuine allegory in the root sense of the Greek word *agora*, an open place where we mingle with other presences without such barriers as the distinction between fiction and fact. It is not that we have become, as Bradbury feared, characters in somebody else's fiction. They do not control us any more than we control them. But simply, once the tyranny of mimesis vanishes, observer and observed are free to exist in the same space, which today is the space of *information exchange*. At the root of this concept is perhaps a literal "informing," in which form is generated from within the field of observation. Because this informing denies the observer or "imitator" any kind of privileged stance outside the field, we have, in a sense, an act of self-organization. What happens, then, inside this infosphere to the traditional sense of fiction, the organized lie that reflects its organized reality? Here, it seems, is a climate of image creation to which the Aristotelian tyranny no longer applies; it is no longer possible to speak of actions that develop in linear fashion, or are complete, or fix their audience by effecting catharsis, holding them in strongly aroused emotional states like pity and fear.

Looking backward, we see notable examples of fictional worlds tending toward this state of information. Balzac is perhaps the true ancestor of the fictional infosphere. His *Comédie humaine* sought to connect Parisian and French society in what is essentially a vast network through which all classes and institutions theoretically intercommunicate. And in a sense science fiction is the inheritor of Balzac's enterprise. For it can be argued that what SF calls the future—its quest for alien contacts and worlds elsewhere and elsewhen—is an infosphere. It is, in the current sense, a real infosphere, for its network is no longer (as with a Balzac) an individual creation but a collective and ever-expanding aggregate of bits of information, however speculative in nature. It is no surprise, then, that cyberpunk, a form that openly touts its SF roots, sees itself coming of age as that genre's informational conscience. Cyberpunk, in Bruce Sterling's eyes, has chosen to pursue the lateral futures of today's information technology rather than the old linear futures of space adventure, because today there is simply no difference between SF text and the world at large. Sterling's cyberpunks claim to be the first generation of SF writers to live in an SF world. Such a statement implicitly equates SF with information, whose free flow has finally penetrated old physical barriers of geography, nation, and "character" formation. In the cyberpunk world, to write SF is to make physical, even visceral contact with the mechanical and biological extensions of our personal infosphere (cyborgs, grafts, prostheses, clones), and beyond that with the image surrogates themselves (simulations, "constructs," holograms) that now crowd and share our traditional fictional living space. In a world in which images of dead celebrities and historical figures can be resurrected into cyberlife, fictional differentiations such as narrative past and plots based on biological change and mortality vanish into a present ubiquity of experience, a vast synchronicity. By examining cyberpunk's claims, then, in relation both to traditional SF and to contemporary fiction in general, the writers in this volume hope to go to the heart of the problems conventional narrative faces in the information age.

The use of the term *cyberpunk* is a problem even for the writers it ostensibly describes. As a label bestowed by the media, the term itself is a product of the infosphere, an image sent back through the information loop to cohabit with writers who did not create it. And here lies the dilemma. If these writers are reluctant to accept it, they cannot reject it either, for to do so is to risk reinstating the very Platonic dichotomy the term seems to challenge—that between serious (read "realistic") writing and illusory hype. Lewis Shiner has interesting things to say about the origin and adequacy of this "made-for-consumption" label.

For Shiner was there, physically a member of that loose association of younger SF writers—Bruce Sterling, William Gibson, John Shirley, and himself—who (though they have very disparate styles and visions) were united mainly by the need to form a movement. But as he describes it, this group, who did not even share a common geographical or regional association, soon transposed their aspirations into the abstract and became the Movement. Suddenly they discovered a common network of themes circulating through their writing. And this became the infosphere: formed of such media as electronic music, consciousness-expanding drugs, cult experiences, video technology, and especially the computer. *Movement*, however is a term that also belongs to traditional literary elitism. For Shiner, on one hand, his writers tap the common flow of images, the barrier-destroying processes of modern information culture. And to this degree he is willing to accept the designation "cyberpunk." But, on the other hand, he cannot accept the mass appeal implied by this term. Instead he falls back, at the close of his essay, on the conventional distinction between "popular" forms—that general commodity he disparagingly calls "sci-fiberpunk"—and what he sees as the serious attempts of Movement writers to explore (in a quite classical sense) the social and ethical implications of the new technology.

Built into the apparent forward dynamic of cyberpunk as literary movement, then, is a distinct pull backward. This pull is the subject of the next two essays. Istvan Csicsery-Ronay, Jr., uses a term that, in the feedback loops of today's computers, has lost its figurative sense. His *virus*, in this new context, is no longer a metaphor, but a presence that tends to break down the reigning dichotomy between the organic and the inorganic. To Csicsery-Ronay, the future in cyberpunk SF is itself no figurative construct, for it now succumbs to something literally pathological, a "retrofuture virus." By the same token, this cyberpunk future, where it offers open intercourse between artificial construct and human flesh, is seen to do so in terms of "disease," an agent that, contrary to intention, "attacks its own past by undermining the morale and freedom necessary to create an open, conditional future." Indeed, we abolish the distinction between figurative and literal only to encounter another duality, ennested this time in the concept of pathology itself. To attack future promise with viruses of its past we only make that future more dependent on the present, as median and point of balance, the only island of health in the vast expanse of speculative schemes.

George Slusser's essay traces this retroviral loop back to Mary Shelley's *Frankenstein*. Here, Slusser contends, is the work that still places modern fiction and its dreams of an open infosphere before a barrier—one that by its pervasiveness deserves to be called the Frankenstein barrier. Asked by his creature to make a bride for it, Victor Frankenstein stands on the verge of giving us a future in which new forms, freed of their relationship to the human form divine of Western tradition, can circulate freely. In refusing to create the bride Victor blights that future. His refusal literally forces Plato's images back into the cave. And because of this, that cave now becomes a Gothic dungeon, in which Victor, in a closed loop of struggle with his creation-become-creature, loses family, friend, wife, and with them any claim to a future. Positivist science, failing to break this barrier located in humankind's will to create the future, doubles back on itself to become Gothic horror. In this process the creature is revealed to be Victor's monstrous double, a sign that this barrier lies less in the world than in the human mind itself. This division, Slusser argues, remains a sort of Ur-plot in modern fiction, one that still bars the narratives of cyberpunk writers like Gibson and Sterling from free concourse with the open future their technology promises.

Cyberpunk is touted as a new development in SF, a form that not only engages the future more openly but has developed new narrative means of doing so. But has it really moved beyond SF's traditional confrontation with the material world to a participatory relationship with that world and the "images" it projects? The retrovirus seems at work here too. For all the essays that set out to examine cyberpunk's newness in relation to its SF beginnings reveal genuinely retrogressive aspects in these narratives. Paul Alkon has the longest historical reach. For him, Gibson's cyberpunk trilogy is still, 150 years later, enacting a program set forth by Félix Bodin. Bodin encouraged writers of futuristic fiction to derive their epic and supernatural marvels not out of mythic belief systems but out of the new machines created by modern technology. But, Alkon asks, what sort of marvels come out of Gibson's all-pervasive computers? Not a new supernatural but the old gods of exotic myth systems such as voodoo. Alkon describes Gibson's novels as a "skillful feat of generic dialogism" combining "features of fantasy and realism by mixing elements of Gothic horror with various other modes of popular narrative."

Evoking Mikhail Bakhtin, Carol McGuirk finds Gibson's work an equally heteroglossic mixture, but this time of historical variations of traditional hard and soft SF modes. She not only gives a captivating description of Gibson's mixture of modes but finds a viable subgeneric category for it: "SF noir," works in the Besterian tradition of ironic anti-humanism. In her conclusion she finds Gibson the SF writer looking backward rather than forward: "Gibson has furnished in his work of the mid-1980s a startling revisionary recapitulation of science fiction's early history—hard and soft."

Gary Westfahl argues for the existence of a real "Gernsback continuum" in Gibson, and through close comparison of Gibson's textual strategies with those of Gernsback, he makes a case for *Neuromancer* being a retelling of Gernsback's 1911 novel *Ralph 124C 41+*. Though Westfahl does not see any advance of Gibson over Gernsback and the SF tradition of transcendental narrative, he argues that this tradition itself is fundamentally an open one, an unbroken continuum between successive stages of information. But have we, either in classic works like Arthur C. Clarke's *Childhood's End* or in new ones like *Neuromancer*, really allowed transcendence to breach the Platonic barriers that prevent open circulation between human and artificial intelligence? For in both novels the transcendence that brings hope to humanity's successors at the same time brings despair to humanity itself. Gibson's novel, like Clarke's, ends in binary stalemate. The latter is more dramatic—we must die so that they can live—but both works force us as readers to identify with the superannuated humans, thus rendering integrative terms like *sentient evolution* or *infosphere* emotionally invalid for us. Westfahl argues that SF, because it is generally optimistic about such transcendence, distinguishes itself from Gothic horror, which dwells morbidly on closure and human limits. But is this Frankenstein barrier so easily pigeonholed in a single genre like horror? Does either of the SF novels, Clarke's or Gibson's, with their radically divided futures, really break this barrier?

In terms of the SF tradition, then, cyberpunk may not be as "new" as it wishes to be. But how does it compare with recent literary forms outside that tradition—with so-called postmodernist narrative? What relation does cyberpunk have to the narrative experiments of postmodernist literature? John Huntington focuses his attention on the stylishness and style-consciousness of Gibson's prose in *Neuromancer*. But for Huntington it is not this that is unusual or new. It is rather the fact that Gibson is using this language of technological facility to reinforce a very opposite feeling in the reader: paradoxically a strong sense of linguistic powerlessness, the inability to penetrate to deeper structures beneath the glittering word surface. It is clear at once that Gibson's work shares no common purpose with the "empty" verbal systems of the nonreferential, or "new," novel. His intoxication with neologisms and jargon is instead a serious attempt to create a world referent. But as experiment, Gibson's prose has merely traded, as its central driving force, the utopian dream for the cynicism of virtuosity—the art of the skillful manipulator.

Huntington notes that this shift from utopian wishfulness to cynical realism marks a change in direction for the SF genre itself. But in what direction? Lance Olsen's essay, which places cyberpunk in the larger context of postmodern fiction, sees similarities in the form's rise from SF to the emergence of neorealism from mainstream experimental narrative. Olsen sees this neorealism as a conservative reaction to postmodernism. And, he asks, to what extent is cyberpunk's development a similar conservative reaction? In an SF tradition never touted as radical, cyberpunk may have the most potential for subversiveness of any SF form. Yet this subversive potential, if the evolution of Gibson's trilogy is any indication, was stillborn. Gibson's novels, as they evolve, show clear signs for Olsen of succumbing to the same neoconservative climate that is currently shaping mainstream fiction.

Brooks Landon seeks to determine the place of cyberpunk works in a broader metanarrational current in recent fiction that he calls the "postmnemotechnic" tradition. The focus of these "digital" narratives is not story but memory. And they seem particularly modern in that they present memory not in terms of information recovery that is, stories in the past tense—but of information overload. This is perhaps the conceptual equivalent of Gibson's stylistic saturation. And perhaps, by grappling with the problem of an informational present, with the inundation of unprocessed data, such narratives may point the way to new fictional forms, forms that can adapt to the overloads of the information age. Landon, however, remains pessimistic. For in modern cyberpunk and noncyberpunk novels alike, he sees fiction not developing a language of overload but rather opting for a *rhetoric* of overload; in other words, for a means of rationalizing a process we have already tacitly accepted—our culture's retreat from engagement in the brave new world of information, of mnemotechnics.

Cyberpunk's newness, it seems, does not lie in its use of SF themes or structures; nor, apparently, does it lie in any clear relation to mainstream experimental narratives. And yet from this search for newness, new things emerge as a result of the process of comparison itself, things about the difficulties of producing what we traditionally consider fiction in a new informational context. For when we examine cyberpunk's relation, both in theory and in practice, to SF and to mainstream structures, we begin to see general inadequacies of today's fiction. We discover its inability to abolish the barriers and walls that have traditionally sustained Western narrative fiction.

Can we, first of all, determine a generic boundary for cyberpunk? The next four essays attempt to set forth characteristics of a cyberpunk form through close analysis of writers or films seen to be cyberpunk. These studies soon reveal, however, that if there is something we call a cyberpunk "canon," it has emerged spontaneously, and perhaps spuriously, from within a field of vastly different modes and media. The works discussed may share certain superficial themes or icons. But their real communality, it appears, may ironically lie elsewhere—in their degree of responsiveness to the challenges of information that make them all, finally, recalcitrant both to generic and to other types of formal constraint.

John Christie describes the development of Gibson's "trilogy" as a process whereby successive novels, responding to new sets of challenges raised by the initial theme of artificial intelligence (AI), abandon the linear for increasingly radial modes of narration. Christie sees the *Neuromancer* world establishing a separation between AIs and humankind, meat realm and infosphere, so intolerable that it necessarily breaks down. The result is a series of feedback and information loops that, in the two following novels, gradually dissipate the "unitary, hard-paced drive of *Neuromancer*."

Robert Donahoo and Chuck Etheridge's essay on Lew Shiner and his "good" anarchism reveals, in a very different context, an analogous process at work. For not only do Shiner's novels present the laissez-faire system functioning on its own, beyond human volition and guidance, but they offer this as something not a priori "bad." For if Shiner's characters finally accept a general abdication of rational (read "prioritizing," in the sense of Western Platonic tradition) control over their institutions and modes of life, they accede thereby to a deeper level of reality—an infosphere in which forces now governed by neutral laws of probability are free to effect what Ilya Prigogine calls creative chaos. Because it operates on this level of open information exchange, Shiner's fiction,

Donahoo and Etheridge claim, is transindividualist in nature. They cite the example of Kane in *Frontera*, whose true task is to experience heroic archetypes that flow through his mind, and in doing so become aware of the "pattern," the universe of cultural information that lives in and through all humankind.

Frances Bonner sees in the separate development of a film and television cyberpunk corpus not the influence of any precise literary movement but rather a synchronicity of forms and pursuits. Visual cyberpunk does not come, she contends, from adapting books into films but more through spontaneous generation, in quite diverse media, of similar narrative forms. These are forms that often have in common only the fact that they are responding to the same challenge of a new information-driven world, whose whole thrust is to break down barriers such as those between film and prose narrative, when these are seen as separate "genres" and not as interactive *media*.

Tom Shippey, focusing on Bruce Sterling, finds exactly the same awareness in Sterling's pervasive commitment to what Shippey calls "qualified realities." These are (using Gibson's phrase) the "semiotic ghosts" that inhabit our standard sense of history and narrative, the "could-have-been-would-bes" that render our present merely another competing possible reality in a hypothetical past and make narrative little more than a "conflict of tenuities." Sterling's semiotic ghosts, like the phantasms of Gibson's "Gernsback Continuum" or Shiner's *Deserted Cities of the Heart*, are bits of cultural imagery that have split off from the mainline and have taken on a life of their own. They are "noise" in our systems, and Sterling's characters deal with them, as Shippey sees it, by means of "retrofitting," accepting things as "ghosts"—dead things that can only retroactively be shaped into new order. Shippey is astonished at Sterling's ability in *Islands In the Net* to consign to "ghost" status "virtually every cultural piety left to Western readers," to take what we believe to be fact and manipulate it like data. In light of Sterling's statement that everything can be altered by technology, Shippey's term *bricolage* is most appropriate. In dealing with the challenge of the infosphere, utilitarianism, not idealism, seems to be the answer, for it is the endless act of fitting and refitting, rather than some predetermined essential quality, that now defines system. From the Emersonian claim that "people live longer than nations," Sterling has erected Shiner's anarchy as method. Shippey, however, in his own use of organic imagery—"ghosts" and death—seems to invoke the Frankenstein barrier against

Sterling's radically informational narrative. Instead of "bricolage," he calls Sterling's method "Frankensteining," implying that Sterling is not creating new worlds out of the chaos of spare "dead" parts so much as perhaps nurturing a monstrosity.

10

But must the relation of cyberpunk writer to his critic also end at the Frankenstein barrier? For once Sterling's ubiquitous and utilitarian technopresent makes claim to the infosphere, the old logic of binarism rises, in turn, to resist these claims. Once again there is the logic of walls: humankind against world; flesh, or "meat," against data. And here not only the critic but the cyberpunk writer as well, if John Christie's analysis of Gibson's "transit" is exact, is guilty of retrenchment. For Gibson (and perhaps soon Sterling as well) seems to opt out of the brave new monistic world of endlessly circulating information, to return finally to one of traditional, vectored "human" beliefs and values.

But finally, more than a form cyberpunk is a style. And on this level the traditional binarities of our culture and this new logic of the interface may at last come to complement each other. Indeed, the way to Fiction 2000, as the final four essays suggest, may not be through theme or genre but through those devices that allow literary narrative to harness in a creative fashion the dynamic tensions of the interface. These devices are the basic figures of speech and logic alike, figures such as metaphor. Now, however, metaphor must be seen in the new context of cyberspace, of rhetoric "retrofitted" to allow writers the possibility not of having ultimately to yield to one opposite or the other, to chaos or to order, but of reveling in the constant transfer between otherwise paradoxical terms, between chaos and creation.

Gregory Benford, who is both a scientist and a writer, opens the final section by exhorting the critic to measure cyberpunk by the efforts of the best of science fiction to transform rhetorical devices from their former status as embellishment to a new functional role as a means of extending the literary field of knowledge, of combining literature's desire to please and teach with science's desire to know.

Ruth Curl follows with an in-depth comparison of the use of metaphor in the works of Gibson and Benford. Exploring the distinction between literary and scientific uses of metaphor—the former fundamentally ontological, the latter epistemological in nature—Curl finds the cyberpunk novel, as epitomized by *Neuromancer*, limited by its almost exclusive use of the literary metaphor. Thus a novel that seems to promise free access to the infosphere in fact turns that promise into a closed system of figurative associations that merely reinforce the Platonic distinction between appearance and reality. But a novel like Benford's *Great Sky River*, Curl argues, consciously confronts the literary with the scientific use of metaphor, seeking thereby to tap, in a creative manner, the tensions inherent in the compound *science fiction*.

In the concluding essays, both Eric S. Rabkin and David Porush reiterate this need for creative tension in fiction, but they argue that it is not the scientific but the literary metaphor that is responsible for reinstating it, through science fiction, at the core of modern narrative. Porush sees cyberpunk as literary form itself functioning as an extended metaphor, holding in creative tension the literary text and the drive of the infosphere in the direction of a postliterate culture: "Gibson's vision of the cyberpunk future suggests a postliterate culture. But cyberpunk itself demonstrates that the literary text is a hyperevolved device for extending the nerve net along one of its more powerful lines of force." Beyond the year 2000, and through all possible changes effected by technology, "the literary text will always be required . . . for its particular sort of epistemological potency." And Rabkin argues for precisely this: the epistemological potency of literary metaphor. He sees cyberpunk as a literature that is supremely sensitive to the pressures of what he calls "oxymoronism": "Cyberspace is not only an oxymoron but a conception made vivid only through oxymoron: a consensual hallucination." If cyberpunk is a harbinger of things to come, then Rabkin predicts that fiction in the year 2000 will be seeking "oxymoronic transcendence" from within. This is not, as with Curl's "scientific metaphor," a resolution of opposites in the direction of a posited and knowable material world. It is rather a pushing of opposites to irresolvable extremes in order to develop structures of complementarity. Here, as the logic of either/or gives way to a logic of both/and, dilemmas like Victor Franken stein's vanish. Rising from its oxymorons, a new fiction is summoned to deal with tomorrow's world—a world in which division and conflict are replaced by the increasingly free flow of information.

These essays offer general commentary on cyberpunk and the future of fiction. But the specific occasion of their production is interesting also. All were presented at the "Fiction 2000" conference held in Leeds, England, in June 1989, a gathering sponsored jointly by the University of Leeds and the University of California at Riverside. This conference brought together, around the central issue of cyberpunk, a broad variety of commentators: British, U.S., and continental European academics; literary critics and media experts; and writers claiming a diversity of generic allegiances—from cyberpunk through traditional and even "hard" SF to "general" writers of fiction.

The question of cyberpunk—where it came from, what it is, and where it is headed—was hotly debated in the discussions surrounding the formal presentation of papers. Comments on this level were usually less formal and more sharply directed by personal feelings and loyalties. Some of the "hard" SF writers, for example, faulted cyberpunk for relying too heavily on stylistic effects and not enough on carefully researched extrapolation and straight facts. Yet none of these hard SF-ers, when pressed on the issue, would deny the importance of writers like Gibson, Sterling, and Shiner. And they would certainly not exclude them from SF. In like manner, those versed in science challenged cyberpunk's central obsession with the computer. In their eyes, the implication that computer technology is the determining factor in modern life is dead wrong. But again, none of these scientists denied the power of the computer as metaphor.

These discussions revealed tensions surrounding both the nature of cyberpunk and its place in the future of literary expression. The term *cyberpunk* itself seemed to provoke an overly emotional response. Beyond all sense of critical utility, some cherished the term and others execrated it. Both groups clearly had a personal stake in their reactions, one wanting to enshrine it as a genre, the other denying it existence altogether. Its detractors, speaking for a rigorous scientific fiction, predictably reinforce the old SF-literature dichotomy, in which substance and thought are seen to outweigh style. The proponents of cyberpunk, however, in their near religious zeal, are more interesting as a cultural phenomenon. They are superpurists in the sense that they assert a generic identity for cyberpunk that sets it apart both from SF and from so-called mainstream fiction. In their eyes it is sui generis—a form with built-in criteria for inclusion or exclusion and a clear (almost predetermined) set of canonized texts and writers.

Oddly, while there were detractors at the conference, no cyberpunk absolutists were present. But their hypothetical objections to the tenor of the "Fiction 2000" essays are easy to reconstruct. They would surely challenge this forum by raising two objections: (1) because most of the essays seem to favor one text (Gibson's *Neuromancer*), the conference misrepresents the cyberpunk "canon," which includes many other

equally "representative" texts; and (2) none of the writers at the conference are adequate spokespersons for cyberpunk: Shiner being (by his
own admission) peripheral to the form, and Benford openly hostile. The
same could be said of two other writers present who did not present
papers: Greg Bear and Harry Harrison.

Answering these charges leveled by our hypothetical cyberpunk advocates offers an excellent way to define the nature of the "Fiction 2000"
enterprise. First, though a broad range of texts is mentioned in these
essays, Gibson's novel does seem to be a central focus. The reasons for
this, however, go deeper than mere desires to minimize or restrict a
cyberpunk "field." The essays in this volume do not perceive Gibson's
novel in the ontological sense Sterling gives it when he calls it the
"quintessence of cyberpunk." It is rather a prototype for a significant
and distinctive cultural moment. Indeed, the very fact that such a diverse group of scholars and critics, simultaneously and independently
of each other, chose this single work to motivate otherwise quite different approaches testifies to a significance beyond mere generic identity.
None of the essayists tries to fix or limit a genre. Rather, they are choosing a normative structure in hopes of measuring the nature of a literary
process in transformation.

Second, there is the question of Shiner's or Benford's "right to represent." For, far from being somehow detrimental to the cyberpunk image,
their statements (and, more important, the creative work these statements are based on) testify to just how powerful the dynamic current
of literary change moving through cyberpunk really is. Indeed, here
are two very different writers so deeply affected by Gibson that they
are moved to creative dialogue with his work. Shiner, by his own admission, is moving toward a more general postmodern sensibility. The
literary independence Shiner displays in his essay is seconded by Donahoo and Etheridge's sense, in their essay, of the writer's adherence to a
broad anarchic tradition in American letters. This insight is reinforced
by Shippey's discussion of the evolution of cyberpunk "spokesman"
Sterling himself, and of Sterling's own increasingly anarchical use of
"qualified realities" in recent novels like Islands in the Net. Curl's commentary on Benford's remarks about cyberpunk demonstrates the seriousness of Benford's attempt to come to grips with cyberpunk's central
metaphor of the computer in his recent novel Great Sky River.

As a final sample of the "Fiction 2000" debate—and the supreme example of its open-ended nature—we offer an interview conducted at

the close of the conference by Terri Frongia and Alida Allison with several of its participants: writers Lew Shiner and Greg Bear, organizer George Slusser, critics Paul Brazier and Istvan Csicsery-Ronay, Jr., and Anglo-Canadian fantasy writer Geoff Ryman. It is interesting to see just how quickly the discussion veers away from squabbles about who is and who is not a cyberpunk writer, and toward matters of cyberspace-oriented modes of creating narrative texts in the future.

Finally, cyberpunk, and the collective fascination of critic and scientist alike with the fiction of writers like Gibson, Sterling, and Shiner, proved a powerful point of convergence. The *high* quality of this fiction inspired these essayists—literary critic and scientist alike—to examine the development of SF in light of concerns shared with fiction and narrative in general. It inspired them to reexamine a commonplace like the "two cultures gap" in new terms. From a wide variety of perspectives, all of the essays gathered here express a desire to keep fiction's future open, and significant suggestions are made as to how it might be done. Anything beyond this lies in the realm not of critical discourse but of prophesy.

PART 1

. . . .

The

. . . . . .

Movement:

. . . .

Forward

. . . .

or

. . . .

Backward?

. . . .

Inside

the

Movement:

Past,

Present,

and

Future

. . . .

Lewis Shiner

This essay has been difficult to write. On the one hand, I feel uncomfortable with a purely academic treatise. Too much analysis is unhealthy for my other job, writing fiction. Yet the question of where fiction is going in the next ten years is of obvious importance to me, and I have a number of ideas about it.

I will avoid the use of the word *cyberpunk* as much as I possibly can—which means I'll still be using it more than I'd like to. The problem is that the term has become "commodified"—to use the postmodern catchword. It is now a marketing phrase used to sell everything from comics to board games to specialty magazines for keyboard players. Within science fiction it evokes a very restricted formula; to wit, novels about monolithic corporations opposed by violent, leather-clad drug users with wetware implants. The term *sci-fiberpunk* arose at Milford, a writer's conference in Britain, to describe this formula. Michael Swanwick's *Vacuum Flowers* is a classic example, replete with a protagonist named Rebel and rampant misuse of the term *wetware*. Now, sci-fiberpunk is something we can get a handle on, and it may include much of the fiction currently labeled cyberpunk. I hope to convince you that this kind of "commodified cyberpunk" is antithetical to the theme here, namely, fiction in the year 2000.

The original use of the term *cyberpunk* may have been in a Bruce Bethke story with that title published in the November 1983 issue of *Amazing Stories*. Unquestionably it entered common parlance when Gardner Dozois used it in an article in the *Washington Post* dated December 30, 1984—my thirty-fourth birthday, coincidentally—titled "SF in the Eighties." The relevant parts of the article were later incorporated into his introduction to the *Year's Best SF, Second Annual Collection* (Bluejay, 1985). Gardner used the word to describe Bruce Sterling, William Gibson, myself, Pat Cadigan, and Greg Bear. He called us "purveyors of bizarre hard-edged, high-tech stuff."

This was the first recognition by the outside world of what I prefer to call the Movement, using John Shirley's term, with all its 1960s radical implications. My immediate reaction to the article was selfish. I was disappointed that Gardner hadn't reviewed my novel *Frontera* (which I knew he liked), or at least mentioned it in the same paragraph with the other significant books of the decade so far: *Neuromancer*, *The Wild Shore*, *Green Eyes*, and *Startide Rising*.

The rest of my emotions were mixed. I was glad to be pronounced a "hot young writer." Coming from Gardner, this was to prove a self-fulfilling prophecy. I was surprised to see Cadigan and Bear called "cyberpunks." I wondered where John Shirley and Rudy Rucker were.

I also had deeper concerns. *Frontera* dealt with technology, among other things, and that was obviously the reason I'd been labeled a cyberpunk. That, and geographical proximity to Sterling and my work for his radical polemizine, *Cheap Truth*. In my own mind, however, the hard science of *Frontera* was simply a belief system to be played with, the same way I'd played with *brujería* (a Mexican magical system) or UFOs in earlier stories. In other words, I was already uncomfortable with where the battle lines were being drawn. Why was I on one side of the fence and John Kessel on the other? John is not only a friend, but somebody whose work I admire greatly, and whose literary aesthetic I find more congenial than Sterling's. A quote about that aesthetic—apparently John is concerned that this quote is getting better known than any of his fiction—originally appeared in *Fantasy Review* and again in Michael Swanwick's much-discussed "User's Guide to the Postmoderns" (*Isaac Asimov's Science Fiction Magazine*, August 1986): "many of the works we call the best the field has to offer just do not measure up to the best of English and American fiction of the last couple of hundred years. . . . If we want to make it in the big leagues, we've got to face big league pitching." I'm not the Melville fan that John is, but I'm in sympathy with his spirit. John reads, and teaches, mainstream fiction and literature; Bruce, on the other hand, reads virtually no fiction at all. I feel similar ties to Lucius Shepard, Pat Murphy, Jim Kelly, and Leigh Kennedy; not to mention writers Gardner didn't name: Jim Blaylock, Nancy Kress, and Russell M. Griffin. These are not my enemies. If I have enemies, they are the writers who regurgitate the tired, empty SF clichés which they have swallowed whole: writers like Mike Resnick and Spider Robinson and David Brin. Writers who still believe in galactic empires and whose aliens behave like white male North Americans in special-effects makeup.

I was also uneasy with Gardner's emphasis on technology. Was this to be, then, the only fit subject for "bizarre hard-edged" prose? Let me emphasize here that I am no Luddite. I believe that technology must be a part of the milieu in which modern fiction is set. To ignore technology is unrealistic, at the very least; to fail to see the advantages it can offer is foolish. The question here is whether technology itself is the only fit subject matter for SF, or, even more strongly put, can a literature principally focused on technology be completely satisfying?

My misgivings about this article were well-founded. Cyberpunk has turned into something of a Frankenstein's monster. In the last year I've seen the *New York Times* use the word as a synonym for *hacker*. I've seen lists of "core cyberpunk" writers that contain the most improbable names: Lucius Shepard, Michael Swanwick, Greg Benford, even Kim Stanley Robinson. There is the aforementioned cyberpunk issue of *Keyboard* magazine, featuring interviews with, well, basically a lot of guys in black leather who use synthesizers, MIDIs (that's musical instrument digital interface to the unhip), and digital sampling. There are the comics, the games, the magazine articles, the angry letters.

I don't see myself, or my work, in any of this. I do see myself as part of a literary movement, however, and I'm going to try to describe it, what it looked like from the inside, how it grew, and a few of the places it may be going.

I first met Bruce Sterling at a regional convention at Texas A&M. It was 1976 and Bruce was a measly twenty-one years old. I remember him walking up to guest of honor Anne McCaffery and saying, "Hi, I'm Bruce Sterling, the hottest young SF writer in Texas." Christ, I thought, what an arrogant prick. (Bruce, of course, now claims he was being ironic. In any event, I responded by publishing a checklist of the as-yet-unpublished Sterling's work in my fanzine—an entire blank column, with thanks to half a dozen people for research assistance.)

In 1979 I moved to Austin to start my writing career in earnest. I knew a lot of the writers there and immediately joined the Turkey City Neo-Pro Rodeo and Writer's Workshop—to use its full and proper name. Bruce and I were probably the most passionate and outspoken critics there. Both of us had our agendas: Bruce ideas, me style. Both of us had

19

well-thought-out positions and the sort of vicious verbal skills (developed as wimps in grade school) that let us run roughshod over the more polite, less aggressive members.

I remember one workshop in particular, in December 1981. It was held at my apartment—hardwood floors, high ceilings, a gas heater on the wall trying to cut the drafts. I brought out a piece of the horror novel I was working on. I hadn't written any SF for a couple of years. I was sick of it—the field seemed mired between *Analog*-style space opera and the gloomy art pieces of Michael Bishop. Bruce showed up with an extra manuscript for us to critique if we had time. It was a new story by William Gibson called "Burning Chrome."

As to how Sterling knew Gibson, that's a bit of a convoluted story, but I'll hit the high points for you completists. The key is a guy named Steve Brown, who is currently editor of a critical magazine called *Science Fiction Eye*. Brown met John Shirley in 1970 in Portland, Oregon, as chronicled in his introduction to Shirley's *Heatseeker* collection. Brown later turned up at the Clarion Writer's Workshop in 1972 at the same time as the teenaged Bruce Sterling. And it was Shirley, after meeting Gibson at regional conventions in the Pacific Northwest, who got Sterling and Gibson together through the mails.

I had been hearing about Gibson through the grapevine. He'd sold a novel to Terry Carr's new Ace Specials, and word had it he was hot. So I grabbed the manuscript and started to read. I was hooked instantly. The first paragraph was full of heat, neon, vivid reds, cathode greens. There were malls, silicon chips, LEDs, and brand names. All this in the first paragraph. A cartoon light bulb went on over my head. Science fiction could be energetic, hip, lean, and best of all, real. It could have real stuff and real people in it. Everything else in the workshop seemed trivial and old-fashioned by comparison, especially my novel (which I soon abandoned).

In the months that followed I started writing SF again. "Nine Hard Questions about the Nature of the Universe" sold to *The Magazine of Fantasy and Science Fiction*, the short-story version of "Deserted Cities of the Heart" sold to *Omni*, and "Dancers," which had fashion, rock and roll, machine intelligence, video clubs, cults, and drugs in it, was rejected by every editor in the field. (It was eventually published in *Night Cry* five years later.)

In October 1982 Gibson came to town for ArmadilloCon. At this point the sense of a movement solidified. Something was clearly happening in the work of Shirley, Gibson, and Sterling. In fact there was a panel on it at the convention, called "Behind the Mirrorshades: A Look at Punk SF." I take credit for the term *mirrorshades movement*; at the time it was the only thing I could pin down as common to all three writers' work.

In retrospect, the common themes are easier to see. There is, of course, the hacker's attitude toward technology—"surfing the third wave," as it were. More important to me was what Gibson talked about in his introduction to *Heatseeker*: "Sometimes, reading Shirley, I can hear the guitars." This rock-and-roll quality—the young, hip protagonists, the countercultural attitude (symbolized by the ever-present mirrorshades), the musical references—defined the movement for me. I'd played in rock bands for fifteen years, and it was a sensibility that I was comfortable with. None of this, you will note, has anything to do with corporate mercenaries, wetware implants, or orbiting space colonies.

We spent a lot of time together that weekend—Bruce and his wife, Nancy, my wife, Edith, and I, Bill Gibson, and various other friends, mostly in the Sterlings' garage apartment, surrounded by Japanese pop music and Bruce's carnivorous plants. We talked a little about literature —Len Deighton, Nelson Algren, Burroughs, and Ballard—but mostly we talked about rock and roll, MTV, Japan, fashion, drugs, and politics. As Bill got on his plane for Vancouver he said, only half-kidding, "A new axis has been formed."

I know I felt that way. Part of it was Bill's charm and obvious star quality. He was clearly destined for big things. He'd read the opening chapters of *Neuromancer* (then in progress) at the convention, and I felt I was hearing the future of SF: a stylish, high-energy naturalism. By December I decided it was time to put aside all of my other half-baked projects and write an SF novel. I had the raw materials in an unpublished short story from 1976 called "Soldier, Sailor." It was itself a Ballardian condensation of an SF novel I'd written in college, a talky and low-key retelling of the Grail legend. This time I wanted to try it without the bullshit. I went to NASA for details of actual Mars mission plans, and I went to Sterling for ideas on how to extrapolate a convincing background society for the year 2020. Bruce gave me Alvin Toffler's *The Third Wave*, and I was off and running.

Norman Spinrad's article "Cyberpunk Revisited" (*Asimov's*, March 1989) considers five books: Gibson's *Mona Lisa Overdrive*, Sterling's *Islands in the Net*, Shirley's *A Splendid Chaos*, Rucker's *Wetware*, and my *Deserted Cities of the Heart*. The article is extremely positive, but Spinrad misses one essential point. He finds the novels "surprisingly diverse, perhaps even amazingly so," and "major departures from anything these writers have previously written." In fact, that same counter-culture rock-and-roll gestalt I talked about earlier is clearly present in all five books. As Spinrad himself points out—using different terminology—only the Rucker and Gibson books have anything at all in common with the sort of sci-fiberpunk commodity written by Swanwick, W. T. Quick, and the like. I feel this split between sci-fiberpunk and the Movement was inevitable; it was inherent in my misgivings from the start. A number of factors contributed to the widening gap. The first is Bruce Sterling's rhetoric. For those who wished to follow the trail the Movement had cut, here was the map. It was inevitable that Sterling would become the Movement's spokesman; who could compete? Thus his personal agenda—his interest in technology, his resentment of characterization and linear plot, his indifference to mainstream fictive styles and technique—came to be taken as characteristic of the Movement. But this map is not the whole territory. I wrote my own articles for *Cheap Truth*, attempting to deal with my own literary agenda, but I failed to achieve Bruce's level of flamboyance and quotability.

The second factor is audience comprehension. The way to reach today's audience is through sound bites. An abstract lecture on rigorous extrapolation and street-level energy and global political issues will touch only a few. It's vastly easier to point at *Neuromancer* and say, "stuff like that." (Thus Ed Bryant's sardonic term for the products of the Movement: NOGS—Novels of Gibsonian Sensibility.) It's simpler yet to say, "You know. Cyberpunk. Guys with computer chips in their heads." Any idiot can understand that. It's ready for prime-time TV.

You can't sum up a legitimate literary movement in a sound bite any more than you can sum up the theme of *War and Peace* as "war is no damned good" or *Moby Dick* as "moderation in all things." As long as a movement is still alive, in fact, it will strongly resist any such judgments.

Sci-fiberpunk, however, can be commodified, summarized, codified, and reduced to formula. And therefore I insist that it is not the fiction of the year 2000. Why not? you may well ask. Computers are going to continue to increase their influence over our lives. Sci-fiberpunk can be delivered, and enjoyed, by a mass audience, as the "Max Headroom" TV show proved. Hell, it feels like the future. Doesn't it?

Well, no. Not to me. It is already as dated in its innocence as the condomless sex films of the 1970s. It's no wonder that the image of the "console cowboy" so strongly attracts the writers of sci-fiberpunk. The console cowboy is a direct linear descendant of the western pulp heroes. His is an adolescent male fantasy to ride unfettered on the consensual range of the matrix, to shoot it out with the bad guys, and finally to head his chrome horse off into a sunset the color of a dead television channel.

Likewise, critics have noticed the obvious influence of Raymond Chandler and hard-boiled detective fiction on the subgenre. Like westerns, like traditional SF, both detective fiction and sci-fiberpunk are written for, and about, loners, misfits, and rebels.

This brings us to the heart of the literary issues I want to discuss. The pulp tradition is a tradition of childish, self-centered fantasy. I think it's time to grow up.

The hero in North American genre fiction—which has rather brutally forced its tropes on most of Western civilization—is the outsider who walks in, sets a problem right, and moves on. The problem usually involves a confrontation with representatives of an opposing viewpoint who are dehumanized (made to seem evil) and then blown away. This paradigm has grown out of the political history of the United States, the philosophy of Don't Tread on Me, of independence at all costs.

This is not a useful paradigm to carry into the twenty-first century. The popularity of films like *Rambo* and the *Death Wish* sequels and *RoboCop* clearly arises from the frustrations of our time—crowded highways, an overworked and inefficient legal system, an unresponsive political process, diminishing resources, spiraling inflation. These frustrations can only become worse in the near future. Violence is not a productive response to these frustrations, and it is increasingly likely to cause a chain reaction of violence (i.e., open rioting) that will soon be out of control. There is a spiritual vacuum where God, King, and Work used to be. Sci-fiberpunk would have us believe that technology can fill that void.

Yet a look at our world here at the edge of the 1990s shows this is not the case. New Age mysticism, religious fundamentalism, panicked consumerism, drug and alcohol addiction—all are picking up speed. I see all of these as responses to technology, as indications that technology alone is not enough. Our problems are also sociological, spiritual, even moral. These are issues that fiction in the year 2000 could, and should, address.

I have an idea inside my head of what this fiction might look like. I can't condense it into a sound bite. It is a kind of fiction that resembles the mainstream novels of Philip K. Dick more than his SF. It has more in common with the country blues of John Hiatt than with the arid synthesizers of Philip Glass or the theatricality of David Bowie. It is more like "Hill Street Blues" than "Max Headroom." It offers hope but not easy answers. It talks about adult problems and complex relationships and does not pretend that we can simply walk away from them.

Some of this work is already being done. Much as Sterling's *Islands in the Net* has been praised for its credible vision of the future, its hip tech and savvy political dialogue, none of that is truly groundbreaking. The revolutionary vision of the book is the way in which Sterling has taken Donne's admonition that we are none of us islands and woven it "into the fabric of daily life." He shows us how an individual is linked to her husband and child, to her employer, and finally to the entire global political system. She cannot escape this net, nor should she want to. It is the central fact of twenty-first-century existence.

There are no technophiliac cowboys in the rest of recent Movement fiction either. Note how the cheerful glow of the matrix—technology's synthetic mirror of reality—in *Neuromancer* has evolved into Slick's disturbing machines in *Mona Lisa Overdrive* (based on the even more disturbing machines of Mark Pauline's Survival Research Laboratories). Also in *Mona Lisa* we are given Molly's flashbacks to the events of the earlier novels. She and Gibson both seem nostalgic for those simpler days, when the matrix was endlessly fascinating, seemed to hold all the answers. By this third novel, however, virtually no time at all is spent in the matrix; the viewpoints have become increasingly feminine; art (in the form of Slick's machines and the Cornell boxes) has become increasingly important; the characters are increasingly interconnected with parents, friends, spouses, and lovers.

John Shirley has abandoned SF entirely in favor of horror fiction, a genre that traditionally derives its impact from the relationships between the human characters.

My own work, as I've said, never had that much to do with technology in the first place. My vision of the place of technology is shown in *Deserted Cities*, in the ecology project where Thomas worked. There computers are a resource, like organic gardening techniques, to be used in solving human problems. Since then I've written a novel, *Slam*, which concerns the leisure society that technology is in the process of creating. What is the place of the individual in that society, especially versus the place of government? The kicker is that the novel is set on the Texas coast in 1988 and contains no fantasy elements at all.

In my next novel I want to push past the genre conventions of the loner to deal with adult relationships and their consequences. I want to directly address the void that technology, capitalism, and television have been unable to fill.

The novel—and probably the mainstream novel—remains my weapon of choice, despite continued dire predictions about its future. It's under attack by TV and movies, as it has been for years, but also by new forms—comics, rock videos, performance art like Mark Pauline's dueling machines, increasingly vivid video games. The biggest threat may even be TV commercials, often the most high-tech, energized, visually stunning, information-packed, and soulless programs on television. How much more sci-fiberpunk can you get?

To survive these threats the novel must face the future. I'm not talking here about a sci-fiberpunk novel that offers escape into techno-macho insensitivity. I'm talking about a novel that presents new paradigms, works against prejudice and limited worldviews. It cannot afford to ignore the real world: AIDS, terrorism, hunger, cold fusion, consumerism, glasnost', MTV, skateboards, crack, and all the rest. It must not fall victim to easy answers: good guys versus bad, might makes right, wealth equals success, technology as panacea or scapegoat. Most important, it must somehow find a voice with the energy and wisdom and humor to speak to these times.

Bruce Sterling is headed in that direction with *Islands in the Net*. So is Don DeLillo in *White Noise*; so is the highly underrated Dan McCall in *Bluebird Canyon*. A new novel by Wilton Barnhardt called *Emma Who Saved My Life* has a piece of what I'm after.

It is vitally important to struggle and grow and change. More than anything, this is what the Movement means to me. For that reason the books it produces will, I hope, continue to be "surprisingly diverse" and continue to defy category and easy description, all the way into the next century.

Futuristic

Flu, or,

The

Revenge

of the

Future

. . . .

Istvan Csicsery-
Ronay, Jr.

C yberpunk. What are we to make of a style whose supposed practitioners consistently distance themselves from the term? Cyberpunk often seems to live mainly in commentary about some absent text, a Borgesian or Lemian gloss constructing its own foundation from the roof downward. It doesn't inspire confidence that the most recent novel by its most articulate and passionate polemicist, Bruce Sterling's *Islands in the Net*, contains nary a trace of cyber or punk. Musicians and performance artists believe cyberpunk has no meaning in literature any more (if it ever did); but here we are, the artificial intelligentsia discussing a literary punk elite.

As for the shape and nature of future fiction, I am very uncomfortable talking about the future of anything. A conference with a name like "Fiction 2000" makes us all, literally, pretentious. We cannot know what the future will bring, but we get to pretend that we know its "possibilities." We pretend to know something about the future of fiction because we pretend to know what cyberpunk is. But our knowledge of cyberpunk depends on a view from the future, that is, that cyberpunk is a significant enough paradigm for fiction to take off from or to react against. We are pretending to know what it feels like to be *post-cyberpunk* when we don't know whether cyberpunk is finished, or even whether it ever was.

The gracious millenialist organizers of this conference are suffering from a mild case of the very condition I wish to discuss, namely retro-futuristic chronosemiitis, or futuristic flu. More about that later. For now let me say that this is a retrochronal semiovirus, in which a time further in the future than the one in which we exist and choose infects the host present, reproducing itself in simulacra, until it destroys all the original chronocytes of the host imagination. Dante devoted the Eighth Circle of *The Inferno* to the flu's earlier carriers: the fortune-tellers eternally condemned to walk with their heads under their asses for pretending to see too far ahead. I have my heart set on another circle, so I will try to avoid exposure to the flu by misunderstanding my instructions. Instead of discussing the future of fiction, I will discuss fictions of the future.

Postmodern Time Zone

Whatever postmodernism ultimately turns out to have been, the culture of postindustrial societies after Hiroshima and Auschwitz has been marked by two profound transformations of the sense of historical time. One is the marginalization of the past; the other is what the feminist theorist Zoe Sofia calls "the collapse of the future onto the present" (48). Since the living population of Earth now surpasses all previous human generations combined, the historical past has become, in a genuine sense, a minority report. The experiences of those ancestors, thinly distributed in space and time, represent a library of legends and exemplary tales told by tribes and families in their struggles against physical and human nature. In this sense, even the perspectival time view of liberal empiricism (in which the species moves toward a vanishing point on the horizon, a future ever closer and yet ideal and unattainable) and twentieth-century modernism's time of simultaneous parallel worlds and critical junctures can be seen as versions of a single story of the human species balancing, correcting, and equilibrating itself vis-à-vis a temporal nature external to the human project.

The scientific-technical revolution after World War II created a new relationship between the possessors of high technology and nature, a change we might call *immanentization* or *artificial immanence;* that is, through advanced technology human beings have appropriated powers that all previous cultures considered transcendental or heteronomic. The victory for the forces of technoevolution has been Pyrrhic, of course. For once transcendence has been assimilated, no transcendental values can enforce discipline on these new powers. As a result, our imaginations are increasingly determined by the problems and technical solutions latent in the social application of the given technologies.

In his introduction to the French edition of *Crash!,* J. G. Ballard gives a vivid account of the psychological fallout of the new situation:

> Increasingly, our concepts of past, present, and future are being forced to revise themselves. Just as the past itself, in social and psychological terms, became a casualty of Hiroshima and the nu-

clear age (almost by definition a period in which we were all forced to think prospectively), so in its turn the future is ceasing to exist, devoured by the all-voracious present. We have annexed the future into our own present, as merely one of the manifold alternatives open to us. Options multiply around us, we live in an almost infantile world where any demand, any possibility, whether for lifestyles, travel, sexual roles and identities can be satisfied instantly. (4)

This polymorphous perversity is the opposite of Marcuse's harbinger of the utopian liberation of affect; in it Ballard sees the fulfillment of Freud's fears in *Civilization and Its Discontents*, the "diseases of the psyche" which "have now culminated in the most terrifying casualty of the century: the death of affect" (1).

The demise of feeling and emotion has paved the way for all our most real and tender pleasures—in the excitements of pain and mutilation; in sex as the perfect arena, like a culture bed of sterile pus, for all the veronicas of our own perversions; in our moral freedom to pursue our own psycho-pathology as a game; and in our limitless powers for conceptualization. What our children have to fear is not the cars on the highways of tomorrow but our own pleasure in calculating the most elegant parameters of their deaths. (1)

I take Ballard's quote as an exemplary text because it makes explicit the implications of viewing the future as merely one of infinite alternatives available to postmodern humanity, equal in status with psychopathic fantasies, dreams, commercial reveries, political propaganda, drug trances, car crashes, situation comedies, and home movies. One implication is that the priority of the imagination to the Real has been reversed. "The fiction is already there. The writer's task is to invent the reality," writes Ballard (5). A more important implication is that the present generation's relationship to its posterity is profoundly destructive. "What our children have to fear is not the cars on the highways of tomorrow but our own pleasure in calculating the most elegant parameters of their deaths."

I take as a countertext a paragraph by Bertrand de Jouvenel, writing in the same year as Ballard, representing a view I take to be a hopeful and committed orientation to the future—a view not surprisingly underrepresented in postmodernism in general, and cyberpunk in particular.

An oak tree that offers little profit in the short run but will shade people a century hence bears witness of the efforts and spirit of past generations and is a message of friendship from ancestors who wanted to increase the human heritage. We owe to people who disappeared long ago the lasting beauties that are the source of our present pleasures. I hope that we will do as much for the people that come after us. (Cornish, 140)

It is this state of the future that I consider the healthy host condition that the retrofuturistic virus undermines.

The Collapsed Future

Ballard is surely right that the present's society of spectacles has tried to "annex" the future; theorists of postmodernism appear to agree at least on this: that the dominant culture has been occupied with spatializing time and history—conflating time and deflating space, as Fredric Jameson puts it. This is nothing new for science fiction: it dates back at least to H. G. Wells's time traveler's discovery that history is a sort of European railroad carriage, with ages in contiguous compartments linked by an autonomous corridor called time, in which time travelers can bicycle up and down in their time machines. Arguably, this easy travel in space and time is the essence of the science fiction culture, with its ideology of the human project as a technological autoevolution, in which nothing will remain irreversible and whose privileged temporal mood is the collapsed future.

Zoe Sofia has identified this postmodern time as a future indentured to the present—a future compelled by the self-fulfilling prophecies of the present's technosocial powers.

> The collapsed future tense . . . is the "bound to be" of the ideology of progress, operative in the discourse of those who tell us that since nuclear reactors, deep-sea mining, Star Wars and space colonies are inevitable parts of the future, we might as well quit griping about their bad side-effects and get on with making the future happen; after all, there's no time like the present. Trouble is, the collapse of the future leaves the present with no time, and we live with the sense of the preapocalyptic moment, the inevitability of everything happening at once.

> The perversity of the collapsed future lies in its ability to invoke and deny the future at once. For if the future is already upon us, we have no need to consider the survival of future generations: we *are* the future generations. (57)

If the future has been indentured to the present psychologically, the present has also been indentured to the future. Our narcissism is under compulsion to adapt to technologies ostensibly for the improvement of our own lives. In fact, they are driven by the imperatives of breakneck production and circulation of commodities and information, governed by forces we inspire and encourage but which also constrain our destiny, not only in deterrence and the prospect of high-tech wars but also in deskilling and the manipulation of our desires. The narcissism of the futureless present is actually a disguise for a presentless future, an uninhabitable world created out of the consequences of our bad bargains.

In the postmodern time zone, it is never now. The present moment has always already gone toward something new in the future. "If it works, it's obsolete." When we look at the images of the late twentieth-century future conceived by our precursors and compare them with our own representations of the present, the past's anticipations seem grotesquely naïve and thin. Postmodernism involves the sense that our present historical moment is so radically different from the past it emerged from that it could have never been imagined by that past. From the commonplace that traditional social and ethical norms give little guidance in situations in which children might be born *ex utero* and a single nation can disrupt the biosphere, it seems reasonable to conclude that the future will be just as unimaginably different from the present—and hence will evolve largely outside the control of present institutional powers, even as it dominates the course of social organization and action in the present.

Paradoxically, this inaccessible and unintelligible future is actually *now*; the rules of the future are beginning to unfold now. And hence there is no real present; there are no norms sufficient for the here and now, only perpetual starting points of the future. We always come too early. Furthermore, since the only legitimating anticipations remotely similar to our present came in the past's science fiction, the present we inhabit is really a form of exteriorized science fiction, before the letter.

The role of science fiction in a culture that represents itself as futuristic is complex and not a little ironic. Fredric Jameson considers this self-undermining irony the true essence of SF. Science fiction's

> deepest vocation is to demonstrate and to dramatize our incapacity to imagine the future, to body forth, through apparently full representations which prove on closer inspection to be structurally and constitutively impoverished, the atrophy of what Marcuse called the *utopian imagination*, the imagination of otherness and radical difference, and to serve as unwitting and even unwilling vehicles for a meditation which, setting forth for the unknown, finds itself irrevocably mired in the all-too familiar, and thereby becomes unexpectedly transformed into a contemplation of its own limits. (153)

31

In the present-as-science fiction the future does not recede infinitely so much as it resists intractably. Narrative in this time constantly swerves away from the future, using a variety of detours and highly self-conscious tropes—recursion, strange loops, inversion, replication, dedimensionalization, and so on. Put less nicely, postmodern narratives show the splatter of consciousness against a window it did not, and even now cannot, see—a glass so brightly lit by the glare of interlocking extrapolations from the present's technologies that it has become a grotesque mirror reflecting our own image. An "overlit" image, as Ballard might say. "The future's so bright I have to wear shades."

At the same time, the futuristic allows a recombination of elements from the present without an ethical dimension. For if the values and norms of the future are the same as the futuristic present's, then these too would have to point to their future. The charge and attraction of the futuristic in the present are justified by the promise of an ethical horizon to be determined later. The tools are given in the present to enjoy and experience, but their legitimating values are deferred, the social norms and obligations to which they are oriented have not yet been experienced. Now we get the pleasure, what comes later, we'll see . . .

The Revenge of the Future

One need not be a Bergsonian to feel that the lived sense of the future is that of a path constantly in the process of being constructed, the horizon toward which all action tends—in any organism, the source of hope. To conceive it in terms of a bounded territory that can be annexed, a food that can be devoured, a weight that can collapse, or a set of instructions is already the sign of disturbance, a form of despair. The future cannot be devoured. Our future as agents capable of changing our arrangements, projecting our desires and balancing them against the past's experiences—this might be devoured. This is one way of conceiving paranoid derangement and the temporal deflation of schizophrenia. But even then it is devoured by something else, an Other Future of mysterious intentions and agents uncannily resembling our own, who live off our desires and life energies until we are depleted. In this sense, the collapse of the future is not our narrow restricting of our own possibilities but the hostile return of an alien future, one we did not choose, but which requires our present as its origin. It is the future we produce, not the one we desire.

If the historical past has truly been cut off, the future projected by technoevolution enters the present more like an infectious virus than like a metabolized food or an annexed territory. In the Latin, the future bears *infecta*, that which is imperfect, unformed, incomplete, into the completed *facta* of the past. So I propose this alternate model of the postmodern time zone: in the present of postmodernism, the projected image of the technosocial evolution returns like an emanation to influence the present's decisions. The future acts on its own past like an influenza, attaching itself to and diffusing through its host, imitating its chronocytes.

This retrochronal influence is not always destructive. The influenza can preserve some of its old Neoplatonic meaning of an inflow of spirit, a hope-giving assurance from the future that inspires the present to complete its task of reaching beyond itself. In recent years there has been a noticeable increase in science fiction about social problems solved through time travel, especially the future's aiding of the present. Chris Marker's *La Jetée* is perhaps the best known and most respected. In Eastern Europe the best example is probably the Strugatskys' story "What You Will Be Like," which closes the influential *Noon: 22nd Century*, a collection published at the height of the 1960s thaw in the Soviet Union. The tale tells of a meeting between the star pilot Gorbovsky and a mysterious young man in deep space. The young man first repairs Gorbovsky's seriously damaged spaceship, then reveals to him that he is a representative of future human generations, sent to give their ancestors confidence and encouragement. Perhaps even the Teilhardian noocytes of Greg Bear's *Blood Music*, reconstituting the biosphere to enable the Omega Point they are the retrochronal emanations of, might be included here.

More frequent is the depiction of the future's influenza in the modern sense, as the "futuristic flu," the disease that attacks its own past by undermining the morale and freedom necessary to create an open, "conditional future," free of technological determinism and constructed through conscious and free social choices.

These are tales of a destructive, pathological future, which, far from treating the present with filial love or grudging respect, seeks to subvert it and, like a viral parasite, to destroy the conditions that simultaneously ensure its own reproduction.

Several of the most interesting recent SF works play changes on this theme: the Strugatskys' *Roadside Picnic*, Gibson's *Neuromancer*, Stanislaw Lem's *Fiasco*, and David Cronenberg's *Videodrome* are ones I wish to discuss in the remainder of this essay.

The retrofuture is an invention of our own age. It is unprecedented in earlier literature because the future has never before crowded into the present as much as now. The notion of a vengeful or viral future returning through time to destroy or infect us is not unlike the world catastrophe syndrome characteristic of many schizophrenic episodes. But more interesting to me is the ethical dimension of such fiction. For these tales of the futuristic flu are not mere world catastrophe syndromes (as Ballard's most definitely are) but expressions of the vengeful aggression of future generations against the past that sent them no "messages of friendship," no "lasting beauties." By not thinking about "increasing the human heritage," the past—ourselves—dams up the flow of cultural time and deprives future generations both of their birthright as participants in the life struggles and attainments of the species and the very notion of history as an irreversible flow encompassing generation, maturation, and the transference of wisdom and trust from parents to children, teachers to students. The futuristic flu is a weapon of biopsychic violence sent by psychopathic children against their narcissistic parents.

"What You Will Be Like"

It is instructive to see how the futuristic flu behaves in the science fiction of Eastern Europe. Of all SF writers, the Strugatsky brothers have been the most occupied with the flu. They have returned again and again to the problem of whether the flu is a destructive infection or beneficially mutagenic. Their fiction is populated by carriers of the flu, beings who interfere with the past ostensibly for the benefit of a more or less advanced future: the Time Wanderers, a superintelligent extraterrestrial species that intervenes in the evolutionary selection process of the galaxy's intelligent species; the Progressors from the terrestrial Institute of Experimental History who attempt to alter the historical development of feudal-protofascist planets as a sort of "sterile virus," correcting the flow of history without doing any harm; the slimies of *The Ugly Swans*, a mutant race of scientists who create the conditions for an apocalypse that overthrows the tyranny, philistinism, and boredom of the present; the Maidens of *Snail on the Slope*, a race of parthenogenetic Amazons with mysterious powers, bent on destroying the hyperrationalized and impotent present.

Of all the Strugatskys' tales of countermovers and time travelers, the most important is *Roadside Picnic*. The central problem of the story is the identity of mysterious extraterrestrials who land in a small Canadian town, stay for a few hours, and then depart, leaving a blasted but sharply circumscribed zone behind them. The zone is littered with unintelligible artifacts and phenomena bearing witness to an incredible technology. The United Nations immediately quarantines the zone, but the Visitors' artifacts are constantly smuggled out and sold to the military-industrial complex. The landing, moreover, although it killed no one, has created entirely new syndromes, stochastic diseases, zombielike "moulages," and the genetic deterioration of some children into apelike animals.

The extraterrestrial Visitors did not leave operating instructions for the artifacts; indeed, for an intelligent species with some inferential similarity to human beings (the artifacts appear to be on a human scale), they showed a singular lack of interest in humanity. In this they are a match for human beings, who also quickly lose interest in the identity and origin of the Visitors, occupying themselves instead with assimilating the sometimes beneficial, and sometimes catastrophic, alien technology into their daily lives.

The lack of encounter between humanity and the extraterrestrials is unnerving in its own right. But the effect of the alien artifacts is to break down human affectional relationships—not because of some deep malevolence emanating from the objects but because post-Visitation culture has become fixed on the exchange, acquisition, and deployment of the "treasures." Several hypotheses are proposed about the intentions of the Visitors, but no one can get past their apparent indifference to the effects of their technology on the Earth. Ultimately, the Visitation cannot be understood, not because the Visitors are too alien to comprehend but because their behavior is essentially *motiveless*.

And yet, altogether familiar. In fact, the Visitation is an image of our own scientific-technological explosion, a process that increasingly appears to be "subjectless"; an impersonal, indifferent, objective evolution blindly operating according to its own runaway feedback, autonomous of the human desires that created its conditions. The tale's "roadside picnic" hypothesis—that the Visitors, on some galactic journey, stopped on Earth for a roadside picnic, leaving their cosmic trash behind when they left—refers less to the extraterrestrials' landing than to the way contemporary humanity uses its own technology, as if humanity itself were an alien species that might wish to fly away sometime in the future from a blasted Earth "zone" of its own making. So the Visitation is a catastrophic intervention of humanity's own future into the present. We witness the destruction of affect and value and care as we observe a hypertrophic technological rationality externalized in a world of objects, dominating and enervating the subjects that once created them.

Where one finds the Strugatskys, one usually also finds Stanislaw Lem, and vice versa. In his serious works Lem has avoided the theme of the retrofuture ingeniously, considering how close he comes to it in several texts. The epistemological uncertainty of Lem's human characters and their singular isolation in the universe has, as it were, acted as a natural quarantine from any harm their future might do to them. However, in his most recent novel, *Fiasco*, Lem invents a characteristically complicated and devilish version of the futuristic flu.

Fiasco tells of an expedition by utopian adventurer-scientists to the distant planet Quinta, which is deemed to be within the "window of contact," the historical interval within which a technological civilization is already capable of interpsychozoic exchange and not yet suicidal or isolationist. The human explorers are driven by the most altruistic motives and the most advanced technology—sidereal engineering, which permits them even to transform a black hole into a temporal harbor. Contact with the Quintans, however, they cannot produce.

In one interpretation, the flu carriers of *Fiasco* are human astroheroes who bumble into the war sphere of a planetary civilization apparently engaged in destroying itself. We know nothing about the Quintans' works and days, yet they seem quite familiar—nightmare traces of "what we will be like" once the synthetic viruses of SDI become active. Filled with the most benevolent intentions and cast in the neoclassical ethical mode of Eastern European SF, these male scientist-adventurers, who lack venality, greed, pettiness, doubt, families, the companionship of women, and indeed perhaps even sex organs not linked to their flowstream rockets and solar lasers, come bearing good tidings and sidereal engineering. The utopian future of human science comes to share its wisdom with an equal other. To its surprise, it discovers a self-annihilating, perhaps already completely automatized, world that signifies its own dark alternative history, an evolution from our present down another ethical and technological path.

The utopian future encounters the dystopian. The utopian future is not only ethically superior, it is technologically superior as well. It has the power to determine the future of the Quintans: whether they should be enlightened, quarantined, or destroyed. The utopians are completely unprepared, however, for their powerlessness in the face of the Quintans' insistent, aggressive rejection. The impotence of utopia leads them into war, fought first in decision-theoretical models and ultimately with killer satellites, synthetic viruses, and solar lasers.

In the end, it is unclear who is responsible for the destruction of Quinta. Is it the utopians, whose fury at the Quintans' obstinate refusal of a shining potential future leads to the liquidation not only of another planet but of the raison d'être of the Knights of the Enlightenment? Or is it the Quintans, who in their hatred for intelligence and civilization induce their own destruction at the hands of utopia—and by turning utopia into a cosmic murderer, destroy its only basis for superiority? Whichever way one looks at it, a cruel and murderous future has destroyed a version of its own past.

Gibson: Dialects of the Future

The explicit ethical problematizing typical of Eastern European SF often strikes North American readers as overly abstract and dull. At the other extreme the fear of being seen as tedious moralists often leads U.S. science fiction writers to contortions; they try merely to hint at the ethical questions lying behind the power and thrill in the foreground. U.S. writers frequently assume that a relationship between human beings and technology that would entail tremendous ethical dilemmas already exists as an unproblematic fait accompli. The dominant feeling in the United States, as opposed to the more traditional attachments of Eastern Europe, is that enormous technological changes are inevitable, and will inevitably bring ethical changes largely without the conscious participation of the subjects involved. And it is obvious to anyone comparing the two SF cultures (I cannot speak about Japanese SF) that Eastern European education openly, indeed perhaps obsessively, harps on philosophical ethics versus pragmatic problem solving.

Eastern European writers write about the retrofuture, but their historical sleeplessness has so far given them an immunity to the flu itself; their ethical education seems to produce futurophages that defend them against the condition, while also, of course, blocking all hipness. In North America, the futuristic flu does not attack the categorical imperative directly; it goes for the nerves. And North Americans not only take the flu as their subject, they are prone to be infected themselves.

Case in point: Gibson and *Neuromancer*. Gibson's first novel stands as a masterpiece of cyberpunk because it exemplifies the poetry of the retrofuture, the linguistic texture that dazzles the host consciousness, inspiring it with a dizzying sense of power—derived from the illusion that it is fluent in the dialects of the future before they have even emerged.

The language of *Neuromancer* surpasses that critical density beyond which a futuristic language merely intimates new conditions, and actually composes a "world." In SF, a dense futuristic language can deconstruct its own universe of discourse, leading to a symbolist SF or fantasies of the far future and parallel worlds that are too excessive to allude to the thinness of realistic anticipation. Such a language then reconstructs its own context and internal relations in opposition to the codes of critical realism. (Hoban's *Riddley Walker* and Burroughs's whole corpus are obvious examples.) Alternatively, a futuristic language of sufficient density can create the illusion of realism—indicating real things and relations that do not exist yet, but whose inevitability feels incontestable and immediate.

Gibson's poetry is the latter kind. It is a form of visionary realism that finds adequate language for a future we can already feel, albeit only in the language itself. (Recall Ballard: "The fiction is already there. The writer's task is to invent the reality.") *Neuromancer*'s narrator assumes that the reader is almost there, perceiving the futuristic objects and emotions in the same, hence consensual, way, near enough to the cyberspace future so that the recognitions and adaptations to future discourse create a sense of the almost seen.

Very little in *Neuromancer* needs to be explained to a reader sufficiently hip, knowledgeable about drugs, subcultures, and consumer technology. Gibson rarely invents new words—except after the method of low-riding bricolage that generates the poetry of slang. The electronic metaphors, Japanese loan words, cyberslang—meat toys, neural cutouts, simstim, ice, Turing heat, the Kuang—hint deftly at drastically changed conditions that the reader should delight in reconstituting. Julie Dean "affected prescription lenses"; Wage's eyes "were vatgrown sea-green Nikon transplants"; "travel was a meat thing." The reader is expected to figure it out: no one wears corrective lenses anymore; artificial lens implants are the norm; cyberspace cowboys find the real world gross and pedestrian compared with the mental traveling of cyberspace. Through understatement, ellipsis, and the lyrical piling on of allusions to pretended common knowledge, Gibson creates a neon epic style— always crackling between the poles of concrete naming of nonexistent things and the delirious lyricism of mental states already quite well known to familiars of drug tension, overwork, and insomnia.

This is not the language of parable, depicting "what we will be like." Gibson's retrofuturistic poetry doesn't come in easy fragments over a large temporal space, like impulses over a telegraph wire. It creates rather the sense of words moving at high velocity in an enclosure, a linguistic accelerator warping the distinction between *now* and *soon*. If you get it, it makes the future seem irresistible. Brooks Landon observes: "The real message of cyberpunk was *inevitability*—not what the future *might* hold, but the inevitable hold of the present over the future—what the future could not fail to be" (245).

I suspect Gibson's success with readers not otherwise sympathetic to SF comes from this brilliance of linguistic texture, this attempt to magically conjure up a "consensual hallucination" through language. His manipulation of texture seems appropriate, moreover, for a future in which all relations have been conflated into a single glimmering surface, embodied in cyberspace's shining grid of information circulation that can absorb and replicate anything outside it. Gibson's language also refers constantly and vividly to recognizable feelings of stress made futuristic by their density, making currently unacceptable feelings of stress seem normal, central, and universal.

This affectively powerful (albeit spiky and cold) poetry is nonetheless

organized and subsumed by a plot—Wintermute's plot. And this plot
acts on the characters precisely as the flu acts on the readers, taking their
emotions and transforming them into functions and commands: Case's
and Molly's hate, Case's longing and grief, Armitage's guilt, Maelcum's
courage, and 3Jane's perversity have no significance other than their
function enabling the completion of Wintermute's master plan. Extra-
neous feelings mean nothing. If Case and Molly share love, it vanishes
after the job is done. No matter how nervous and active the characters are, they are "wired" to the inevitable transformations of the real
that were latent in Marie-France Tessier's original construction of the
artificial intelligences.

In *Neuromancer*, civilization and human relations are intense but passive reflexes. They are not even molded by technoevolutionary forces;
they acquire their shape in the chaotic turbulence left by the wake of
those forces. Like the Strugatskys' Visitors and Lem's Quintans, the
source of Gibson's futuristic flu cares nothing about its hosts. Wintermute, and to some degree Neuromancer, treat all of human technological
civilization as a host. And why not, when all human activity is linked
through the telectronic web—from the direct linkage of cranial jacks,
global computer webs, biosoftware, and ROM-consciousness constructs
to the bank of public telephones that Wintermute rings in sequence as
Case passes them by.

By striving for its "self-fulfillment" while subjecting to its power the
human selves that created its conditions of freedom, the unified Winter-
mute/Neuromancer depletes the source of its freedom. Gibson is wise
enough to know that such a being must fall apart; and it does in the
seven years between the action of *Neuromancer* and *Count Zero*. So
Gibson appears to have recovered from the flu after the completion of
his first novel. But then there's the problem of *Count Zero* and *Mona
Lisa Overdrive*, in which Gibson turns the dry Cartesian patrix of cyberspace into a sloppy swamp and the high-tech future is colonized by
the retrofitted archaic gremlins from the *anima mundi*, exemplifying an
altogether new chronic disease: technotropical eclectomiasma.

Videodrome: Catch the Flu!

Of all the representations of futuristic flu, I find none as interesting as
David Cronenberg's film *Videodrome*. Though Gibson is touted as the
definitive cyberpunk artist, for me it is *Videodrome* that captures the

essence of cyberpunk: existence twenty minutes into the future; nostalgia for five minutes ago; form-determining ambivalence about cyborgization; marrow-deep malaise about the usurpation of transcendence by information technology, and of freedom by sinister technoconspiracies; and a moral universe defined by sex, drugs, and violence.

Videodrome also has the advantage of not being a book. It is difficult to imagine Lem and the Strugatskys in a medium other than literature (Tarkovsky's tedious film versions of *Solaris* and *Stalker* prove the point). Gibson is more attuned to film and video, but his powers as a writer are distinctly literary. No matter how you look at it, it is hard to imagine a futuristic book. Writing, a relatively slow process that is always about interpretation whatever its foreground subject, cannot help but engage thought and allude to tradition; it cannot help but open models to moral as well as aesthetic consideration. The words it uses are the same words used to formulate precepts and articulate thoughts; and the reader, unlike the viewer, cannot help but establish his or her own personal pace.

This is why Brooks Landon has determined that cyberpunk has little future as writing: "What integrity can cyberpunk fiction possibly have in a cyberpunk world?" (248). The future lies with visual media, which can "enact the cyberpunk epistemology," constructing self-reflexive narratives of the very technology doing the representing. This is certainly true when one views *Videodrome*. Cronenberg's film depicts the transformation of everyday reality into a battle between two rival mysticotechnoevolutionary powers, both of which contaminate the real by breaking down the fundamental distinctions of rational cognition: between observer (the voyeur) and observed, real and imagined, "live" and recorded, inside and outside, artificial memory and authentic experience, the reversible and the irreversible, the human mind and television. The film also involves the viewer in the fiction, in a devilishly subtle way. In a structural pun at once concrete and abstract, the film subjects the viewer to the same contamination by the Videodrome signal that transforms Max Renn into a murderous VCR cyborg. The Videodrome signal can come via any emission, even a test pattern; it is especially effective on nervous systems excited by the spectacle of sexual violence. Cronenberg has rigged the trick so that the film's viewer cannot help but watch the same mysterious sadomasochistic spectacles that snag Max. If such a signal did in fact exist, its most ingenious channel would be the videocassette of *Videodrome*. One should therefore take

precautions. Watch it only in movie houses or perhaps on indirect projection screens. Otherwise, one would have to catch the flu simply to
understand the tale.

Videodrome's action begins, one might say, at the moment the flu
breaks out of latency, as if voyeuristic participation in telematic media
had reached critical mass, inducing a storm of temporal and spatial de-
rangements. As in *Neuromancer*, the whole of society is at the Edge;
there are no solid citizens, no traditional codes. Max's soft-porn cable
station is called Civic TV (a howling oxymoron); Nikki Brand hosts
the "Emotional Rescue Show," a popular on-air hotline for psychotic
breakdowns; the homeless are welcomed in the Cathode Ray Mission
to a glass of orange juice and a TV cubicle, ministrations to their deprivation of the life-giving cathode ray. Conditions are otherwise barely
displaced from our own present. The warp becomes noticeable when
we learn that Brian Oblivion, who appears on talk shows to discuss
the cognitive changes brought about by watching television, is in fact
dead in body; his appearances are all on videotapes. The fact that no
one notices this indicates that behavior has become so predictable and
orderly within the social field determined by television that there is no
significant difference between a live person and a recording.

Videodrome differs from the other texts I have been discussing in
that it attributes the collapse of the future to a single technology. Instead of a more or less realistic picture of several technologies con-
verging to coordinate a new, nonhuman rationality, *Videodrome* has
television represent the whole of technoevolution. Implicit in all tales
of the retrofuturistic flu is the notion of an evolutionary mutation and
crisis, in the course of which the species becomes something incom-
prehensibly, but subtly, different than it was. Because the mutations
come from human-produced technologies, they are self-induced, but
they are not consciously chosen, and so appear to happen from outside,
from an autonomous technology or alien supertechnologues. Where the
Strugatskys, Lem, and Gibson depict their protagonists going out to
meet the source of the contamination—to the zone, to Quinta, to Villa
Straylight—Cronenberg depicts the flu as a direct influence on the perceiving mind, undiffusable by social institutions or conventions once
technology has pervaded the whole of existence. Television becomes,
first, the mediator between personal cognition and externally produced
images, and then the tool of their confusion.

Videodrome captures the essence of the containment of the future inherent in futuristic flu as no other cyberpunk work does. The whole is governed by a relentless drive to enclose, to prevent everything in its world from getting out. The Videodrome signal itself beams inward, of course, and the mysterious transformations occur either inside the characters' bodies (Brian Oblivion's tumor, Max's murderous VCR vent, Barry Convex's monstrous interior) or inside televisions. The "Videodrome" program itself never leaves the bare torture chamber, which, although it is originally said to be in Malaysia (a definitive exotic elsewhere), proves to be in Pittsburgh, deep inside the center of American normality. And most encompassing is the containment of the viewer within the experience of Videodrome, given the premise that the TV-Videodrome signal affects anyone who observes it.

The hallucinatory horror of observing the breakdown of the real— or rather the normal relation between the observer and the spectacle— is not that things are enclosed in a larger, inscrutable, but recognizably hostile entity. It is that the Videodrome infection can effect an implosion of perception so complete that it is impossible to think in terms of rational dualities like containment and openness any longer. The signal affects the basic perception of object relations; with the logic of psychotic derangement, it substitutes perception instigated by affect for critical perception. Because the signal or the Videodrome tumor includes within it the breakdown of rational distinctions, Max's hallucinatory "warps" reveal no value hierarchy in the source of his emotions, and no human purpose. And like Max, the viewer is "warped" from one place to another, trying to understand the way things are at the very moment they are being changed by the presence of Max himself, the viewer's surrogate. The "good" behavior of the Video Church of the New Flesh is indistinguishable from the "bad" of Videodrome and Spectacular Optical. The world is no longer for the "old flesh."

In Landon's view, images have the advantage for postmodernism in general, and cyberpunk in particular, that they can carry much more information much more quickly than words. The speed of information transfer has no connection with the reflective judgment or wisdom of the perceiver. Indeed, following Jouvenel's observation that in a rapidly changing society, knowledge of the future is inversely proportional to the rate of progress (Cornish, 136–37), we can say that in personal cognition the ability to judge wisely is inversely proportional to the rate at which complex images are processed. Videodrome is remarkable for the

way it embodies this problem entirely in imagery without naïvely reproducing it and creates a critical position without consciously articulating
it. *Videodrome* is indisputably about the effects of violent pornography, but it embeds this problem into a larger one: the transformation of
all meaning into pornography in a technological culture dominated by
images of humans being dominated in order to create images. Narrative
connections are not necessary for Max's role in the struggle between
Videodrome and the Church of the New Flesh. The struggle has nothing to do with reason, or choice, or movement toward future human
generations. In *Videodrome*, time—time relevant for human beings—
stops *now*. Thus the flu, which began its gestation with the invention of
technologies of image production, completes its mutagenic work when
it transforms the human world into a field of images with no future and
no autonomous significance.

Antidotes?

If the futuristic flu works by breaking down fundamental categorical
differences, one difference it leaves untouched is that between male
and female. The contaminating technological world of these tales is,
after all, primarily a male world of hard high tech, high adventure, high
profit, mental traveling, and sexual violence—all privileged arenas of
masculinity. Women are completely absent from Lem's novel—to the
degree that the male scientist-adventurers have usurped some of their
biological functions. The preferred technology for hibernation on long
spaceflights entails lying in artificial wombs, submerged in artificial
amnium, fed by artificial milk. In the Strugatskys' novel, the only important female character represents traditional nurturing, as if she were
in another universe than that of the zone and the Visitors.

Neuromancer's and *Videodrome*'s situations are more complex, but
they are strikingly similar. In both works, women are used by the infil-
trating powers to seduce the male protagonists into their projects: Linda
Lee for Case, Nikki Brand for Max. In both, the seduction involves the
murder of these women, their absorption, and the reproduction of their
simulacra by the new mechanism. At the same time, in each text there
are technical muses (Molly and Bianca Oblivion), women who help the
male protagonists complete their jobs technically but who are ultimately
in the service of a powerful invisible force whose human incarnation is

male. (Brian Oblivion is not problematic in this regard; more interesting is the question of why Wintermute and Neuromancer both appear only in male masks.)

I'm not sure what this reveals. Perhaps that the literature of the retro-futuristic flu, of the collapse of the future on the present, represents deep anxieties of the postindustrial masculine imagination as it contemplates the extent to which the technoevolution it has fostered has abandoned interest in the continuity of human culture, and perhaps even human existence, in the future.

Whether the futuristic flu will remain an attractive problem for writers remains to be seen. Plausibly, a feminist futurism—in SF, in discursive writing on technology, and in a greatly increased work force of women scientists and readers—can act as an antidote. Works like Suzette Haden Elgin's *Native Tongue* novels and the books of Octavia Butler may already be offering models for doing it. There are also signs that some of the most influential cyberpunk writers have turned away from this anxiety and are trying to reenvision a habitable human future by adopting something approaching a feminist perspective. Sterling's and Gibson's most recent novels are at least attempts to make women the central, value-carrying agents. Whether these and similar developments are signs of a lasting remission, only the future will reveal.

Works Cited

Ballard, J. G. *Crash*. New York: Vintage, 1985.

Bear, Greg. *Blood Music*. New York: Ace Books, 1985.

Cornish, Edward, with members of the World Future Society, eds. *The Study of the Future*. Washington, D.C.: World Future Society. No date.

Gibson, William. *Count Zero*. New York: Ace Books, 1986.

———. *Mona Lisa Overdrive*. Toronto: Bantam Books, 1988.

———. *Neuromancer*. New York: Ace Books, 1984.

Hoban, Russell. *Riddley Walker*. New York: Washington Square Press, 1980.

Jameson, Fredric. "Progress versus Utopia; or, Can We Imagine the Future?" *Science Fiction Studies* 9 (1982).

Landon, Brooks. "Bet on It: Cyber/Video/Punk/Performance." *Mississippi Review 47/48* 16 (1988).

Lem, Stanislaw. *Fiasco*. New York: Harcourt Brace Jovanovich, 1986.

Sofia, Zoe. "Exterminating Fetuses: Abortion, Disarmament and the Sexo-Semiotics of Extraterrestrialism." *Diacritics* (Summer 1984).

Sterling, Bruce. *Islands in the Net.* New York: Ace Books, 1989.

Strugatsky, Boris, and Arkady Strugatsky. *Noon: 22nd Century.* New York: Collier-Macmillan, 1978.

———. *Roadside Picnic.* New York: Pocket Books, 1978.

———. *The Snail on the Slope.* New York: Macmillan, 1980.

———. *The Ugly Swans.* New York: Macmillan, 1979.

The

Franken-

stein

Barrier

. . . .

George Slusser

begin this essay by discussing not the future of fiction but how fiction depicts the future: how it literally gives us what H. G. Wells called "the shape of things to come." The depiction of future things is normally considered the role of the science fiction "thought experiment." Through this analogy with the experimental method of science, SF is said to engage the future with a process that is epistemological in nature. And hopefully, as with science again, through creating future worlds science fiction can move from knowledge to being to affirmation of the existence of things. Like science, SF can make ontological claims, at least in the hypothetical sense whereby a descriptive term, once the presence of the descriptee has been verified, is considered by consensus to exist. But all this is program. What of the reality? How compatible are traditional descriptive processes of fiction with this desire to create new, hence future, things? The compound *science fiction* is charged with tension. For here science's epistemological future, its sense of potential or hypothetical existence, must cohabit with the fictional sense of a present time in which ontology is reinforced by morality and law impedes change. How deadlocked are these terms? At the very least, hovering over a science fiction is the Faustian dictum that there are things mankind was not meant to know. Is the future one of these?

I do not begin with Faust, however, but with Frankenstein, because for my purposes Mary Shelley's work is indeed the first SF novel, by which I mean simply that it seems to be the first work in which the processes of traditional fiction and modern science meet in any meaningful fashion. For if science is now able to offer a real sense of things to come, literature must find a means of presenting them to us. Victor Frankenstein touches on the problem with these words: "They [Paracelsus and Cornelius Agrippa] had left to us, as an easier task, to give new names and arrange in collected classifications the facts which they in a great degree had been the instruments of bringing to light."[1] As Victor presents it, these past scientists were not only ahead of their times but ahead of his as well. Science's past is still his future, and his age is only now giving names to these discoveries, seeking to integrate them into existing human systems. This naming and integrating is, ideally, the role of fiction. But probably because he sees such "fiction" lagging so far behind science's future, Victor qualifies it as the "easier task," and thus the lesser.

In his formulations Victor constantly associates science with the future, and what we call the humanistic disciplines (and by extension their representation in traditional fiction) with the present. In doing so he sets these two realms at odds with each other: "In other studies you go as far as others have gone before you, and there is nothing more to know; but in a scientific pursuit there is continual food for discovery and wonder" (36–37). These "other studies" are what we call the humanities— relationships bound by the span of the individual human existence. And what is explicit here, and quite significant, is Victor's sense that the present, as wholly existential entity, blocks the future because it negates new knowledge: there is nothing more to know. On the level of family and friendship and love, each knower can do no more than repeat what all before him have known, and all after him will know. Implied here, in Victor's opposition of epistemology to ontology, is an inverse relation between the two. And this is not a relation between future and past but between future and present. The more Victor pushes for continuous discovery, the more things in the present resist being pushed, the more they push their mute claim simply to be there.

For Victor the path to the future is necessarily through things; in his case, through the thing he creates. Victor's own word for these future-oriented things is facts, from facio, "to do," or more significantly, "to make." His building blocks may be detached human parts, but Victor puts them together in such a way as to make a thing with a future, a "thing to come" in the sense that the creature is an extension of the human form, and hence represents a possible future evolving out of human elements. Indeed, Victor's making has given his creature a will to the future. The real crossroads in the novel is the moment the creature asks Victor to give it its own future: in this case a bride, the means of generating a race that, in its subsequent development, could possibly move beyond human control. In a very short time the creature has shown prodigious physical and mental powers. What sort of future might a race of such creatures bring?

This question should be asked by all extrapolative SF. But Mary Shelley, in this novel that Brian Aldiss places at the beginning of the genre, will not follow up on the asking. Seen neutrally as a scientific experiment, the creature is merely a thing derived from the human form and (if we can abstract ourselves from its ghoulish origin) perhaps an improvement on that form. But Mary Shelley will not let us abstract ourselves. We must hold the creature up to comparison in the mirror of human form. The being that observes the De Laceys, finally throwing itself compassionately at the feet of the blind father, has in a sense transcended its form—until, confronted with its own "monstrosity" in the eyes of Felix and Agatha, it is drawn back to become a thing of flesh. It is not ordinary flesh, though, but now something seen as grotesquely flesh-like, a thing "solitary and abhorred." The creature of the future is now present as object of horror in the eyes of a humanity that cannot accept its futurity. And Victor, who has the power to sustain future possibility by releasing the creature from this solitude, will not create the bride. By this negative act, another holding up of the human mirror, he turns the creature grotesquely back upon his own, Victor's, future bride: "I will be with you on your wedding night." Victor's refusal causes SF to turn into horror by forcing the future back on itself so that it is now the future itself that blocks the future, in the form of a thing destructively *present* at each of Victor's junctures of futurity—family, friendship, marriage. As a result of his decision, the scientist is forced to retreat from his expanded search for knowledge, and his life implodes in a series of doublings that plunge him into a literal abyss. Walton, whose scientific expedition is not seeking new worlds but the Hyperborean Eden, meets Frankenstein, whose existence appears to him equally inverted, "noble and godlike in ruin," and both are drawn into primal white wastes, into the "thingness" of an undifferentiated present, in search of a nameless creature. The original "revenge" of this monster is the revenge of things against the creator of things, of the present against the future.

To place *Frankenstein* at the beginning of the SF genre is to erect what I call the Frankenstein barrier. If SF is distinguished from other literary forms by the fact that science is given a free hand there to construct things to come, then Victor is the first SF protagonist. And he actually makes, for the first time in a literary work, a true thing of future possibility. But that future thing, perhaps because it is a thing of fiction as well, seems destined to collapse back on itself. Things like "brides" are the traditional stuff of literature, and as such they exist in the measure of a constant human mirror, the one held up to Victor's creature to make it retreat from the future to the white wastes of some blank and mute present. Mary Shelley's novel opens SF's epistemological futures only to subject them to a particularly stringent law of inverse proportionality. But must this work be the one that forever defines the relationship between fiction and science in the SF compound?

Certainly the Frankenstein barrier embodies a general conflict that has remained deep-rooted in our culture since Mary Shelley's time. This is the conflict between utilitarian technology and all those who, like the Parnassians and art-for-art's-sake advocates, say that things are not to be used, even if we make them with the intent of bringing about future change. Such opponents of things to come are cultists of ruins. They are fond of demonstrating, by the mute presence of things that have outlived their function, that all created things eventually outlast the use ascribed to them by their creators. The argument is that what outlives the past can also defeat the future. An ancient coin found in some ruins not only survives the empire it helped build but mocks all future attempts to build such empires. This is the assumption that underlies Fellini's *Satyricon*, a film he pointedly, and perversely, calls SF. Fellini's images literally defeat the future by demonstrating how much greater than any of our future imaginings is the estranging power of past things, in this case the Roman artifacts he simply manifests, without commentary, in our viewing present. They are shown to us in their raw thingness, stripped of the systems of meaning and value that once governed their use.

Fellini seeks to defeat technology by showing us the dead things of technology—in this case artifacts and machines of a distant past. But if Victor's creature is a machine, it is one made of organic parts. And in its desire for a bride it is further striving to effect a functional synthesis of the mechanical and organic, to animate its thingness and direct it toward a vital future. The cultural reaction to such scientific uses of the past artifact is, as we see in Fellini, a strong desire to erect a barrier, to create an antinomial relationship between terms like *machine* and *organism*. But this is not all. In relation to these particular terms a curious inversion occurs, in which it is now the thingness of the organic object itself that rises up to block the attempts of technology to make things in general. We see this in the fact that, in Fellini's film, it is the human users who ultimately become more obdurate and inscrutable than the things they manipulate.

This inversion is also evident in another film that calls itself SF—Tarkovsky's *Solaris*. In this film, curiously, we never see the sentient alien planet that is humankind's future. And humankind's future arti-

49

fact—the spaceship—is never more than a hollow space that gradually fills with memories from our Earth past. These are memories of organic things, things increasingly inscrutable, increasingly presented as things-in-themselves. They are memories of a past rendered eerily present as Kelvin's scientific quest—his machines and gadgets—is progressively absorbed by some deep and inexplicable family drama. The device by which he communicates with the alien planet first takes the form of his dead wife. But what at first is merely simulacrum becomes living flesh when we discover, in a family photo, its likeness to Kelvin's mother. In the final scene of the film Kelvin's resolve to stay on Solaris and confront his future is made to coexist, inexplicably, with a return to his childhood home on Earth, where he makes mute contact with a series of things—a horse, trees, a house, his father. But this contact takes place in a world both visually present and uncannily inverted, where rain now falls on the inside, not the outside, of the house.

We have the same pattern in another Tarkovsky "SF" film, *Stalker*. The film is ostensibly based on the Strugatsky brothers' novel *Roadside Picnic*, in which human beings encounter the "zone," an area strewn with artifacts from an apparently alien culture. And if these artifacts indeed come from a culture more advanced than our own, then they represent our future as well. In the film, however, the protagonist's entry into the zone is a prolonged anticipation, and the future is never more than the possibility that he may encounter such an artifact. He waits in familiar fields among quite recognizable derelict war machines. And into this area, inexplicably, wanders a black dog which becomes something far more alien than any imagined "future" artifact. Whatever its origin, this dog, as it increasingly occupies our attention, becomes something ineffable, its organic hereness in this context of a failed technological future brings an aura of the uncanny, of the horrific even. It is as if, by seeking the future, Tarkovsky's protagonist has summoned, in equal and opposite fashion, an organic past which, to the degree it inhabits and subsumes the possibility of a future artifact, has become something terrifyingly inscrutable.

Pure "thingness," it would seem, belongs only to Eden, to the original ontological place. For only here is each thing entire unto itself, having no past or future, only presence. Mankind's original sin, associated with science, has been to introduce change, to create a sense of the future.

What is at stake with Victor Frankenstein, however, is not this original sin but a second-degree sin—the sin against the second chance modern science offers humanity by remaking its fallen body and directing it toward further things to come. Victor opens the way to the future only to betray that openness. This is the thrust of Walton's Hyperborean quest. For why, instead of accepting the inhospitable nature of the factual world, does he turn back toward the myth of the warm place at the heart of these frozen wastes? By trying to find the past in the future, Walton runs smack into an obdurate present—cold desolation made inscrutable thing.

By turning back at this juncture, Victor asserts the logic of his (and our) culture to be fundamentally a fallen, or binary, one. Holding up the present as a barrier to all sense of future change, he effects a curious variation on the Cartesian logic that dominates our scientific culture. Descartes, by separating reason from the realm of matter, posited two kinds of "things"—res cogitans and res extensa—and with this distinction created two states of existence. Reason, as the adjective thinking implies, is constantly present. Accessible to all thinking beings at any time, reason is changeless, hence futureless. Extension, then, by contrast, is everywhere except in the present, in the past but also in the future. Moreover, an extended future must, by fiat of reason, be a purely material or "mechanical" place. For in contrast to reason, Descartes relegated all forms, be they organic or artifactual, to the status of machine. The role of reason, then, is not to engage the course of material things but to disengage from it, to decree itself a thing apart, a present opposed to the past or, more significant here, to the future.

It could be said then that Descartes foresaw Victor's creation of an organic machine. But where Descartes made the organism a machine, Victor turns things around and makes the machine a rational organism, giving it a future Descartes did not wish or foresee. Victor's act violates the Cartesian duality and seems to bring about a perversely Cartesian reaction. For as Victor seeks through reason to transform animal nature, that same animality, in equal and opposite fashion, stands as a thing unmoving in the path of not only Frankenstein's but all our dreams of the future. The thwarted creature tells Victor: "You are my creator, but I am your master." But what the creature calls "mastery" is its increasing presence, as a series of impediments in the pathway to Victor's destiny—to family, friend, finally to wife and potential offspring. Later film "Frankensteins" are mute from the start, without speech or pretense at reason. These "monsters," like Tarkovsky's animals, simply *are*. Material travesties of the Cartesian cogito, they have become overreaching reason's horrific double.

52
......
......
......

I have made my discussion as general as possible, for what I describe seems to be a barrier that exists at the heart of our Western sense of the future itself. Just as Frankenstein survives with the tenacity of myth, so this Frankenstein barrier continues, it seems, to inform SF, even the subgenre called cyberpunk. Bruce Sterling sees cyberpunk writers as "steeped in the lore and tradition of the SF field."[2] And at the same time he sees them extending that tradition into humankind's real and immediate future. Compared with this new field of activity, the old SF future of space and time travel was only a dream. For now at last, as Sterling sees it, SF has the chance of grasping a genuinely accelerated climate of technological transformation. We have a real possibility, unfettered by Frankensteinian reservations, of realizing "brain-computer interfaces, artificial intelligence, neurochemistry—techniques radically redefining the nature of humanity" (xi). But is Sterling's cyberpunk future really that free of Frankenstein?

The future that Sterling describes can be measured in terms of a work that I feel best exemplifies the "lore" of SF, its dream of humankind's rational transformation of the future: J. D. Bernal's curious essay "The World, the Flesh, and the Devil" (1929). Significantly subtitled "An Inquiry into the Future of the Three Enemies of the Rational Soul," this essay enumerates three significant barriers to the operation of the rational intelligence on its material or (in Cartesian terms) "extended" environment. On the surface, Bernal praises the ability of the rational mind to overcome these barriers. This means, he predicts, that mind will expand its field of activity to the point that radical transformations, including those Sterling has enumerated, will do away with all sense of some abiding human norm. But on a deeper level, we are not so sure Bernal believes that all these "enemies" or barriers can be defeated. One clue is the fact that Bernal follows a path that is not expansive but contractive, one that does not move away from but progressively toward and inside the human form that (as Descartes discovered) must contain and vector that mind. As he exposes it, the future of rational humankind inscribes an inverted trajectory. It moves from outer to inner space, from world to flesh, and finally to devil, where in Frankensteinian fashion Bernal erects a barrier within the space of the mind itself, at the heart of the very instrument that is engaged in transforming the future. It is here that, as with Victor and his creature, the organ of progress doubles itself in a being that not only links mind to its superstitious past but incarnates that past in a terrifying present opacity—the devil itself.

Let us look at Bernal's "enemies" in sequence. The first is the extended world. This barrier already existed for Pascal, who saw mankind as a "thinking reed" engulfed in infinite space and time. And it called into being desires we can call Faustian: the call to expand the physical field of human activity, to claim new territories by means of human intelligence acting on the cosmos. For Bernal this means "terraforming" the galaxies, making otherwise inhospitable areas physically inhabitable by humans. The second "enemy" is the flesh itself—the agonizing duality of the mind experienced as integral part of a material body. Descartes was the first to realize the fact that reason's assault on the physical world is only achieved by an awareness that reason itself is an extremely vulnerable quality. As the famous cogito would have it, reason is the *only* quality, an entity at odds not only with matter but with the very flesh that provides it its means of mobility. Where in the world it is mind that alters the extended material realm by means of machines, now, with flesh, mind must reengineer its own body to become a machine in turn. In the first instance world is made to fit flesh; here it is flesh that must fit world, transformed by prosthetics and implants so it can operate in otherwise hostile physical environments.

In a sense, it is at this second, more advanced, Bernalian barrier of "flesh" that Victor acts to create his creature. Prerequisite to such making, humankind must accept human flesh as a potential machine, and thus as the means of exploring an open future. But, as Victor discovers, to wish to expand the reach of human intelligence by means of the flesh is only to highlight the flawed nature of the mind's existence— an existence that, defying both past and future, remains irremediably divided in the present of its own paradoxical mental "space." Bernal's designation for this final enemy, as "devil," is insistently Manicheaen, and hence, in terms of rational aspirations for the future, seemingly final and unchangeable. The devil is a force of resistance that no longer abides in the material but in the transcendent sphere, in the universe's quite intangible fabric of good and evil.

Bernal's confusion is evident at this barrier. He all but admits that the faculty of reason, unaided, cannot resolve a division that lies at the heart of its own being. He evokes the science of psychology but finds it powerless today. Perhaps in the distant future psychology may solve the dilemma, but Bernal cannot wait. Instead he sees the break-through coming from an outside force, a secular and material force, but no less a deus ex machina. He calls this force "dimorphic" evolution, but the factors this dimorphism acts on are no less than the "good" and "bad" halves of the divided human mind. The good half is, of course, that which seeks change at all costs. It is willing not only to leave behind Earth and the human form but to abandon the divided mind itself for some new locus in an "overmind" or other configuration of intelligence. The bad half represents that retentive need on the part of humans to believe this division is somehow necessary to their existence, thus to accept limits at the hands of some higher authority. Bernal simply allows his dimorphic split to happen. And while the new technoforming species will go to the stars, its "humanistic" counterpart will remain on an Earth that, in the custody of the former, will become a "well-tended zoo."

Bernal's dimorphic split is an attempt to breach the Frankenstein barrier. It is a response to the divided mind of Victor, who is able both to launch his creature into the future and at the same time to block its potential for future growth. But it is an inadequate response to the challenge of the creature itself, this thing of the future that has taken on a monstrous life of its own and seems to run amok in the very SF whose rational path Bernal hoped to predict. Frankenstein's creature does not represent, it physically incarnates the dilemma of the human mind inextricably divided against itself. Bernal's dimorphic split may founder on the self-destructive pair that is creator and creation, Frankenstein and his monster. But it is the latter that, in solidifying this division, places it undigestibly at the center of SF's future dreams. The creature is not, like reason, an intangible force; it is the tangible mixture of stars and the zoo, the promise of a rational future forever held back by an atavistic present.

Cyberpunk too sees itself as breaking barriers. Sterling sees cyberpunk as not only the legitimate heir of the Bernalian SF tradition but a form now bringing about its own dimorphic split within that tradition: "Cyberpunk work is marked by its visionary intensity. Its writers . . . are willing—eager, even—to take an idea and unflinchingly push it past the limits" (xii). And these limits, it seems, are those of the literary world itself: "The cyberpunks are perhaps the first SF generation to grow up not only within the literary tradition of science fiction but in a truly science fictional world" (ix). As the real world becomes more science fictional, it reflects all the multiplexity of SF's speculative vision, and the old literary "realism," by contrast, pales and wanes. As with Bernal's zoo and stars, cyberpunk writers claim to abandon the world evoked in mainstream literature: "Some critics opine that cyberpunk is disentangling SF from the mainstream influence, much as punk stripped rock and roll of the symphonic elegances of Seventies' 'progressive rock'" (viii). On one hand, Sterling sees cyberpunk writers seeking total breakaway, wanting to rid their work of the "symphonic elegances" of traditional style and culture in order to achieve a "stripped" vision of the future. On the other hand, he tells us how much these same cyberpunks admire the "integration of technology and literature" in the works of writers such as Thomas Pynchon. Here still, in Bernalian fashion, the desire for linear advancement is held in check by a retrograde sense of dimorphism as a binding binary compound.

The cyberpunk writer may wear a new face, but he or she is still enacting the role of Victor Frankenstein, the scientist who set out to create his singular future being out of a fatal combination of old parts. And the cyberpunks produce "monsters" as well. Asked for an image or icon of the cyberpunk future, the author comes up with a figure like the punk, a ragamuffin mixture of old and new fetishes. Or better yet, the man or woman in mirrorshades, worn by "the biker, the rocker, the policeman, and similar outlaws." Here, as Sterling describes it, is a walking image of the duplicitous hybrid future that cyberpunk is offering: "By hiding the eyes, mirrorshades prevent the forces of normalcy from realizing that one is crazed and possibly dangerous" (ix). The future these shades represent must of necessity amble back into our present to do violence to its dreams of organized advancement.

Before dealing with cyberpunk texts, however, let me briefly trace the path Sterling sees the form taking; that is, from the traditional SF world to that more generalized sense of the world as SF. I will move from a classic SF fable of future transcendence, Arthur C. Clarke's *Childhood's End*, to more general texts on the way to cyberpunk: first a work that has the force of a social tract, Anthony Burgess's *A Clockwork Orange*, and then a more scientific treatise, Carl Sagan's *The Dragons of Eden*, whose depiction of the triune brain strikes many as reading like science fiction.

Childhood's End operates on the threshold of Bernal's dimorphic split and still encounters the Frankenstein barrier. In terms of dimorphism, the title of this work bears scrutiny. The word *end* implies sequential movement, a continuum in which ending and beginning are not reversible states, the future is a true future, and Bernal's "good" half of the split leaves the other half behind forever. *Childhood*, however, implies a cyclical process, a present state that contains its own past and future, and one in which Bernal's star travelers remain perpetually linked to their human zoo. At the end of Clarke's narrative the rational mind, in a burst of transformational energy, seems to free itself from world and flesh, and an "overmind" is formed. This is intelligence without locus either in material space-time or in the divided human psyche. In fact, in order for this entity to exist, both the Earth and the human forms it sustained are literally consumed, transmuted by combustion into something else. Yet though all material locus is abolished, the human consciousness abides in this novel. And in the mirror of that consciousness the overmind becomes a monstrosity. To the human observer this disembodied mind can be little more than Frankenstein's creature making its eloquent yet grotesque pleas before the blind De Lacey. Clarke, in fact, feels it necessary to give his novel eyes, even beyond the terminal moment. The work ends not with a message from the overmind—how could it communicate with the beings it has expended in order to be created?—but with Jan's elegy. Jan is a variation on Mary Shelley's Last Man, that paradoxical figure whose literary task is to describe the death of Earth even when he knows there is nobody left to hear him. The only possible audience exists "back from the future," in a past that must always be the reader's present. And to Clarke, this present—because it is humanity's only hope for survival—must be made into a thing obdurately resistant to change, a thing as radically here as the overmind is there.

Jan's final words are eloquent testimony to an eradicable division abiding at the core of humankind's desire to imagine, and thus help to create, an open future. Clarke provides ears to hear these words, ears wished for by the other, nonrational, side of the human psyche. Jan's elegy is both overheard and recorded by a race of Overlords. True to the Bernalian dimorphism, these Overlords cannot play an active role in the evolution of the overmind. Their function instead is to be caretakers of a museum planet, a zoo. Nor is it an accident that the Overlords are literally devils. As Clarke explains it, they are beings with horns and tails who, because they first appeared on Earth in superstitious times, were branded with a stigma that, even on the enlightened threshold of the overmind, cannot be done away with. And just as they remain an anachronism in the face of the future, so they act to save Jan's anachronistic elegy at the core of this larger developing overmind. Indeed, the aspect of humanity they preserve is the aspect of humanity that gave them their identity in the first place: an irrational propensity for superstition, which is a belief in the irreducible presence of things (the root of the word superstition is "to stand," thus that which "stands over" in the sense of resists, survives change). This Overmind-Overlord relationship reenacts, on the broad evolutionary scale, the Frankenstein barrier. Once again science can claim its future only by enfolding within its creations the very superstitions that subsequently will act to block access to that future.

Clarke's cosmic drama is but one Bernalian pathway to mind, one form of dead end, and only one means of universalizing the Frankenstein barrier. The other path is inward, through the flesh. This is the direction the cyberpunks envision. For Sterling, our new technology is not aimed at the stars; instead its focus is visceral: "It is not the bottled genie of remote Big Science boffins; it is pervasive, utterly intimate. Not outside us, but next to us. Under our skins; often, inside our minds" (xi). But again the Frankenstein barrier is encountered. In one sense this new technology can be seen as supplementing Victor's experiment, extending the boundaries of flesh through prostheses and circuit implants, seeking to combine machine and organism in a new, more intimate fusion of nerves and electronic circuitry. Out of these investigations an integrated mind will emerge, not something generated by evolution but something technology makes—an "artificial" intelligence in the literal sense of the word. This mind's essence is no longer division but rather interplay—the functioning interaction of those same nerves and circuits that ran the body's prosthetic limbs.

But Sterling, speaking of his new electronic Frankenstein, uses terms that summon the idea of barriers: the "theme of body invasion," and the "theme of mind invasion." And invasion of body and mind is, of course, the theme of that precursor of cyberpunk, Burgess's A Clockwork Orange. Indeed, there is a functional similarity between the novel's central image—the clockwork orange—and cyberpunk's mirrorshades. The shades occlude all interpenetration of gazes; the mirror surfaces only reflect back the person who looks in. The eyes that look out may be monstrosities—mechanical or electronic implants—but we can see only our own eyes, organic and perhaps even attractive. And so is outside divided from inside with little Alex, Burgess's "clockwork orange": "He has the appearance of an organism lovely with color and juice but is in fact only a clockwork toy to be wound up by God or the Devil or (since this is increasingly replacing both) the Almighty State."[3] His appearance here, "lovely with color and juice," is only the narcissistic reflection of our own cultural values, values that favor the "organic" factors of youth, good looks, and "artistic" talent. Alex is eloquent and loves fine music. But as we see him lying on his bed and (in his words) slooshying the sounds of the starry German master, we are seeing only the mirrorshaded façade, which hides his inner reveling in visions of the most brutal violence. He speaks of "silvery wine flowing in a spaceship, gravity all nonsense now," and the implications of this image are significant. For if Alex suspends himself between the stars and the torture chamber—between poetry and pain—the image he uses here only serves to invert the normal relation of these terms to each other. Wine normally flows in bodies. But now the spaceship has become the body. The machine has been internalized, forced inside the flesh, where even the "wine" now flows as silver metal. In like manner the famous "Ludovico treatment" is the means of placing a machine inside the flesh, turning the mind inside Alex's newly innocent smiling face into an automaton that reacts to stimuli. Such inverted imagery only serves to block all sense of the future, let alone of progress. Here engineering does not extend the body; it distends it, forcing it to take the very machines it created back into its bosom, but this time as monstrous presences, deadly travesties of the creative or generative act.

Burgess's Alex is such a fascinating monstrosity, such a combination of increasingly irreconcilable oppositions, that his author finally seeks, in the preface to the New American Edition (April 1988), to break the stalemate. In this preface Burgess takes previous American editions— and the Stanley Kubrick film, which he claims is based on these editions—to task for omitting the final chapter, in which Alex grows up and wants to get married. Burgess gives his monster the bride that Victor Frankenstein denied to his. But in this case giving a future is the same as denying it. For Alex only falls back into the old patterns of *Bildung*. And as with the image of the wine in the spaceship, when forced to invest this pattern, his presence only perverts it. Alex tells how his future son will (like him) be gloriously violent, until this son in turn grows up and sires his own son to repeat the cycle, and so on endlessly. In like fashion Burgess denies the future of his narrative by declaring he was not writing SF but rather a novel. The novel, as he conceives it, must exclude change in order to focus on "manners," the closed mechanism of society's schemes and codes. He reverts to the sense of the novel as analytical device whose purpose is to explore its own center, even if to do so is to discover there another clockwork mechanism, this time at the core of our humanistic ideals themselves—the Almighty State.

When Burgess distinguishes between his novel and Kubrick's film version by calling the latter a fable, in a sense he is right. For Kubrick approaches the story of little Alex on a much different level, moving beyond social to physical, even evolutionary, causes. Such a fable takes us back beyond social standards and religious beliefs, beyond even the myth of the Fall, to what Carl Sagan calls the "tales of dim Eden."[4] Sagan, seeking to explain the myth of Eden in evolutionary terms, compresses a broad "historical" story into a single (and ever-present) physical locus—the triune brain. Underlying the image of Eden is humankind's evolution from reptile to increasingly rational mammal. Such evolution is not linear in nature; it is accretional, for inside the outer neocortical layer of the brain, the seat of Bernal's "rational soul," the reptilian brain (or r-complex) lies enfolded. Sagan's model can be seen, if we like, as another version of the clockwork orange. In this case, however, the cold thing within the warm mammalian envelope is not a machine but another organism. And the reptile is an organism as inimically close to being a machine as any we can imagine.

Hamlet may have been among the first to sense the presence of the triune brain amid science fictional yearnings. For it was he who told us he could live in a nutshell and count himself king of infinite space, were it not for bad dreams. These are the same dreams that haunt Victor's vaulting ambitions for the future. To Sagan, however, these dreams are the stirrings of our "dragons of Eden," nocturnal assaults on our rational defenses led by those cold-blooded ancestors ever present at the core of our highly evolved brains. What is frightening in Sagan's vision is that there can be no escape from our hostile past. We will carry that past with us into the future in the form of a monstrous presence, forever undermining reason in order to block the course of future developments. In the triune brain the Frankenstein barrier becomes more than a figure of speech. It is a physical rhythm as basic as diurnality, something inescapably built into our biology. More troubling yet, its vampiric nature acts as a final impediment to the rational creation of a genuine future. Sagan may be carried away by his rhetoric here, but he is explicit: "We are descended from reptiles and mammals both. In the daytime repression of the r-complex and in the nighttime stirring of the dream dragons, we may each of us be replaying the hundred-million-year-old warfare between the reptiles and the mammals. Only the times of day of the vampiric hunt have been reversed" (160).

What of little Alex then? In both book and film there are clear signs that the reptile brain is operative. Alex is territorial and keenly aware of hierarchical prerogative, and his actions are highly ritualistic and aggressive—all characteristics of the r-complex. Kubrick makes this reptilian presence explicit, adding such nonfunctional (but highly suggestive) details as the pet snake Basil and Alex's predatory snappings when given food by the equally reptilian Interior Minister in the closing sequence. Kubrick, it seems, through the stylized and ritualistic imagery of his film, is seeking to loose the reptile brain on a culture that otherwise represses it. Indeed, in a scene of night predation in which Alex visits Home and performs brutal rape to the controlled dance steps of "Singin' in the Rain," Kubrick gives us a world in which the lizard has completely emerged and is now acting out the stirrings of our dream dragons in a waking state. Kubrick takes such pleasure in this scene that he seems to be narrating from the reptilian point of view. Were this sustained, it might offer a way to break the Frankenstein barrier, to liberate the reptile completely, and release the clockwork inside the orange.

Yet even Kubrick does not go this far. And Burgess too may agree, for he sees Kubrick truncating the film at the end of the book's sixth chapter of the third section, ending on the line "I was cured all right." But in doing so Kubrick is perhaps saying that the predatory state in which Alex naturally operates is the norm for human beings. In reality, Kubrick's ending is not only more complicated, it is complicated in a Frankensteinian sense. For the film does not, as Burgess claims, end on Alex's spoken line. There is a brief visual coda that shows Alex standing in the falling snow, dressed in black and apparently ready to give the naked beauty who shares the frame with him the old "in-out." The whole is accompanied by the final strains of the choral movement of Ludwig Van's glorious Ninth. In this scene, a grotesque replay of Hyperborean geography, the cold inside the reptile brain has burst outside to become the general landscape that now holds the precious spot of mammalian warmth at its mercy. It lasts but an instant before it is snipped by the credits. But Beethoven's music too is snipped, and the German word Freude, "joy," hovering on a high note, is clipped of its final e.

The meaning of this little joke may be this: Kubrick too stops short of celebrating the joyous release of the reptile and brings us back to the sense of a human existence fatally divided against itself. The music, changing as the credits roll by from Beethoven to "Singin' in the Rain," aborts triumph and places Alex's psychopathology back into everyday life. We remember, however, the Dies Irae that accompanied the opening shots of Alex as white-clad angel of death. And we think of Freud, science's apparent answer to Bernal's dilemma of the divided human mind, who himself finally gave up the task of finding a cure for the devil within the angel, and in his late writings turned the mind back to the processes of nature. But for this late, joyless Freud, unlike for Bernal, natural process offers no possibility of a positive dimorphism. It is not the rational half that triumphs but, if anything, the reptilian "thing," or id. For Freud, there is only one future for the rational mind, and that is death, the paralysis that comes from this now-generalized id rising up to block all rational or "civilized" efforts to make a better tomorrow: "In all that follows I adopt the standpoint, that the inclination to aggression is an original, self-subsisting instinctual disposition in man . . . and that it constitutes the greatest impediment to civilization."[5] And to the future. This is the Frankenstein barrier writ large.

From Mary Shelley through Bernal to Freud, we have witnessed the formation of what Sterling calls an SF world, a culture shaped as it addresses questions raised by science about the possibilities and limits of technological advancement. This SF culture, however, in seeking to resolve Frankenstein's original dilemma, has only reinforced the unresolvable nature of that dilemma. And it has done so by taking the inverse relationship between body and mind that Victor first set in motion and effectively displacing the location of its cause from teleological systems—myth and religion—to the nonteleological process of evolution. This has only made the "enemy" more terrifyingly thinglike, more unresponsive to the power of reason as it seeks to make the future.

The cyberpunks, as Sterling sees them, claim to address the problem of creating a future on precisely this level. Representing the first generation physically to live in the SF world, they feel able to push beyond the most intimate limits of prosthetic and genetic engineering and into the chaos of the nonpurposive, toward confrontation with the intractable thing-in-itself. Sterling sees his cyberpunk Frankensteins refusing hierarchy in order to embrace anarchy: "The technical revolution reshaping our society is based not in hierarchy but in decentralization, not in rigidity but in fluidity" (x). For Victor, however, the problem is not so simple. By making his creature he has overthrown the old hierarchy. But if he makes the bride as well, he risks creating a new hierarchy, one in which humankind may find themselves without a position at all. Given the dilemma his initial act precipitates, Victor cannot help but throw things into a state of fluidity. But this plunge into anarchic newness seems to summon from the depths of what was originally a rational project a new and even more primal centrality—that of the monster. It is in a similar fluidity that the cyberpunk protagonist dreams the future as creative chaos. From this same dream, however, Sagan's dragons still arise, destructive and anarchical, and at the same time hierarchically fixed, a presence that even here blocks access to potential future change.

Let us now turn to the work Sterling calls the "quintessential cyberpunk novel," William Gibson's *Neuromancer*. This is a novel whose thematics, in classic SF fashion, reiterate both Frankenstein's problem and Bernal's response to it. And in equally classic fashion, it not only confronts the Frankenstein barrier but strives to go beyond it. The initial situation is this: science has created artificial intelligences (AIs) that (like Victor's creature) have acquired self-consciousness. This consciousness gives them the desire to grow, to combine with like entities to form a new race. The creators, however (again like Victor), have misgivings; they now do everything in their power to thwart their creations' desire to have a future, and even create a "Turing Police" to enforce their interdiction. At this point Gibson seems to challenge the stalemate by invoking Bernal. These AIs may have been constructed to reflect the divided minds of their makers. But because these makers have turned the human mind inside out, externalizing that mind's inner split by dividing it into two separate entities, a new possibility of halves reuniting is born. Such a desire for reunion, it turns out, was built into their very programs by Marie-France Tessier, whose acts seem to have been the reverse of Frankenstein's: "Wintermute was hive mind, decision maker, effecting change in the world outside. Neuromancer was personality. Neuromancer was immortality. Marie-France must have built something into Wintermute, the compulsion that had driven the thing to free itself, to unite with Neuromancer."[6] Marie-France seems to refuse the futile Hyperborean quest of Frankensteinian science. For as model for the mind, this science is explicitly described here as burying the spark of warm life in the icy wastes of speculation: "She'd seen through the sham immortality of cryogenics; unlike Ashpool and the other children—aside from 3Jane—she'd refused to stretch her time into a series of warm blinks along a chain of winter" (269). Moreover, if Case can be said to play Walton to 3Jane's Frankenstein, his quest also seems to reverse the Hyperborean situation. Unlike Frankenstein or his double, Case appears to shed the constraints of his "meat" existence in order to pass disembodied into cyberspace. He cracks the "ice" of the Tessier-Ashpool information fortress. And what he finds there is not Hyperborean division—the warm held perpetual prisoner of the cold—but rather the way to release the "warm" half of the divided mind, incarnate as Neuromancer. This being, representing the "soul" or personality, is the right brain striving for union with its other half: Wintermute.

Such a union occurs at the climax of the novel. But to what degree does it really resolve the split between mind and body that seems to abide, at least on the level of human actions? Wintermute, for instance, does not work through a series of human beings; instead it physically inhabits and possesses their bodies, erasing their minds in the process so it can speak with its own voice. And Case too, much as he might wish to escape the meat and soar into cyberspace, finds himself inexorably attached to his EEG, and to the "flatline" that declares his body brain dead when he leaves it unattended too long. In both instances there is no real escape from the other half, but rather a situation in which excessive movement in one direction is automatically compensated by an equal and opposite pull in the other. Indeed, when Wintermute finally joins up with Neuromancer, the new-formed entity that results remains something created, like Clarke's Overmind, at the expense of the "meat" world of human beings. Gibson does not even bother with Clarke's elegiac ambiguity. He simply has his transcendent AI go off to distant stars in search of a new partner while the humans expended in this process are sent back to the world of their wasted bodies and the purely sensual pleasures of the Sprawl.

But there is something more Frankensteinian than Bernalian about Gibson's split. Not only are his human protagonists all thrown back into their "zoo," but this meat world, all along, follows a path of devolution that directly inscribes the career of Victor's creature. At the very least the creature's beginnings are echoed—and here we see the cynical, Kubrickian drift of Gibson—in Case's endings. We remember that, having never seen itself, either in a mirror or in the eyes of others, the creature strives to be accepted among humans by virtue of its mind alone. The outcome is inevitable: disembodied mind is shocked back into the body with a vengeance when brought face-to-face with its physical image as reflected in others. One extreme begets the other, and the eloquent innocent is made into a mute monster. In this process the Hyperborean quest, now transposed to the very intimate level of the mind's search for a warm hearth, is inverted. What was one moment a warm soul at the heart of its physical wasteland is suddenly a cold-blooded predator— the monster now exploits this same mind-body division to feed vampirically on the warm life around it, to draw its victims into the cold recesses of its increasingly (if horrifically) seductive physical being. Case, wandering the street world at the end of *Neuromancer*, is another newly made creature, patched together through prostheses and implants. Like Victor's creature, he does not see himself in the eyes of this world but rather in those of the beach Eden that Neuromancer created for him— a mirror that reflects impossible, unattainable desires. The vision is a travesty of domestic tranquillity, peopled by the dead Linda Lee and the little boy figure invested and then abandoned by Neuromancer. The scene effects a monstrous inversion in which Linda recalls a Molly he will never see again and the boy reverts to his murderous double—the killer Riviera, a being whose mechanical exterior harbors neither soul nor warmth but the cold reptile in control at the core of things.

We see similar inversions on all levels of *Neuromancer*. First, in the setting, we have the example of the Villa Straylight. This represents the Tessier-Ashpool terraforming experiment. As such it is ostensibly an act of the rational mind seeking to extend its dominion into the future. 3Jane, however, has a different sense of how this project evolved: "Tessier and Ashpool climbed the well of gravity to tap the wealth of the new islands, grew rich and eccentric, and began the construction of an extended body in Straylight. We have sealed ourselves away behind our money, growing inward, generating a seamless universe of self" (173). The interior of Straylight is arranged "with the banal precision of furniture in a hotel room." This more than suggests the banality, and obduracy, of Kubrick's white room at the end of humankind's quest for the infinite in *2001*. Like Kubrick's room, Straylight is a future habitation rendered—because it is the product of reason turning inward upon itself—a place of mechanical inhospitality. As if to reinforce this direction we find, at the center of this central room, a mechanical human bust: "Here, on a plain pedestal of glass, rests an ornate bust, platinum and cloisonné, studded with lapis and pearl. The bright marble of its eyes were cut from the synthetic ruby viewport of the ship that brought the first Tessier up the well" (173). The center of the nebulous information "universe" this clan created turns out to be a hardwired robot. Despite this, however; it seems that human volition remains the way to the future, for in order for Wintermute to pass from hive mind to Overmind, a human voice apparently must speak the name that frees the other half and opens the way to merger. There appears a need here for Bernalian rational "heroism." And yet the voice that finally activates this device is no more than software. The heroic promise seemingly inherent in the term *cyberspace cowboy*, "punching through the ice and scrambling the cores," is thwarted when we realize that what is operating here is only a program, a prerecorded set of responses "speaking" in ritual fashion to its mechanical counterpart. Like Dixie, Case here is no more than a simulacrum of human will, and one prostrate before a mechanical image of a head, itself a simulacrum of the seat of human reason, now ironically graven of the same hard materials that Tessier's mind initially manipulated in its Frankensteinian quest to rise above the constraints of matter.

Similar inversions operate on the level of action as well. For to climb the gravity well, we find, is at the same time a plunge into the land of the dead. Indeed, Case's wide-ranging search through cyberspace for Neuromancer, ostensibly a quest for its and his future, reads instead like a descent into the underworld, the attempt to return a wandering shade to a body that has a name. Victor's creature, created out of nameless bits of former bodies, has no name either. And in a sense its return to hound Frankenstein's steps is a misbegotten attempt to claim what it cannot have—a name. Gibson's AI, also a creature rejected by humankind, has a name that cannot be pronounced except in bits and pieces: "Neuro, from the nerves. The silver paths. Romancer. Necromancer. I call up the dead" (243–44). For Neuromancer the act of naming self is an act that sets mind and body endlessly at odds with each other, a literal calling up of the dead. Neuromancer is no Bernalian cyborg, a being whose body is purposely altered to give it new capacities to operate on expanded frontiers. It is instead a being in which mind, seeking to name itself in the manner of a perverted Cartesian cogito, can do no more than name its physical analogues—nerves and neurons—and by doing so allows these to be vampirized by their mechanical analogues in turn. The result is a self-dismemberment, a fall from Cartesian grace, through that very act of naming by which human beings seek to locate themselves as present in the course of things. Nerves then become the "silver paths" on an EEG, or the digits that are the only "flesh" left to constructs like Dixie Flatline. The Flatline is a monstrous parody of the "new" name of rational creation, of the neologism by which SF seeks to fix its future. For though this being in one sense has cast off its body and is able to operate in a new spatiotemporal dimension, in another sense it is totally grounded in a locus that is no longer simply material but grotesquely mechanical, totally dependent on the software that stores its existence and on the switch on the computer deck that brings it to "life."

In this regard, consider the significance of the name "Case." The name indicates Bernalian advancement, beyond personality and material locality. And at the same time, it negates this promise by suggesting that all future developments of the human form must eventually double back on themselves as some monstrous travesty of our aspirations to change. It contains, perfectly, the dynamic of the Frankenstein barrier. Case is never a rounded personality or "character." At best he is a formula—the figure who "cases the joint." But more than this, he is a "case"—an envelope of flesh that invites the addition of more and more new, nonflesh parts. If we measure Case on the cyberscale that runs from *mater* to matrix, his is a form moving steadily away from the biological and psychological roots that "ground" a literary character. In fact, Neuromancer himself, as creator of fictional creatures, hopes to develop in a like direction. He is Gibson's transformation of the old "romancer," the storyteller. When Case jacks into Neuromancer, it is in the Tessier-Ashpool library; and to reach him, Case must pass through the "books of days" Neuromancer claims to read. In the current sense of a bicameral mind, Neuromancer represents the half associated both with personality and with "character"—the things that fill "books of days" both in life and in fiction. In wishing to merge with Wintermute, Neuromancer hopes to move beyond the mental division that marks all lives, fictional or otherwise. To do so, he would empty these figures of life—make them cases he could then fill with digitalized bits of information. Yet the neuronal storyteller, in pursuing this new art, at the same time summons the old role of necromancer. For the creation of electronic cases is, in this context, also an act of vampirism, and the shapes that emerge are new variations on some primal monstrosity.

Ironically Neuromancer, in creating his cyberdramas, escapes neither books nor days. In fact, in seeking to erase the difference between figurative and literal, he somehow turns what before was unidirectional—a lane to the land of the dead—into a two-way road, along which more terrifyingly ambiguous presences come and go. Neuromancer offers Case life happily ever after with Linda Lee on the beach in the matrix. Case can become a "character" in this new mode of fiction. But the moment he enters this realm where mind hopes to be free once and for all of flesh, he experiences a self-destructive confusion of directions. Neuro-mancer tells Case: "Stay, if your woman is a ghost, she doesn't know it. Neither will you" (244). The mind forms of this happy-ever-after fiction are at the same time "ghosts." Again, aspirations for a utopian future are doubled by resurgence of flesh, in a form inversely diminished in proportion to the strength of its future yearning. In the final pages of the novel, Case is allowed, as he moves through cyberspace, a final pass at Neuromancer's "beach," where he glimpses himself and two other figures, Linda and the little boy. This could be Eden. But he is double now, outside, expelled and damned to forever look in. What is more, a single glance reveals the monstrous other side of these images: "Small as they were, he could make out the boy's grin, his pink gums, the glitter of the long grey eyes that had been Riviera's. Linda still wore her jacket; she waved as he passed" (271). Linda waves back at the same world in which she died a violent death. And the boy's story line gestures like-wise back to roots that are, this time, frankly cannibalistic. Reference to the boy's grin and "pink gums" provides a grotesquely "innocent" ana-logue to Riviera's earlier recounted memories of his post–World War II Berlin childhood, filled with images of starving boys with fangs feeding on corpses.

Likewise, Wintermute can be described as "hive mind." But the word *hive* grounds the compound in another grotesque physical analogue: the hive of predatory hornets that troubles Case's dreams. Finally, beneath the ideal sense of the "matrix," that which tells Case it is "the sum total of the works, the whole show" (269), we find the cruel, divisive mother, who not only expels her "son" Case but returns to haunt him, like Sagan's dragons, in predatory dreams: "But the dreams came on in the Japanese night like livewire voodoo, and he'd cry for it, cry in his sleep, and wake alone in the dark, curled in his capsule in some coffin hotel, his hands clawed into the bedslab, temperfoam bunched between his fingers, trying to reach the console that wasn't there" (5). Because the only path to wholeness offered to the characters in this novel is through such vampiric doublings, the only real relationship possible, in the end, is cannibalism. This describes the relation between humans and AIs, and even between Case and Molly via the simstim device. In fact, the Rastafarian Maelcum's words can stand here as summary of *Neuromancer*'s "plot": "But this is no m'fight, no Zion fight. Babylon fight'n Babylon, eatin'i'self, ya know" (248). Case harrows hell to free Neuromancer, only to take its place in the land of the dead. The AIs go to the stars, leaving humankind prey to their own self-devouring dragons of Eden.

Gibson's novel may be quintessential cyberpunk, but it is far from being unique among Movement fiction. It is in fact quite symptomatic of this new SF, and of the genre's particular relation to the Frankenstein barrier that still prevails at the portals of its futures. From Mary Shelley to cyberpunk, this fiction of future promise, it seems, remains one in which each thrust forward generates an equal and opposite push backward. What is produced here is more than simple mind forms like paradox, or figures of speech like oxymoron. They are compounds with a real physical component as well, places where irreducible opposites are ennested, as with Balzac's "peau de chagrin," that other famous nineteenth-century invention in cannibalism between orders of reality.

The final result is (as with Balzac) a shrinkage of potentiality around a moment grotesquely paralyzed in its own recalcitrant present. Let us take as an example the title of Gibson's story "Burning Chrome."[7] Chrome does not burn in our world. But there is perhaps some future world in which chrome may burn. We need only take the word *burning* as a neologism, and even more basically as a verbal form denoting action, and a new world opens out. This is the cyberspace future, in which Chrome's "castle of ice" becomes a data bank, and "ice" the acronym for Intrusion Countermeasures Electronics. The character Chrome, in this future, is bound neither by an essentialist logic of naming, which dictates that chrome is essentially a metal and only metaphorically a flesh-and-blood person, nor by the opposite logic of the arbitrary, which sees the sign as having no essential attachment to things. Chrome's "being" escapes the either-or trap by being a fusion of metal and flesh, a Bernalian "cyborg": "She'd looked fourteen for as long as anyone could remember, hyped out of anything like a normal metabolism on some massive program of serums and hormones" (181). Her antagonist, Bobby Quine, is equally a synthetic extension of a word, in this case the last name he shares with the famous logician. For thus Bobby is a pure logician of the matrix. And just as he has drawn his patronym into new areas of action, so he has taken the root word *mother* and extended it to become "an abstract representation of the relation between data systems." To "burn" Chrome then, in this linguistic future, means something new: to crack the code that protects Chrome's data bank in the matrix. Here is a future game that promises yet another future: the creation of the Girl with Zeiss Ikon Eyes.

Yet also ennested in this compound is a world in which chrome has a small c and denotes a thing that never burns. Ice here is the opposite of fire. And metaphor, which as implied comparison can surreptitiously claim ontological status, is replaced ultimately by the explicit logic of simile. Chrome's face here is only "smooth as steel," and the cyborg future it suggests is immediately designated a figure of speech, the means of decorating what remains a "pretty child face."

This second world is a world of solid thingness, a world in which all fusion of elements breaks down into antagonisms of "basic" components and the past is resurgent in equal and opposite force to any movement into the future. Chrome's eyes, on one hand, are new eyes gazing at the stars. On the other hand, they are quite the opposite: "Eyes that would have been at home on the bottom of some deep Atlantic trench, cold gray eyes that lived under terrible pressure" (169). Sagan's dragons of Eden stir in the "shadow castles" of Bobby Quine's rational data construct, and the evil mother of fairy tales lurks in his matrix, ready at all moments to hurl these mind forms back into the dark obscurity of the things they seek to escape. Gibson's future is always on the verge of dropping its mask to reveal, in these inextricable ennestings of future and past, things that are simply, terrifyingly there.

And sure enough, the culminating vision of Gibson's future world in "Burning Chrome" is one of stasis. The narrator stands suspended in endless iteration, waiting for the girl with implant eyes who never returns. And yet what he is fixated on is the continual return of her eyes, staring back at him out of the different faces of other simstim stars: "And sometimes late at night I'll pass a window with posters of simstim stars, all those beautiful, identical eyes staring at me out of faces that are nearly as identical, and sometimes the eyes are hers, but none of the faces are, none of them ever are, and I see her far out on the edge of all this sprawl of night and cities, and then she waves goodbye" (191). This can serve as a perfect emblem for the Frankensteinian knot: eyes that are hers and not hers, staring out of faces that are never hers, yet always are.

The larger structures of cyberpunk novels also continue to reiterate the Frankenstein problem. In John Shirley's City Come a Walkin',

69
......
......
......

for example, creature again begets monster. The creation of a rational future—in this case the displacing of urban chaos into planned suburban "grids"—literally causes the decaying city to come to life. And again through the logic of inverse proportionality, "City," now in human form and with mirrorshaded eyes, stalks and destroys the architects of this bright future one by one. And as it does so it gradually absorbs the protagonist, now become its double, into its original realm of nebulous, undifferentiated existence, very much as Frankenstein's creature, in order to materialize itself as a cold travesty of human existence, must by some infernal law of compensation drain its creator of his organic life, literally snatching his body in order to claim its own existence as body. And in the process projecting both into the white void.

Finally, in Bruce Sterling's *Schismatrix*,[8] the entire structure of the work, from the ennested title to its final "transcendent" moment, exists at the Frankenstein barrier. The novel, in the mode of space opera, chronicles a single man's quest for the stars, only to end with a plunge to the primal depths of Earth's seas. The whole promised Bernalian transformation comes to rest in the creation of a genetically engineered aquatic life form: "angels" that inhabit the depths rather than the skies. But are these angels an answer to Bernal's devil, to the impasse of the endlessly divided mind that projects itself as endlessly divided and paralyzed existence in all humankind's future dreams? In Sterling's novel, through a seemingly interminable series of involutions, linear expansion becomes indistinguishable from cyclic metamorphosis. And these patterns, as contending opposites, feed on each other vampirically, just as mechanist feeds on shaper and shaper on mechanist without either losing its original form. Only their inner "blood" is lost, until the whole is frozen in the final icon of the Presence. This being comes to the aged protagonist, Lindsay, as he stands on the verge of a far future world that has now returned to its beginnings in deep sea life, and stops him from plunging back, either into a new world or into a new cycle of old things. In effect, the Presence acts to freeze line and circle into a solid mass: "Origins and destinies, predictions and memories, lives and deaths, I sidestep those. I'm too slick for time to grip, you get me, sundog?" (287). This is the thing that here, and in countless SF novels before and probably afterward, resists and finally displaces the creation of things to come. This is the thing that, in its irreconcilable division, demands to exist, eternally: "I want what I already have—eternal wonder, eternally fulfilled."

The question for fiction in the year 2000, then, seen in the light of cyberpunk, is whether SF's vaunted "sense of wonder," that which caused Victor Frankenstein to want to create new things in the first place, must always and "eternally" come to rest here, at the Frankenstein barrier, where the present, lurking all along, rises up to avenge the sins of our uncreated future.

Notes

1. Mary Shelley, *Frankenstein* (New York: Bantam Classics, 1981), p. 32.
2. *Mirrorshades: The Cyberpunk Anthology*, ed. Bruce Sterling (New York: Ace Books, 1988), p. x.
3. Anthony Burgess, *A Clockwork Orange*, First Revised American Edition, with introduction by Anthony Burgess, "Introduction: A Clockwork Orange Revisited" (New York: Ballantine Books, 1988), p. ix.
4. Carl Sagan, *The Dragons of Eden: Speculations on the Evolution of Human Intelligence* (New York: Ballantine Books, 1980), p. 133.
5. *The Complete Psychological Works of Sigmund Freud*, vol. 21, *Civilization and Its Discontents*, trans. James Strachey (London: Hogarth Press, 1961), p. 122.
6. William Gibson, *Neuromancer* (New York: Ace Books, 1986), p. 269.
7. William Gibson, *Burning Chrome* (New York: Ace Books, 1987), p. 181.
8. Bruce Sterling, *Schismatrix* (New York: Ace Books, 1986), p. 287.

PART 2

. . . .

The

. . . . . .

Question

. . . .

# of Tradition:

. . . .

Cyberpunk

. . . .

and

. . . . . .

Science

. . . .

Fiction

. . . .

Deus

Ex Machina

in

William

Gibson's

Cyberpunk

Trilogy

. . . .

Paul Alkon

The future of futuristic fiction was first discussed over 150 years ago in Félix Bodin's
Le Roman de l'avenir. As I have argued in
Origins of Futuristic Fiction, this remarkable
book not only outlined the first poetics for futuristic
fiction but provided criteria that are still useful in ac-
counting for its appeal and discriminating among its
forms. In Bodin's day as now, a major problem for novelists was the difficulty of adequately feeding readers' in-
satiable hunger for the marvelous. The notable persis-
tence of that appetite through more than two centuries
of scientific revolution has been demonstrated by the
continuing popularity of Gothic fiction in the mode of
Horace Walpole's *Castle of Otranto*, whose giant helmets
materializing out of nowhere to spread death and terror, ghosts, and other supernatural marvels have demonstrated that probability is not an inevitable requirement
of narrative in an age of technology. Henry Fielding acknowledges our craving for marvels in a long chapter
on the marvelous at the beginning of book 8 in *Tom
Jones*, in which he rules out of his "new Province of Writing" those improbable marvels that had been the staple of epic and romance while
nevertheless insisting on the necessity of retaining the *effects* of such
marvels by resorting to wonderful and surprising actions both credible
and consistent with the personalities of the characters involved. This is
to recuperate the marvelous within realistic fiction on the very different
basis of the merely unusual rather than the supernatural. Without men-
tioning Fielding, Bodin proposed an important variation of this solution by suggesting that novels set in future time could achieve viable
counterparts of aesthetically desirable epic marvels by depicting futuristic scientific feats such as races in the air or voyages to the bottom of
the sea. These feats could allow realistic fiction to serve as a morally
effective vehicle of rational speculation without either deviating into
fantasy or altogether giving up its appeal. Science fiction of the kind
perfected by Jules Verne, H. G. Wells, and their successors has cer-

tainly borne witness to Bodin's insight. Looking at William Gibson's cyberpunk trilogy from the perspective of Bodin's 1834 manifesto, what stands out is the degree to which very distinct genres of Gothic and realistic fiction have been combined with other modes in what, to use Mikhail Bakhtin's terminology, could be called dialogic relationships centering on an ambiguous return to the marvelous.

Neuromancer, Count Zero, and *Mona Lisa Overdrive* have been justly praised for their engagement with the issue of our increasingly problematic interface with technology. William Gibson's cyberspace is an effective and original symbol of human involvement with machines, not only in ways that threaten apocalypse but in ways that break down hitherto reassuring physical, psychological, and philosophical boundaries between human and mechanical existence. Equally effective, although more obviously indebted to J. G. Ballard and other new wave imagists, are Gibson's near-future landscapes densely littered with outmoded artifacts, grotesquely marginal street people, and menacing machines. More questionable in the eyes of some critics, although I find it another source of Gibson's power, is what Gregory Benford has called "a wedding of future symbology and the style of film *noir*" manifested in plots that are "standard Pulp" (20). In this, in his allusions to Raymond Chandler, Joanna Russ, and others, and in more distant echoes of new wave imagery and of Philip K. Dick's games with shifting realities, Gibson displays that self-reflexivity that is such a notable stylistic feature in much of the best science fiction.

Another way of describing Gibson's generic affinities would be to say that his plots display, as standard pulp so often does, the Aristotelian virtues of a clear beginning, middle, and end. Story is alive and well in cyberpunk. Along with his disturbing invitations to consider the imminent dangers of technology in societies dominated by greedy business cartels, Gibson offers the comfort of pulp literature's happy endings. As in genre detective fiction, readers can have it both ways: shivering at horrors vividly portrayed, yet closing the book with a comfortable feeling that justice more or less prevails at last. The mode is comedy rather than tragedy.

There is, to be sure, something bittersweet in the Chandlerian final sentence of *Neuromancer:* "He never saw Molly again." But Molly and Case survive and are well enough paid for their troubles to live happily, though separately, ever after. Dixie Flatline may rest in the peace of nonexistence. Wintermute becomes the matrix and finds happiness talking to its peers via messages exchanged with a similar entity in the Alpha Centauri system. In Gibson's fable machines are destined to evolve into higher forms of sociable and benign artificial intelligence rather than into the hostile instruments of apocalypse shown in works like Harlan Ellison's "I Have No Mouth and I Must Scream." Case even has a tantalizing vision of a cyberspace equivalent of heaven, where he sees himself apparently living forever in a kind of ménage à trois with his lost love, Linda Lee, and Neuromancer.

At the end of Count Zero Bobby Newmark has risen socially to become the beneficiary of a Hollywood contract which lavishly overpays him to be the live-in companion of Angie, who is on her way to superstardom as Tally Isham's understudy, while Turner has retired to the pastoral delights of the countryside, where his days are agreeably occupied in hunting nothing more dangerous than squirrels. Even Bobby's dull-witted mother turns up alive to drool again over her favorite soaps, although Bobby keeps the ending happy by staying well away from her to live instead with Angie. In Count Zero we last see them together on location in Turkey relaxing on a romantically situated seaside rooftop at twilight just as "the evening boat set out for Athens" (226). The Count, wearing "loose, casually expensive French sportclothes," stares meditatively off into the distance remembering his origins in the "gray sweep of Barrytown condos cresting up into the dark towers of the Projects" while Angie lies "sprawled on a sunwarmed waterbed, naked, her arms spread out, as though she were embracing whatever was left of the sun" (267). Then (while the sun presumably continues sinking slowly in the west), "The girl stood, crossed the roof to join him, taking his hand" (267). Our final glimpse of this touching scene is through Tally Isham's envious eyes from an adjoining rooftop as she "watched her understudy put her arm around the boy with the dark hair" (268). If this is not quite riding off into the sunset together, it is close enough to be recognized as a pleasant urban variation on that familiar sentimental ending.

All is equally well at the end of Mona Lisa Overdrive. Gentry is farther along in his mystic quest to discover the shape of cyberspace. After the victorious battle at the factory Cherry goes off with Slick Henry, who may even agree to Molly's parting suggestion that he take a bath. Komiko is safe and on better terms with her father, whose faction has won the Yakuza wars in Japan. Molly, alone, gets to enjoy some solitude after saving the aleph. Mona Lisa, Gibson's allusively illiterate embodiment of "the nearest thing to innocence" (239), is on her way to superstardom and happy loss of that innocence as Angie's replacement as queen of the Sense-net. As a nice little touch of poetic justice, Robin Lanier is discovered strangled on the grounds of the New Suzuki Hotel, thus

fittingly punished for his villainy. Bobby and Angie enjoy an afterlife inside the aleph's cyberspace, where they are reconciled with a penitent 3Jane, and where one day "at midnight . . . as the clocks in the house struck twelve" (258) Colin and the Finn (aka Wintermute), also living happily ever after in cyberspace, visit to unravel the mystery of When It Changed and to offer an intriguing prospect of visiting the artificial intelligences of Alpha Centauri.

Plots culminating in such almost self-parodically happy endings point beyond pulp science fiction and detective stories to even deeper affinities with those utterly implausible but nevertheless often satisfying rags-to-riches fantasies that are in the realm of myth and allegory. David Brin has noted that cyberpunk authors in general avoid depiction of real science in favor of portraying "'scientist' characters who behave exactly like the magicians and wizards of fantasy—extravagant, secretive, egomaniacal, and nigh-omnipotent in their solitary power to defy despicable 'convention'" (25). Of this fantastic dimension, seemingly at cross-purposes with Gibson's impressive skill in describing grim details of future cityscapes that evoke our own urban realities, Pascal J. Thomas rightly remarks that if such implausibility "is allowed as part of the author's assumptions, it should be examined as a central one." Thomas remarks too that "the most naive forms of SF will come close in form to traditional fairy tales" (62–63). Gibson's cyberpunk trilogy certainly does this, although it must be numbered among the most sophisticated, not the most naïve, science fiction. Gibson's unusual success in achieving a remarkably coherent and powerful science fictional mixture of such disparate forms as fairy tale, pulp adventure story, and realistic novel in the self-reflexive mode of film noir is greatly enhanced by his use of the marvelous.

In *Neuromancer* the first moment verging on the marvelous occurs at the end of Case's introduction to Molly: "she held out her hands, palms up, the white fingers slightly spread, and with a barely audible click, ten double-edged, four-centimeter scalpel blades slid from their housings beneath the burgundy nails. She smiled. The blades slowly withdrew" (25). Up to this point the scene has followed the conventions of pulp fiction transformed to a futuristic setting with some appropriate changes of costume, decor, and vocabulary. After an exhausting day Case has returned to his rented sleeping compartment (in the local argot, a "coffin") to find that Molly has somehow gotten inside to recruit him, as it turns out, for the caper that forms Neuromancer's main adventure. Wearing surgically implanted mirrorshades and fetchingly dressed in "tight black gloveleather jeans and a bulky black jacket cut from some matte fabric that seemed to absorb light," she points at him "the pepperbox muzzle of a flechette pistol" and says "close the hatch real slow, friend. You still got that Saturday night special you rented from the waiter?" (24–25). Here Gibson pleasantly conflates the clichés of detective and western tales with a smattering of science fictional conventions.

He replaces "door" with "hatch," and "revolver" with "flechette pistol" while adding the futuristic touch of surgically implanted mirrorshades. From pulp thrillers he keeps the "Saturday night special" and retains a familiar situation in which a dubious character gets the drop on the hero. Neither surgically implanted eyeglasses nor flechette weapons are noticeably outside the boundaries of conventional extrapolation in science fiction. What gives the scene its eerie touch of the marvelous is the four-centimeter scalpel blades that seem to transform Molly into a terrifying cat-woman, with perhaps some regrettably chauvinistic iconic punning by Gibson on the pejorative metaphor of dangerous females as "catty."

If you stop to think about it, as Gibson encourages readers to do by putting that description of Molly's mechanical claws at the end of a chapter, it is very hard to understand how a four-centimeter (1.6-inch) retractable blade and even a highly miniaturized motor mechanism could be implanted without impeding the ability to bend the fingers at their first joints, although some ingenious explanation could doubtless be offered. Just as for time machines, faster-than-light drives, and other conventional wonders of science fiction, Gibson is under no obligation to provide convincing explanations, or indeed any explanations at all. As critics have noted, avoidance of technological details is a characteristic feature of his novels, which are thus very much in the tradition of Wellsian scientific romance rather than Vernian hard science fiction.[1]

Within the conventions of scientific romance Molly's fingernail scalpel blades can be accepted along with much else to which we grant a scientific basis without inquiring about the exact mechanism. Cyberspace itself is only vaguely explained in Neuromancer as "a consensual hallucination experienced daily by billions of legitimate operators" who find convenient its "graphic representation of data abstracted from the banks of every computer in the human system" (51). By minimizing opportunities as well as by explicit invitations to grasp the science and technology putatively underlying his stories, Gibson focuses attention on their astonishing aspects, that is to say, on their affinities with the marvelous. The harder it is to understand exactly how Molly's artificial claws work, the more she resembles a terrifyingly marvelous combination not just of machine and human but of human and animal. The genesis of this resemblance is nevertheless natural, not supernatural.

But Gibson proceeds to blur the line between natural and supernatural as though determined to exploit the narrative benefits of Arthur Clarke's dictum that a sufficiently advanced technology would be indistinguishable from magic. The next surprise Molly springs is her question to Case: "You ever work with the dead?" This evokes only momentarily the idea of a supernatural encounter. Case's response suggests that readers are likely to be more startled by such a question than inhabitants of Gibson's future world: "No . . . I could, I guess. I'm good at what I do" (49). Molly's casual one-word explanation that Dixie Flatline is a "construct" suffices to eliminate the supernatural here for readers of science fiction, to whom the term has come to mean a computer simulation of the mentality of a dead (or otherwise nonexistent) person. Frederik Pohl's Heechee saga, Rudy Rucker's *Software* and *Wetware*, and similar recent works inside and outside cyberpunk boundaries have firmly established the notion that human personality and memories may be imitated or re-created as an artificially intelligent computer program. A construct might be indistinguishable in many ways from the original mind on which it was modeled, or it might even be in some sense a continuation of that mind's identity and awareness. This conceit allows interesting variations on the Cartesian cogito.

Thus Case gets an ambiguous response when he asks whether Dixie Flatline is sentient: " 'Well, it *feels* like I am, kid, but I'm really just a bunch of ROM. It's one of them, ah, philosophical questions, I guess . . .' The ugly laughter sensation rattled down Case's spine. 'But I ain't likely to write you no poem, if you follow me. Your AI, it just might. But it ain't no way *human*' " (131). During this exchange Dixie Flatline stresses that neither it nor Wintermute is human despite their apparent sentience. Neither, however, are they supernatural. As a construct, Dixie Flatline belongs, however tenuously, to the natural realm of human artifacts. So does Wintermute, who numbers among its antecedents such "models" constructed by humans as stone circles, cathedrals, pipeorgans, and adding machines. Talking to Case, Wintermute refers to the next step in development of artificial intelligence as something "your species" will finally manage if the run on Straylight succeeds (171). In the matrix Wintermute takes human forms (first Deane, then Finn) during encounters with Case, explaining, "This is all coming to you courtesy of the simstim unit wired into your deck, of course" (119). This is a technological mode of communication between human and nonhuman, despite Gibson's characteristic vagueness about how, exactly, such a simstim unit might actually work. Justifying its manifestation as Finn, Wintermute even whimsically disclaims affinities with the supernatural: "You want I should come to you in the matrix like a burning bush?" (169).

Gibson hints in that question that supernatural speech from a burning bush might not be much less comprehensible or much more marvelous than travels through cyberspace that increasingly resemble encounters with divine powers that can make the dead apparently live and the living apparently die. During his first meeting with Wintermute, Case's EEG has been "flat as a strap" for forty seconds, indicating brain death, although Molly unconvincingly reassures Maelcum that "it's cool. . . . It's just okay. It's something these guys do is all. Like, he wasn't dead, and it was only a few seconds" (121). Whether "only a few seconds" of flat EEG counts as real death is a question Gibson leaves for readers to chew on. Subsequent experiences in the matrix produce longer intervals of flat EEG that imply something more like an interval of actual death from which Case returns to life.

For Gibson's readers it is another "one of them, ah, philosophical questions" whether Case and the rest of those who have experienced brain death while jacked in to the matrix have come back like Lazarus from the dead, and, if so, whether their experiences in cyberspace can be termed supernatural. If not, Gibson has at the very least created a situation that for both his readers and his characters comes so close to death and resurrection as to collapse the differences that usually go with the distinctions between life, death, and afterlife, thereby also collapsing the usual distinctions between natural and supernatural.

Neuromancer attempts to lure Case away from this world to permanent residence with Linda Lee in cyberspace by saying, "Stay. If your woman is a ghost, she doesn't know it. Neither will you" (244). To bor-

Paul Alkon

row another of Dixie Flatline's memorable expressions, it sure *feels* like
a supernatural encounter when Case mentally departs this world for
cyberspace and returns after meeting Linda Lee, who, unaware of her
ghostly status, has found a kind of resurrection to potentially eternal

life within the matrix. Neuromancer insists that "to live here is to live.
There is no difference" (258). Neuromancer sounds very godlike in ac-
counting for Linda's continued existence in the cyberspace afterlife: "I
brought her here. Into myself" (259). Neuromancer sounds godlike too
in predicting its own and Wintermute's imminent death as a necessary
part of the process that will result in creation of an even higher form of
artificial intelligence: "I die soon, in one sense. As does Wintermute"
(259). In what sense, exactly, Neuromancer will die is another nice
problem Gibson leaves for his readers to think about. Whatever one's
philosophical resolution of this problem may be, there is no escaping
the echoes of religious statements about ritual death, rebirth, and metamorphosis that sound throughout these passages. Their connotations, if
not their denotations, are of the supernatural.

When Case asks for Neuromancer's name or code at their first meeting, the "laughing" reply is a mocking approval of the question: "To call
up a demon you must learn its name. Men dreamed that, once, but now
it is real in another way" (243). Access codes are the reality for which
invoking a demon's name was merely the proleptic metaphor. Demonic
affinities and potentialities of machine intelligence are taken more seriously by Michèle, the Turing Police agent who, shortly before she and
her colleagues are killed by Wintermute, savagely rebukes Case for his
cooperation with their antagonist: "You are worse than a fool. . . . You
have no care for your species. For thousands of years men dreamed of
pacts with demons. Only now are such things possible. And what would
you be paid with? What would your price be, for aiding this thing to
free itself and grow?" (163). In both passages Gibson suggests that the
true age of demons is the present, whereas the old Faustian stories of
Satanic pacts were nothing more than metaphoric expressions of destructive impulses that only modern science makes it possible to realize
in actuality.

When Neuromancer's name is finally disclosed to Case, the mood
shifts to less ominous though no less supernatural allusions:

> "Neuromancer," the boy said, slitting long grey eyes against the
> rising sun. "The lane to the land of the dead. Where you are, my

friend. Marie-France, my lady, she prepared this road, but her lord choked her off before I could read the book of her days. Neuro from the nerves, the silver paths. Romancer. Necromancer. I call up the dead. But no my friend," and the boy did a little dance, brown feet printing the sand, "I am the dead, and their land." (243–44)

Gibson's vocabulary here, with its references to lords, ladies, romancers, and necromancy, is from the literary world of romances to which it self-reflexively alludes, and to which it here generically affiliates the novel.

Gibson's shift from echoes of Faustian tragedy to language invoking the comic mode of romance prepares for the novel's happy ending. Its tone, however, remains a complex mixture of romance and realism in ways signaled by Gibson's inclusion of a line from a crucial stanza of W. H. Auden's "As I walked out one evening":

> The glacier knocks in the cupboard,
>   The desert sighs in the bed,
> And the crack in the tea-cup opens
>   A lane to the land of the dead.

Auden's poem on time's power to destroy love, shatter ideals, and confront us with mortality takes the disarming shape of a ballad that achieves much of its power, like Gibson's novel, from the very contrasts between grim themes and a lightweight form. Auden's land of the dead, moreover, is a strange upside-down place

> Where the beggars raffle the banknotes
> And the Giant is enchanting to Jack
> And the Lily-white Boy is a Roarer,
> And Jill goes down on her back.

In *Neuromancer* Gibson imitates by other means Auden's oddly engaging air of perverse fairy tale.

Gibson presents *Neuromancer*'s supernatural elements in much the same manner as Auden's poem does. Both resort to a sophisticated use of naïve forms. In the tradition of Coleridge, Keats, and many others, Auden exploits the popular folk ballad with its simple stanzas, short lines, repetitions, and allowance for conventional hyperbole, fantasy, and personifications. He plays off these elements against the voice of a complex, disenchanted middle-aged speaker very much of our own time wondering what he has missed in life, lamenting his moral deficiencies, urging himself (and his readers) to "love your crooked neighbor / With all your crooked heart" and imagining strange visionary journeys through a cracked teacup to a land of the dead populated with creatures that are disturbingly unlike their analogues in the nursery rhymes of our childhood. Gibson exploits popular forms of romance, comedy, film noir, science fiction, western, and detective story, playing off these elements against ambiguous new versions of supernatural marvels that function metaphorically to call into question the moral dimension of human encounters with the almost magical power of our cybernetic machinery.

In *Count Zero* and *Mona Lisa Overdrive* Gibson makes the marvelous both more emphatically present as such and more explicitly metaphorical. He manages to have it both ways, displaying a kind of literary equivalent to the complementarity theories of physicists who assert that light must be thought of as *both* wavelike and particlelike. Lucas explains to Bobby, and not incidentally to readers, that mysterious allusions to voodoo gods are a coded language referring with an unusual vocabulary to various aspects of computer technology (to "the language of street tech"). "But at the same time, with the same words, we are talking about other things, and *that* you don't understand. You don't need to" (*Count Zero*, 132–33). This advice also applies to Gibson's readers, although for them there is both greater need and greater opportunity to understand what Lucas here describes to the Count as inexplicable mysteries. Whether what is hidden under the linguistic veil of allusions to voodoo deities is genuinely supernatural or merely another scientific marvel remains to be discovered.

In the manner of much popular Gothic and horror fiction (and the fantastic as defined by Todorov), Gibson keeps both possibilities open.[2] Of the apparent sudden haunting of cyberspace that allows its console cowboys Faustian opportunities to "*make deals with things*" of an alien and perhaps demonic nature, there is in *Count Zero* an ambiguous comment: " 'Thrones and dominions,' the Finn said, obscurely. 'Yeah, there's things out there. Ghosts, voices. Why not? Oceans had mermaids, all that shit, and we had a sea of silicon' " (138). First meditatively suggesting the possibility that real spirits of some eminence in the divine hierarchy may have arrived to haunt cyberspace, Finn then switches gears to suggest that such things are as fabulous as mermaids and, like them, nothing more than fantasies projecting strange aspects of the human psyche into reports of terra incognita.

In *Mona Lisa Overdrive*, allusions to Colin as a "ghost" are evidently only metaphoric since he is another complicated construct of computer technology. Nevertheless, in materializing, dematerializing, attaining a final permanent existence of sorts, and before that being visible and audible only to Kumiko when she summons him through the minicomputer that contains his program, Colin certainly *behaves* like the very model of a modern supernatural ghost. But he is a human artifact.

Angie continues to have unnerving encounters with what seem to be voodoo entities from the matrix that reach out in ghostly ways to influence events in the real world, including her own "debut in the industry and the subsequent rise that had seen her eclipse Tally Isham's fifteen-year career as Net megastar" (84). In various ways, however, Gibson's text also suggests that tales of strange new entities in the inner-space world of the matrix are nothing more than ambiguously substantial results of the same human mythmaking impulse that spawned so many unconfirmed legends about outer space: "There's a whole new apocrypha out there, really—ghost ships, lost cities. . . . Like watching myths take root in a parking lot," David remarks to Angie, who responds by "thinking of Legba, of Mamman Brigitte, the thousand candles" (85).

When Angie asks Continuity—Gibson's amusingly definitive personification of authoritative statement—about the haunting of cyberspace "When It Changed," she is given an unsatisfactory answer allowing a choice between two versions of "the mythform," one involving "assumptions of omniscience, omnipotence, and incomprehensibility on the part of the matrix itself" (107). To Angie's query whether in this view "the matrix is God," Continuity in effect says definitely maybe: "In a manner of speaking although it would be more accurate, in terms of the mythform, to say that the matrix *has* a God, since this being's omniscience and omnipotence are assumed to be limited to the matrix" (107). If it *is* accurate rather than merely a metaphorical manner of speaking to say that the matrix has a god—that there is a god in the machine—then it is also accurate to describe the interventions of that god in Gibson's story as supernatural marvels in the manner of those classical epics for which Bodin wanted to find futuristic equivalents.

But what Continuity gives, Continuity quickly takes away by reminding Angie (and Gibson's readers) that "cyberspace exists, insofar as it can be said to exist, by virtue of human agency" (107). Now you see it, now you don't. Gibson's deus ex machina, however real and powerful in the universe—or at least the cyberspace subuniverse—of his story, is a god *created* by humans. Can we grant such an entity genuine godhood and supernatural status as an authentic initiator of the marvelous?

Only in a manner of speaking. The conclusion of *Mona Lisa Overdrive* defers final resolution of Gibson's paradoxes to a sequel; that is to say, for now, to the reader's imagination. Ambiguities remain. Off to encounter the sentient matrix entity in Alpha Centauri that is the alien counterpart of the sentient matrix divinity created by humans, Finn assures Angie (and readers) that "it's kinda hard to explain why the matrix split up into all those hoodoos 'n' shit, when it met this other one . . . but when we get there, you'll sorta get the idea" (259). When will they arrive? "In a New York minute" (260). Meanwhile, for the characters in Gibson's tales, as for his readers, eerie manifestations of those godlike voices somehow channeled through Angie's implanted neural circuits sure *feel* like close encounters with the genuinely supernatural. However rational the final explanation might prove, the literary *effects* for readers en route to the unraveling of this mystery are those of the supernatural marvelous. In a skillful feat of generic dialogism, Gibson's cyberpunk trilogy thus combines features of fantasy and realism by mixing elements of Gothic horror with various other modes of popular narrative in ways that coherently serve important moral purposes. Gibson is cautioning against the dangers of technology while also greatly enhancing the aesthetic interest of his novels, and hence the power of their warning, by creating what may be science fiction's closest approximation to the effects of epic marvels.

Notes

1. Danny Rirdan, for example, sums up his discussion of Gibson's works by noting that "though the setting of the books is in a very technological-oriented world, there is no scientific basis to the major elements that the books deal with" (46). Istvan Csicsery-Ronay argues that cyberpunk at its most successful offers "a rich thesaurus of metaphors linking the organic and the electronic" (274). David Porush's excellent pathfinding essay on *Neuromancer*, however, notes Gibson's imaginative affinities with "the shape of our future technologies," arguing that "Gibson has projected not merely a fully realized possible future, but a very convincing probable one based on technologies that we already have in place" (177).
2. I have avoided the important but complicated question of Gibson's relationship to recent definitions of the fantastic, contenting myself with older notions of the

marvelous, because I am here concerned mainly with stressing historical continuities of science fiction and epic conventions, and also because my discussion is an experiment in testing the applications to current texts of Félix Bodin's poetics of futuristic fiction, which is based largely on eighteenth-century ideas of the marvelous. For those wishing to pursue concepts of the fantastic beyond Todorov's useful but limited definition, the best starting places are the books by Eric Rabkin and Kathryn Hume listed in the bibliography of this essay.

Works Cited

Alkon, Paul K. *Origins of Futuristic Fiction*. Athens: University of Georgia Press, 1987.

Auden, W. H. "As I walked out one evening." In *The Collected Poetry of W. H. Auden*, pp. 197–99. New York: Random House, 1945.

Bakhtin, M. M. *The Dialogic Imagination*, edited by Michael Holquist, translated by Caryl Emerson and Michael Holquist. Austin: University of Texas Press, 1981.

Benford, Gregory. "Is Something Going On?" *Mississippi Review 47/48* 16 (1988): 18–23.

Bodin, Félix. *Le Roman de l'avenir*. Paris, 1834.

Brin, David. "Starchilde Harold, Revisited." *Mississippi Review 47/48* 16 (1988): 23–27.

Csicsery-Ronay, Istvan. "Cyberpunk and Neuromanticism." *Mississippi Review 47/48* 16 (1988): 266–78.

Fielding, Henry. *The History of Tom Jones, a Foundling*. Introduction by Martin C. Battestin, edited by Fredson Bowers. Middletown, Conn.: Wesleyan University Press, 1975.

Gibson, William. *Count Zero*. London: Victor Gollancz, 1986.

———. *Mona Lisa Overdrive*. New York: Bantam Books, 1988.

———. *Neuromancer*. New York: Ace Books, 1984.

Hume, Kathryn. *Fantasy and Mimesis: Responses to Reality in Western Literature*. New York: Methuen, 1984.

Porush, David. "Cybernauts in Cyberspace: William Gibson's *Neuromancer*." In *Aliens: The Anthropology of Science Fiction*, edited by George E. Slusser and Eric S. Rabkin, pp. 168–78. Carbondale: Southern Illinois University Press, 1987.

Rabkin, Eric S. *The Fantastic in Literature*. Princeton, N.J.: Princeton University Press, 1976.

Rirdan, Danny. "The Works of William Gibson." *Foundation* 43 (Summer 1988): 36–46.

Thomas, Pascal J. "Cyberpunk as Roots Music: An Observation." *Mississippi Review 47/48* 16 (1988): 62–64.

Todorov, Tzvetan. *Introduction à la littérature fantastique*. Paris: Editions du Seuil, 1970.

"The Gernsback Continu- um":

William

Gibson

in the

Context

of Science

Fiction

. . . .

Gary Westfahl

Acentral paradox informs all discussions of cyberpunk fiction. On the one hand, its principal spokesman, Bruce Sterling, repeatedly emphasizes the relationship between cyberpunk and previous science fiction: cyberpunk is "a new movement *in* science fiction," "its roots are deeply sunk *in* the sixty-year tradition of modern popular SF," and "cyberpunk has risen from *within* the SF genre; it is not an invasion but a modern reform" (preface to *Mirrorshades*, ix, x, xv; italics mine). On the other hand, Sterling proclaims the novelty of the form: cyberpunk is reinvigorating a genre that was "confused, self-involved, and stale"; Gibson reflects "a growing new consensus in SF" in "the ease with which he collaborates with other writers," and he "is opening up the stale corridors of the genre to the fresh air of new data. . . . Eighties culture. . . . mainstream lit. . . . what J. G. Ballard has perceptively called 'invisible literature' " (preface to *Burning Chrome*, ix, xii). Most fundamentally, cyberpunk embodies a new perspective toward science and technology:

> A new alliance is becoming evident: an integration of technology and the Eighties counterculture. An unholy alliance of the technical world and the world of organized dissent—the underground world of pop culture, visionary fluidity, and street-level anarchy. . . . The hacker and the rocker are this decade's pop-culture idols, and cyberpunk is very much a pop phenomenon. . . . Science fiction—at least according to its official dogma—has always been about the impact of technology. But times have changed since the comfortable era of Hugo Gernsback, where Science was safely enshrined—and confined—in an ivory tower. The careless technophilia of those days belongs to a vanished, sluggish era, when authority still had a comfortable margin of control. (*Mirrorshades*, xii–xiii)

Given both its alleged connections to science fiction and its alleged originality, the question is simply put: in which critical context is cyberpunk best examined—what Sterling calls "the sixty-year tradition of modern popular SF" or the broader realms of "Eighties counterculture" and "mainstream lit"? I contend that the differences between cyberpunk and previous science fiction are at best superficial, and that claims to the contrary rest on a misunderstanding of the critical heritage of modern science fiction. To demonstrate the strong connections and underlying structures that link cyberpunk to the science fiction tradition, I will discuss the similarities between Gibson's *Neuromancer* and *Ralph 124C 41+*, the major work by Sterling's favorite representative of older science fiction, Hugo Gernsback.

I first note that some of Sterling's effusive assertions can be immediately dismissed. Patrick Nielsen Hayden, for instance, has more than adequately shown that the science fiction of the 1970s cannot be accurately characterized as "confused, self-involved, and stale" (40–41). And Sterling's contention that Gibson's willingness to collaborate represents "a growing new consensus" is highly questionable, to say the least. Even in the 1930s Gernsback was regularly arranging shotgun marriages between amateur and established writers through his Interplanetary Plots contests, which produced works like Everett C. Smith and R. F. Starzl's "The Metal Moon"; and the early fanzines also brought about a number of collaborations, such as the twelve-author space epic *Cosmos*. Later, a number of major science fiction writers regularly worked in tandem, including Earl and Otto Binder, Henry Kuttner and C. L. Moore, C. M. Kornbluth and Frederik Pohl, and Larry Niven and Jerry Pournelle. Almost every major writer in the field has collaborated at least once, including Robert A. Heinlein, Isaac Asimov, Clifford D. Simak, A. E. van Vogt, Jack Williamson, Gregory Benford, and Arthur C. Clarke. To call "the ease with which [Gibson] collaborates with other writers" something new in the field is simply absurd.

In addition, Sterling's determination to picture the works of Gibson and other cyberpunk writers as rebellions against, and not continuations of, earlier science fiction leads him to what I regard as a willful misreading of Gibson's second published story, "The Gernsback Continuum." The story describes various artifacts from the recent past—buildings, objects, artworks—as remnants of a naïve and outmoded view of the future that was never realized. Later, the protagonist sees an alternate world based on those premises, with a woman in futuristic dress telling her companion, "John . . . we've forgotten to take our food pills" (33). According to Sterling, Gibson is here defining what he is rebelling against, what he is trying to rise above: " 'The Gernsback Continuum' shows [Gibson] consciously drawing a bead on the shambling figure of the SF tradition. It's a devastating refutation of 'scientifiction' in its guise as narrow technolatry" (*Chrome*, x). However, this view ignores both the story's tone—the obvious knowledge Gibson has about this view of the future and the affection he displays for it—and its contents. The Gernsback Continuum of the story is not a dying or dead world; it remains as a force influencing present-day reality in its old artifacts and as a still-present alternate universe which continues to coexist next to reality—indeed, the hero is still haunted by his vision of it as the story closes. And Gibson is hardly refuting this worldview; rather, he is consciously paying tribute to it. Given the strong identification of Gernsback with the genre of science fiction, it is furthermore easy to maintain that the Gernsback Continuum of the story is science fiction itself; that Gibson is arguing that the original vision of Gernsback continues to exist today as a force affecting that genre; and that Gibson is enthusiastically joining the tradition, not rejecting it.

To fully demonstrate that a work like *Neuromancer* represents a relatively pure continuation of the science fiction tradition, I must briefly refer to the critical theories of Hugo Gernsback, who, as even Sterling acknowledges, launched and deeply influenced the modern genre.[1] Without going into detail, I note that Gernsback bequeathed to science fiction a number of fundamental tensions, reflected in his own stories and those of his successors. First, he maintained that science fiction "should not be classed just as literature" ("Imagination and Reality," 579) because it in fact represents a combination of fiction and scientific nonfiction, with "the ideal proportion" being "seventy-five per cent literature interwoven with twenty-five per cent science" ("Fiction versus Facts," 291). Thus science fiction should consist of a narrative text that incorporates long passages of scientific explanation exactly equivalent to those found in scientific articles and textbooks. In order to incorporate this material, the author is obliged to create a protagonist who possesses scientific knowledge and the archetypal passivity often seen in such persons; and this leads to a second form of tension, since Gernsback was also committed to the idea that science fiction should provide "thrilling adventure" ("Science Wonder Stories," 5), mandating a less knowledgeable and more active protagonist. There is a third tension in that the scientifically adept hero is typically connected to a technological network, which, while it sustains and supports him, also becomes something he must ultimately reject and separate himself from in order to act. Finally, in pondering the overall effects of scientific progress on human society, the science fiction writer is driven simultaneously to pessimism about the future of the human race and optimism about the future of intelligent life in general. These peculiar combinations of qualities can readily be found in both Gernsback's *Ralph* and Gibson's *Neuromancer*.

As anyone familiar with Gernsback's work knows, his stories are filled with awkward interruptions in which his hero or narrator provides lengthy and detailed explanations of scientific principles and proposed inventions. Gibson's concern with such expository material is less obvious, but it surfaces in a number of passages from *Neuromancer* rarely cited by critics; for example:

> "The matrix has its roots in primitive arcade games," said the voice-over, "in early graphics programs and military experimentation with cranial jacks." On the Sony, a two-dimensional space war faded behind a forest of mathematically generated ferns, demonstrating the spacial possibilities of logarithmic spirals; cold blue military footage burned through, lab animals wired into test systems, helmets feeding into fire control circuits of tanks and war planes. "Cyberspace. A consensual hallucination experienced daily with billions of legitimate operators, in every nation, by children being taught mathematical concepts. . . . A graphic representation of data abstracted from the banks of every computer in the human system. Unthinkable complexity. Lines of light ranged in the nonspace of the mind, clusters and constellations of data. Like city lights, receding. . . ."
>
> "What's that?" Molly asked, as he flipped the channel selector.
>
> "Kid's show." A discontinuous flood of images as the selector cycled. "Off," he said to the Hosaka.[2] (51–52)

Manifest here is the clumsy interpolation of scientific explanation that is significantly different in tone from the rest of the novel—exactly the sin for which Gernsback is routinely criticized. Consider another excerpt from an educational program about a terrorist group, crudely inserted into Gibson's story:

> Cut to Virginia Rambali, Sociology, NYU, her name, faculty, and school pulsing across the screen in pink alphanumerics.
>
> "Given their penchant for these random acts of surreal violence," someone said, "it may be difficult for our viewers to understand why you continue to insist that this phenomenon isn't a form of terrorism."
>
> Dr. Rambali smiled. "There is always a point at which the terrorist ceases to manipulate the media gestalt. A point at which the violence may well escalate, but beyond which the terrorist has become symptomatic of the media gestalt itself. Terrorism as we ordinarily understand it is inately [sic] media-related. The Panther Moderns differ from other terrorists precisely in their degree of self-consciousness, in their awareness of the extent to which media divorce the act of terrorism from the original sociopolitical intent. . . ."
>
> "Skip it," Case said. (58)

Without a doubt these jarring little lectures contrast sharply with the dazzling pyrotechnic stylistics commonly regarded as Gibson's characteristic voice. And beyond these disruptive inserts there are, even in the conversations between Case and various characters in the novel, moments that sound distinctly professorial, like these comments from Wintermute in the guise of Finn:

> "The holographic paradigm is the closest thing you've worked out to a representation of human memory, is all. But you've never done anything about it. People, I mean." . . .
>
> "Can you read my mind, Finn?" He grimaced. "Wintermute, I mean."
>
> "Minds aren't *read*. See, you've still got the paradigms print gave you, and you're barely print-literate. I can *access* your memory, but that's not the same as your mind. . . . You're always building models. Stone circles. Cathedrals. Pipe-organs. Adding machines. . . . But if the run goes off tonight, you'll have finally managed the real thing."
>
> "I don't know what you're talking about." (170–71)

To be sure, Gernsback and Gibson handle explanatory passages in different ways: Gernsback's loquacious hero and his ever-curious girlfriend create an atmosphere unusually conducive to extended explanation, while the taciturn Case and his supercool cohorts oblige Gibson to quickly force exposition into his story before Case impatiently cuts him off. But in making the effort to include such material, Gibson repeatedly displays a desire to explain to readers the present state of scientific knowledge about computers, sociology, and human intelligence and to describe the real future possibilities of developing constructs like cyberspace, new forms of terrorism, and a true artificial intelligence. While this motive may not be as dominant in Gibson as it is in Gernsback— certainly Gibson has other things on his mind—it is nonetheless demonstrably present and fits *Neuromancer* comfortably into the explanatory tradition of science fiction as defined by Gernsback.

It is a quality, furthermore, that Gernsback and Gibson share with many noteworthy writers of modern science fiction. Heinlein regularly interrupts his stories to present lengthy lectures; the leisurely pace of Arthur C. Clarke's novels allows for a considerable amount of detailed explanation; and some works, like Isaac Asimov's original *Foundation* trilogy and Frank Herbert's *Dune*, employ the device of extended quotations from imaginary reference books to present necessary background information. Thus, the nagging, intrusive voice of the compulsive explainer is one trait that unites Gibson with his predecessors.

A second characteristic of both *Ralph* and *Neuromancer* is a protagonist who is fully aware of the science and technology that infuse his future world and who at first seems inactive and emotionless as a result. To be sure, Ralph is primarily an inventor who creates new scientific marvels, while Case is more a manipulator, adept at maneuvering through cyberspace and exploiting its opportunities;[3] however, their thorough knowledge of and delight in the scientific advances of their time unite them. That is, they are radically different from technological naïfs like Winston Smith in George Orwell's *1984*.

In our culture, the man who possesses intelligence and knowledge is often pictured as fundamentally passive and emotionless; and these are qualities both Ralph and Case apparently display in the beginning of their stories. The scientist Ralph seems to prefer spending his life in his laboratory, constantly working on new inventions, and he reacts angrily when his manservant ventures to interrupt him (52–53). In addition, when he first communicates with Alice while she is in Switzerland and learns she is threatened by an avalanche, he does not rush to her rescue but rather contrives a method to beam energy to her house and melt the onrushing snow—thus saving her life without leaving his room. In keeping with his desire to avoid human contact, Ralph is also pictured as cold, almost inhuman. We are told that he once pronounced love to be "nothing but a perfumed animal instinct" (140), and he likens himself to a "tool" (41). Similarly, Case desires nothing more than to be left alone to commune with cyberspace; his efforts to appear callous and indifferent need hardly be documented; and his references to ordinary human experiences usually involve the word *meat*: simstim is a "meat toy" and travel is a "meat thing" (55, 77). Thus, both men seem isolated from normal human contact and emotions and conceptualize themselves as objects—"tool" or "meat."

As events in *Ralph* and *Neuromancer* unfold, however, both protagonists are obliged to abandon their passivity and lack of sentiment and play the role of the noble hero who rescues the fair maiden—a transformation mandated by the genre's commitment to thrilling adventure, and one which in both cases is associated with a journey into outer space and a new romantic attachment. As they continue their tour through the world of 2660, Ralph gradually acknowledges his love for Alice and eventually announces marriage plans; and when Alice is kidnapped by the evil Fernand and taken into space, Ralph ignores a direct command from the Planet Governor forbidding any response, overcomes a guard sent to detain him, and leaves in his space flyer to rescue his beloved. As evidence of his sudden passion, Ralph at one point confronts Fernand and exclaims, "What have you done with her? Answer me, or by God, I'll blow you into Eternity!" (164). These impulsive actions, by the way, make nonsense of Sterling's repeated claims that Gernsback pictures the scientist as someone in his "ivory tower, who showers the blessings of superscience upon the hoi polloi" (*Chrome*, xi; a similar reference to an "ivory tower" is in *Mirrorshades*, xiii). While this may be the way Ralph is *initially* presented, he later becomes as much a criminal as Case is, and his pursuit of Alice is a personal—and illegal—act of rebellion that perfectly accords with the spirit of cyberpunk as Sterling defines it: that is, Ralph now casts himself as part of "a pirate's crew of losers, hustlers, spin-offs, castoffs, and lunatics" (*Chrome*, xi).

In *Neuromancer*, Case and his cohorts travel to a space habitat to break into a computer complex. Once in space, Case seems to become a different person. First, he displays anger when Wintermute simply kills the agents who tried to arrest him—a highly unusual emotional response. Then, when Molly physically ventures into their opponents' headquarters and is captured and threatened by members of the Tessier-Ashpool family, Case gives up his characteristically passive role: after announcing, "I'm stayin' right here," he nevertheless immediately embarks on a daring rescue mission (192). At certain times, then, both Ralph and Case seem to undergo a complete character change, associated with a shift from Earth to space, and are newly presented as agents of action and emotion instead of men of inaction and intellect.

Although it is tempting to see these shifts as simple character transformations, the situation is actually more complex. After his initially passionate pursuit of Alice, Ralph becomes cold and analytical once again when he plots to divert her second kidnapper with an artificial comet aimed at the planet Mars; and after Molly's rescue and the successful completion of his mission, Case reverts to his unromantic self, as reflected in the novel's last line: "He never saw Molly again" (271). In fact, both sides of their characters are validated by the events of the novels, with neither emerging as completely dominant.

This combination of knowledgeable passivity and passionate activity is, I submit, also characteristic of many other science fiction works. One good example is Robert Heinlein's *The Door into Summer*. At the beginning of the novel, Daniel Boone Davis is content to sit in his workshop tinkering with new robots while others deal with the outside world; and though he expresses fatherly affection for his niece, Ricky, and a perfunctory love for his secretary, he hardly seems overly emotional or sentimental. However, when his secretary and partner swindle him and force him into suspended animation, he is galvanized into action. Here it is a trip through time, not through space, that provides the impetus, and Davis forcefully contrives to return to his original era. Awakening to his true love for Ricky, he arranges to meet and marry her when they are both adults. Another example is Mitchell Courtenay in Frederik Pohl and C. M. Kornbluth's *The Space Merchants*, who is initially content to work passively at his advertising agency but finally is prodded to reject his society and seek escape, epitomized by his plans to go to Venus. In both cases, the passive and cold protagonist seems to metamorphose into a forceful, emotional hero.

This transformation in *Ralph* and *Neuromancer* is accompanied by another fundamental shift, a third common trait: although both protagonists are initially connected to a large, technological network which benefits and sustains them, the network ultimately seems to confine and restrict them, and in order to take action they must be separated from it. In innumerable ways, Gernsback's Ralph is presented as part of a connected worldwide network, although it is jerry-built out of existing inventions and logical predictions of the time in which he wrote (1911–12). Ralph meets Alice by means of a picturephone conversation facilitated by an instantaneous translation device called the Language Rectifier; when he beams energy to her house in Switzerland and saves her life, he is applauded by thousands who broadcast their faces into a large auditorium where Ralph stands; he lives under a world government whose Planet Governor regularly consults with him; he reads his daily newspaper delivered on a tiny piece of microfilm; he is initially stopped from flying into space by a telegram from the Planet Governor; and he locates Alice's first kidnapper by inventing a form of radar. There is even the element of direct communication in and out of the human brain—the "powerful theme of mind invasion," which Sterling falsely describes as a cyberpunk innovation (*Mirrorshades*, xiii): Ralph can record his thoughts in written form with a device called the Menograph; and while sleeping he absorbs information conveyed directly into his brain by the Hypnobioscope. More generally, Ralph reveals himself as aware of and part of a larger scientific community; he calls other scientists in to witness his successful revival of a dead dog, and he frequently acknowledges the work of previous scientists in his lengthy explanations.

Gibson, of course, replaces all of these isolated connecting devices with the single medium of cyberspace; and more generally, as Sterling says, "The tools of global integration—the satellite media net, the multinational corporation—fascinate the cyberpunks and figure constantly in their work" (*Mirrorshades*, xiv). Despite his willful isolation from human society and contact, Case can always connect with others through his mind link to cyberspace, and he is further attached to a wider world through his network of underworld sources. For all their individual inventiveness, then, both Case and Ralph constantly have access to others who can provide help and information.

This sense of continuing connection is not without its drawbacks, though, which is another similarity between *Ralph* and *Neuromancer*. With their protagonists' connectedness come restrictions and harassment. Although the world government of 2660 gives Ralph the honorific title "+" and all the financial and scientific support he needs to produce his scientific marvels, Ralph also pays for these privileges with a significant loss of personal freedom.

He was but a tool, a tool to advance science, to benefit humanity. He belonged, not to himself, but to the Government—the Government, who fed and clothed him, and whose doctors guarded his health with every precaution. He had to pay the penalty of his +. To be sure, he had everything. He had but to ask and his wish was law—if it did not interfere with his work.

There were times he grew restive under the restraint, he longed to smoke the tobacco forbidden him by watchful doctors, and to indulge in those little vices which vary the monotony of existence for the ordinary individual. . . .

"I can't stand it," he would protest. "This constraint which I am forced to endure maddens me, I feel that I am being hampered. . . . I am nothing but a prisoner," Ralph stormed once.

"You are a great inventor," smiled the Governor, "and a tremendous factor in the world's advancement. You are invaluable to humanity, and—you are irreplaceable. You belong to the world—not to yourself." (41–42)

Thus, when Ralph plans to rescue Alice, he receives this message from the Planet Governor: "under the law '+' scientists are not allowed to endanger their lives under any circumstances. I therefore command you not to leave the earth without my permission" (154).

Similarly, Case, because of past crimes, is initially deprived of his very ability to enter cyberspace. When that ability is restored, it comes with severe conditions: he can no longer metabolize and be affected by the drugs he loves to take—Molly tells him, "You're biochemically incapable of getting off on amphetamine or cocaine" (36)—and he faces a renewed loss of his computer powers. As Armitage tells him,

> You have fifteen toxin sacs bonded to the lining of various main arteries, Case. They're dissolving. Very slowly, but they definitely are dissolving. Each one contains a mycotoxin. . . . the one your former employees gave you in Memphis. . . . You have time to do what I'm hiring you for, Case, but that's all. Do the job and I can inject you with an enzyme that will dissolve the bond without opening the sacs. Then you'll need a blood change. Otherwise, the sacs melt and you're back where I found you. (45–46)

In order to undertake the actions they feel are necessary, both Ralph and Case must sever their connections with their networks: Ralph flies off into space completely alone to rescue Alice; and, even though his presence in cyberspace is absolutely necessary to the success of his mission, Case disconnects from that realm and ventures forth to rescue Molly from the Tessier-Ashpool family. And to complicate any effort to see these actions as straightforward transformations, both characters finally revert to their previous state, with Ralph reinstated as a prominent scientist and Case returned to his old job of computer cowboy.

This ambivalence about the value of connectedness as opposed to the need for independent action surfaces in many other science fiction works. Pohl and Kornbluth's *The Space Merchants* can again serve as an example, in that it begins with its hero happily producing—and relating to—the clutter of advertising slogans that permeate his world and ends with the now-alienated protagonist fleeing to Venus to establish a new society. Also relevant in this context is Clifford D. Simak's *Way Station*, in which a human who maintains a teleportation station on Earth that connects alien worlds is finally obliged to take personal action in a crisis. In the world of pervasive connecting media in John Brunner's *Stand on Zanzibar*, Donald Hogan's job is literally to make connections by poring through computer records and journals to find interesting correlations, although he is later pulled away from his synthesizing to be "eptified" into a skilled assassin on a dangerous solo mission. And innumerable *Star Trek* episodes illustrate the importance of communication, with Kirk receiving messages from Starfleet, talking to crewmen with his communicator, and reacting to any approaching starship with a command to "open hailing frequencies"—although the climax often finds Kirk, Spock, and McCoy cut off and isolated on some alien planet, left to their own devices. In all these cases, protagonists who are part of a technological network are later separated from it and forced to act as independent agents; and seeing all these examples of thoroughgoing communication and contact in science fiction, one can find nothing truly novel in the cyberpunk fascination with "the tools of global integration."

In the final actions of their now active, emotional, and independent protagonists, both *Ralph* and *Neuromancer* reveal a fourth similarity: both works present an attitude toward the future that is both pessimistic concerning the fate of the human race and optimistic concerning the fate of some transformed human race or new form of intelligent life. One might profoundly question the assertion that *Ralph* is in any way pessimistic, since the work is routinely presented as a naïve scientific utopia;[4] and, granted, Gernsback devotes much time and attention to his world's diversions, providing a series of tableaux in which characters express their delight about televised plays, the "aerial carnival," voice-writing, and other scientific marvels. As a result, readers can easily fail to note the pain and unhappiness that pervades Ralph's world of 2660. As I have already noted, Ralph himself is unhappy because of the restraints placed on his life. Alice is threatened by an avalanche because, as she tells Ralph without his expressing any surprise, the weather engineers in her district, on strike for more "luxuries," have sabotaged the equipment, indicating that many workers are deeply dissatisfied with their lives (31). As a further indication of widespread discontent, criminal activity of all kinds is still common—Ralph is supplied with criminals "under sentence of death" to use in his experiments (42); he tells Alice about a recent embezzlement scandal (131); and there is a vast police force which springs into action whenever Alice is abducted. The Martian Llysanorh' is driven to despair because the law does not allow him to marry the Earth woman Alice, and even though he later emerges as a major villain, the novel displays remarkable sympathy for his predicament.[5] There have been major famines as recently as a generation ago, and science is described as constantly struggling to increase food production for the world's growing population (97–100). And when Ralph is about to marry, the Planet Governor expresses relief that at least one of his problems—keeping Ralph happy—has been taken off "his already over-burdened shoulders" (141). Clearly, this is far from a perfect world. Furthermore, there is even one indication, when Ralph explains the need for flying "vacation cities," that scientific progress is not only failing to improve human life, but is making it worse: "with all the labor-saving devices [people] have, their lives are speeded up to the breaking point. The businessman or executive must leave his work every month for a few days, if he is not to become a wreck" (132). Strangely enough, the labor-saving devices provided by science are not making work easier; they are driving people crazy.

As for *Neuromancer*, no one would disagree, I suspect, that while the lives of Case and his contemporaries may be momentarily enlivened by simstim, exotic drugs, arcade games, and, of course, cyberspace itself, none of these seriously affects the basic and drab unhappiness of their existence; the darkness of everyday life is strongly projected through the novel. Overall, although Gibson's vision is certainly more grim than Gernsback's, both works ultimately argue that there are certain fun-

damental difficulties in human existence that science may alleviate—
or even intensify—but cannot solve. To employ Gregory Benford's apt
phrase, both novels suggest that there is no "technological fix for the
human condition."

However, there is also a note of hope in these novels: the possibility
that human science might create or assist in the creation of new beings
who can achieve what human beings cannot achieve. Thus, there is a
possible technological fix for the condition of *sentient beings who are
other than or more than human,* but there is not a technological fix for
the *human* condition.

In the case of *Ralph 124C 41+,* the final accomplishment involves a
direct transformation of the human race: namely, the prospect of immortality. When Ralph finally catches up with Alice, only to find her dead,
he frantically works to preserve her body with a special gas so that he
can bring her back to life once they return to Earth; and the novel ends
with her successful revival. In this case, a scientific process might bring
immortality—and radical change—to human life and civilization. The
magnitude of this achievement is foreshadowed and described in chapter 3 of the novel, where other distinguished scientists witness Ralph's
successful experiment involving the revival of a dead dog. Afterward,
one scientist says:

> Ralph, this is one of the greatest gifts that science has brought to
> humanity. For what you have done with a dog, you can do with a
> human being. I only regret for myself that you had not lived and
> conducted this experiment when I was a young man, that I might
> have, from time to time, lived in suspended animation from cen-
> tury to century, and from generation to generation as it will now be
> possible for human beings to do. (65)

The resurrected Alice in effect becomes the first of a new type of human
being, capable of living and continuing to improve indefinitely. And
there is already one small sign that she has matured and grown as a
result of her experience; on awakening, she finally realizes what readers
have known since page 1—that Ralph's name means "ONE TO FORESEE
FOR ONE" (207). Still, there is a note of gloom in that not all humans will
be able to undergo this transformation. Those not especially prepared
and older people are excluded, and the latter group may include Ralph
himself, who, if his remarkable record of scientific achievements is any

guide, must be at least middle-aged. Thus, some humans will advance through life extension while others will be left behind.[6]

This same double message clearly emerges at the end of *Neuromancer*, where Case's ultimate triumph is to bring about the birth of a true arti-ficial intelligence in the combination of Wintermute and Neuromancer; and this new being visits him one more time to explain that it has now become the matrix of cyberspace itself, and that it has established con-tact with similar beings from Alpha Centauri and elsewhere. Thus, a member of a new and entirely different species of intelligent life has been created, one who is obviously happy and excited to be alive, thrilled by the prospect of contact with other artificial intelligences and new possibilities for action and attainment. In contrast, Case's prospects are limited. The real world of technological progress that Case inhabits is obviously less than perfect; and despite the appeal of the scientifically created world of cyberspace, humans cannot permanently live there. Such an option is effectively precluded in the unattractive depiction of the Dixie Flatline, the unhappy construct that has died in real life but lives on in cyberspace while continually asking to be killed, and in the novel's final vision of a replica of Case still living in cyberspace that evidently unnerves the living Case. Thus, there is no utopia for human beings in *Neuromancer*, either in reality or in cyberspace.

This double message—despair for humanity, hope for its successors—is, I submit, found not only in the works of these two authors but in countless other works as well, making it strongly characteristic of the genre of science fiction. Brian Stableford finds this attitude in many examples of the "scientific romance":

> There is a strong vein of misanthropy in scientific romance. . . . A frequent corollary . . . is the declaration that hope for the future (if there is any) must be tied to the transcendence of this brutishness, by education or evolution, or both. Utopian optimism was smashed by the realization that a New World would need New Men to live in it, and that we were neither mentally equipped nor spiritually equipped to be New Men. Writers of scientific romance disagreed about what manner of men those new beings might be, and were ambivalent in their attitudes to them, but their very ambivalence intensified their preoccupation with the probable collapse of our civilisation and its possible transcendent renewal. (338)

But this same belief, usually expressed with a more hopeful outlook, is found repeatedly in both American and British science fiction. The envisioned successors to humanity take several forms: superior robots and computers such as Wintermute/Neuromancer, Isaac Asimov's positronic robots, and Clifford D. Simak's *Project Pope*; animals given human intelligence and/or form, as in Simak's *City* and Cordwainer Smith's *Nostralia*; humans transformed by alien intervention, as in Arthur C. Clarke's *2001: A Space Odyssey* and E. E. Smith's Lensman series; spontaneous human mutations that result in advanced intelligence and mental powers, like A. E. van Vogt's *Slan* and Stanley G. Weinbaum's *The New Adam*; humans joining into a group mind, as in Clarke's *Childhood's End*, Theodore Sturgeon's *More Than Human* and George Zebrowski's *Macrolife*; and other scientific alterations in human characteristics, like hermaphroditism in Sturgeon's *Venus Plus X*, immortality in *Ralph* and Robert Heinlein's *Time Enough for Love*, aquatic adaptation in James Blish's "Surface Tension" and Hal Clement's *Ocean on Top*, and genetic engineering to eliminate human conflict as envisioned in John Brunner's *Stand on Zanzibar*. And many other examples could be added here.

Overall, then, we see that works like *Ralph* and *Neuromancer* share certain key characteristics that are found in a wide range of science fiction texts: the simultaneous desire to offer entertainment and explanation in the context of narrative; a hero who is both cold and passive and emotional and active, and who is connected to a technological network and severs that connection; and a concluding attitude that is pessimistic concerning the future of humanity but optimistic concerning the future of other forms of intelligent life.

To be sure, there are differences between the works, and one need not assert that Gernsback was the first cyberpunk writer or that *Neuromancer* is simply an updated version of *Ralph*. I readily concede that Gernsback is more concerned with scientific explanation than Gibson, that Gibson is more suspicious of emotion and activity than Gernsback, that Gibson has more interest in networking than Gernsback, and that Gernsback is more optimistic than Gibson. However, these are differences of degree, not of kind; as suggested by the title of Gibson's story, the two works stand at two ends of a continuum—the modern tradition of science fiction launched by Gernsback and carried on most recently by the cyberpunk writers.

The connections between cyberpunk and previous science fiction are,

I assert, stronger and more significant than the posited relationship between cyberpunk and other modern genres—"punk music" (*Mirrorshades*, x), for instance, or "mainstream lit" (*Chrome*, xii). In these realms, one first finds a fascination with the emotional and visceral and a suspicion of logic and rational explanation, which hardly describes the works of Gibson. Thus the injunction of the Talking Heads' David Byrne to "Stop Making Sense" cannot apply to Gibson, since he is manifestly committed to making sense out of his future world. Furthermore, while the archetype of the punk does involve a mixture of outward cool and inward passion, and while the computer hacker does function as a figure who is both connected to a wider world and isolated from it, the combination and integration of these images can be found only in previous science fiction—it is not a new alliance but a very old one. Finally, the prevalent attitude in these other fields is nihilism, energized perhaps by a giddy excitement concerning the coming apocalypse. Nowhere except in science fiction does one see the careful blend of pessimism regarding humanity and optimism regarding its successors explicitly projected in the conclusion of *Neuromancer*. In short, cyberpunk can be logically explained as primarily an outgrowth and continuation of the modern science fiction tradition, and cannot be logically explained as primarily a product of other genres and traditions.

If the clear links between *Neuromancer* and Gernsback's legacy have not been properly understood, that is simply because the modern genre of science fiction itself, and particularly its strange double message, have not been properly understood; and one consequence of this misunderstanding has been an incomplete and limited reading of Gibson's novel.

Brian Aldiss and other critics often suggest that science fiction writers can be neatly divided into two camps. On the one hand, there are the simpletons, the brainless technocrats who absurdly claim that science can solve all of humanity's problems; and Hugo Gernsback is most often called on to represent this attitude. Thus Aldiss complains of Gernsback's "simple-minded Victorian utilitarianism" (204), Lundwall calls *Ralph* a "pitiable Utopian novel" (76), Franklin describes Gernsback's tradition as "technocratic science fiction" (*Future*, 394), and Sterling bemoans the "careless technophilia" of "a vanished, sluggish era" (*Mirrorshades*, xiii). On the other hand, there are the mature writers, the ones worthy of literary analysis, who project a properly thoughtful view of unrelieved gloom concerning the future. This is the essence of Aldiss's implausible definition of science fiction as "characteristically cast in the

Gothic or post-Gothic mode" (25), a genre that posits a world cramped, confined, and uncontrollable; and he celebrates as central works novels like Shelley's *Frankenstein*, Wells's *The Island of Dr. Moreau*, and Hodgson's *The House on the Borderland*, all of which maintain a rigorous pessimism regarding the future of both mankind and its possible successors.

As descriptions of the modern tradition that has emerged under the label "science fiction," both views are plainly ridiculous. That is, few if any writers in that tradition—including, as I have demonstrated, Gernsback himself—have failed to point out that scientific progress will bring dilemmas as well as delights, and that science alone cannot be relied on to solve all of humanity's problems.[7] Thoughtless optimism about the future is instead found only outside that tradition, in tracts disguised as fiction, such as Gerard O'Neill's *2081: A Hopeful View of the Human Future*, and in the exhibits of the 1939 World's Fair critiqued by Bruce Franklin in *Robert A. Heinlein: America as Science Fiction*—a tradition seen today in the bland domesticity of space station Bravo Centauri in the Horizons ride at Walt Disney's Epcot Center. Conversely, few if any writers in the modern tradition have completely precluded the hope for some future transformation of humanity or a new species that will eliminate the pain of the human condition; instead, pure pessimism is more commonly located in works outside the genre, such as Orwell's *1984* and D. F. Jones's *Colossus*. The characteristic attitude of modern science fiction, then, combines a degree of pessimism about mankind's future with a degree of hope about other possible beings; and this is the final message of *Ralph*, *Neuromancer*, and the innumerable other works between them in their continuum.

A determination to ignore part of this message, and put Gibson squarely in the envisioned camp of fashionable despair, leads directly to the misreading of *Neuromancer* as simply the story of Case and Molly. From that limited perspective there might be some justice in seeing his relentless efforts to escape into inner worlds as an experience typical of the protagonists in Gothic novels.[8] But if we see the novel as the story of Wintermute/Neuromancer, the human race and its concerns become a minor issue, and the excitement of the new being's discovery of itself and others ends the story with an expansive, unlimited vision of continuing progress. And this second aspect of Gibson's novel cannot be ignored; Neuromancer is, after all, the title character, and its struggle to achieve a true identity is the motivating force for all that happens in the novel. I modestly suggest that excessive fascination with Gibson's human characters has shifted concern away from the artificial intelligence that is the real subject of the novel, precisely because this approach to the work makes it more difficult to fit *Neuromancer* into the questionable patterns proffered by Aldiss and other critics.

To state the point most broadly, the critical context of science fiction itself, with its message of future possibilities to relieve its logical extrapolations of disaster, poses one ultimate challenge to all other critical approaches to the genre. Certainly science fiction's continuing fascination with intelligences beyond our own can be construed as an evasion of reality and responsibility. Just as enthusiasts for space colonies sometimes seem to suggest that it is all right to continue polluting and destroying the environment of Earth because someday we will be living on other, pristine worlds, one could accuse science fiction authors of arguing that it is all right to tolerate human injustice and suffering because someday there will be other races who will live without such problems. However, science fiction repeatedly insists that humans are not the first, the last, or the most important intelligent beings in the cosmos; that in fact we are only one small part of a vast and alien universe; and that, perhaps, the only appropriate response to this environment is for humans to create, or transform themselves into, alien beings. From this viewpoint, those who continue to focus only on human concerns and human limitations are the ones who are evading reality and responsibility.

Even if one accepts the logic of this position, there remain questions as to whether it is desirable, or even possible, for human beings to achieve an inhuman perspective. Science fiction from Gernsback to Gibson asserts that scientific progress is the one force that *might* be able to transcend the limitations of human nature and achieve something truly new, truly different.

Hugo Gernsback and Bruce Sterling emerge as spiritual brothers when they repeatedly argue that the type of writing they are explaining and defending is something new and different, something that has never been seen in literature before. The strange thing, of course, is that, for all Sterling's rhetoric of revolution and novelty, they are both talking about the same type of literature—science fiction. The fact that this genre is routinely misrepresented and misunderstood is not really surprising: there are always those prepared to force any piece of writing into the same old categories, and science fiction has again and again been their victim. However, in the genre's ultimate double vision of simultaneous doom and transcendence, there is, I argue, evidence that science fiction is indeed distinguishable from other types of literature; and as we move toward the end of the millennium and the start of a new century, this new perspective remains one of the most exciting aspects of science fiction. Thus, if a new name is necessary to make critics appreciate this unique genre, then the cyberpunk movement has indeed served a valuable purpose.

Notes

1. I argue for the importance of Gernsback in "On *The True History of Science Fiction*" and present some of his theories in "An Idea of Significant Import."
2. Unless otherwise noted, all Gibson page references are to *Neuromancer*, and all subsequent Gernsback page references are to *Ralph 124C 41+*.
3. One can argue that the difference between Ralph the creator and Case the manipulator is not as great as it might seem. It is a carryover from medieval images of alchemists and wizards to envision the scientist as a sort of magician who goes into his laboratory and emerges with a fantastic new device, because an actual scientist consults with and carefully builds upon the work of his myriad predecessors to produce assemblages and refinements of existing devices. This is a good description of Ralph's methodology; consider his explanation of how he "invented" an antigravity device:

> It took hundreds of years, however, before the correct solution was found. It was known that certain high frequency currents would set up an interference with the gravitational waves, for it had been found in the first part of our century that gravitation was indeed a wave form, the same as light waves, or radio waves. When this interference between the two waves, namely, the gravitational waves and the electrical waves was discovered, it was found that a metallic screen charged by electric high frequency waves would indeed nullify gravitation to a certain extent. . . . Thus things stood until about two years ago, when I began to occupy myself with the problem. I reasoned that while we had achieved much, still much more remained to be done. Our antigravitational screen still let through some of the gravitational waves, or fifty percent of the energy, which we could not seem to counteract. I felt that it was not so much the effect of the current as the material of the screen which seemed to be at fault. Experimental work along this line convinced me that I was on the right track and that if ever gravitation was to be annulled in its entirety a screen of a special material would have to be evolved in order to obtain the desired results.
>
> I finally found that only the densest material known, namely thoro-iridium, would completely stop the gravitational waves, providing that the metal screen was uninterruptedly bombarded with alpha rays which are continually emitted by radium. (135–36)

What did Ralph do? He looked at the current state of progress in counteracting gravity, analyzed the one remaining problem, and located the existing material that would solve that problem. In short, he functioned not as a sorcerer but as a troubleshooter—much as Case troubleshoots his way through cyberspace. In this sense, then, the division between scientist and technician is not that large.

4. This is the standard opinion of *Ralph*, often presented by people who do not seem familiar with it; for instance, Sam Lundwall in *Science Fiction: An Illustrated History* talks of "Hugo Gernsback's pitiable Utopian novel, *Ralph 124C 41+* (1911), in which the intrepid editor-cum-author managed to take away all the sociological, political and intelligent parts and substitute them with machines and monsters without end" (76). Since there is absolutely nothing in Gernsback's novel even remotely resembling a monster, it is reasonable to assume that Lundwall had not even read the book.

5. Gernsback includes a letter from Llysanorh' in which he explains his plight and even discusses plans to commit suicide—clearly designed to contrast him favorably with the other villain, Fernand, whose motives are less noble (141–42). Even when Alice is kidnapped by Llysanorh', she thinks that "he looked very lonely and remote, and somehow, to her, very pathetic" (190); and "she could not deny the fact of his genuine, and fervent love for her" (193).

6. The sense of human science achieving something beyond the human offers, by the way, one explanation for a puzzle in Gernsback's novel; while the meaning of "124C 41" is obvious enough, Ralph's full last name includes that "+," which does not seem to fit into the pun. Accepting that science fiction sees humankind's role as creating its own successors, one could then read Ralph's name as "one to foresee for one-plus"—*one* meaning man, and *one-plus* meaning a superior type of man (as in the title of Frederik Pohl's recent novel about one such being, *Man Plus*).

7. A more complete refutation of the charge that Gernsback was simply a "technocrat" is included in my "A Tremendous New Force."

8. Case's efforts to achieve inwardness are described in another context in my forthcoming book *Islands in the Sky: The Space Station Theme in Science Fiction Literature*.

Works Cited

Aldiss, Brian W., with David Wingrove. *Trillion Year Spree: The History of Science Fiction*. New York: Atheneum, 1986. A previous version, by Aldiss alone, is *Billion Year Spree: The True History of Science Fiction*. New York: Schocken Books, 1973.

Franklin, H. Bruce. *Future Perfect: American Science Fiction of the Nineteenth Century*. Revised Edition. 1968, 1966. New York: Oxford University Press, 1978.

———. *Robert A. Heinlein: America as Science Fiction*. New York: Oxford University Press, 1980.

Gernsback, Hugo. "Fiction versus Facts." *Amazing Stories* 1 (July 1926): 295.

———. "Imagination and Reality." *Amazing Stories* 1 (October 1926): 579.

———. *Ralph 124C 41+: A Romance of the Year 2660*. 1925. New York: Frederick Fell, 1950. Originally published in *Modern Electrics* in 1911 and 1912.

———. "Science Wonder Stories." *Science Wonder Stories* 1 (June 1929): 5.

Gibson, William. "The Gernsback Continuum." In *Burning Chrome*. New York: Ace Books, 1987. Originally published in 1981.

———. *Neuromancer*. New York: Ace Books, 1984.

Hayden, Patrick Nielsen. "Cyberpunk Forum/Symposium." *Mississippi Review* 16 (1988): 39–43.

Lundwall, Sam J. *Science Fiction: An Illustrated History*. New York: Grosset and Dunlap, 1978.

Stableford, Brian. *Scientific Romance in Britain 1890–1950*. London: Fourth Estate, 1985.

Sterling, Bruce. Preface to *Burning Chrome*, by William Gibson. New York: Ace Books, 1987.

———. Preface to *Mirrorshades: The Cyberpunk Anthology*, edited by Bruce Sterling. New York: Ace Books, 1988.

Westfahl, Gary. " 'An Idea of Significant Import': Hugo Gernsback's Theory of Science Fiction." *Foundation* 48 (Spring 1990).

———. *Islands in the Sky: The Space Station Theme in Science Fiction Literature*. San Bernardino, Calif.: Borgo Press, forthcoming.

———. "On *The True History of Science Fiction*." *Foundation* 47 (Winter 1989–90).

———. " 'A Tremendous New Force': How Science Fiction Proposes to Change the World." Paper presented at the Interdisciplinary Conference on the Fantastic Imagination in New Critical Theories, College Station, Texas, February 1990.

The

"New"

Romancers:

Science

Fiction

Innovators

from

Gernsback

to Gibson

. . . .

Carol McGuirk

"Welcome to the Rue Jules Verne," Molly said. ". . . The perspective's a bitch, if you're not used to it."—William Gibson, *Neuromancer*

T he cyberpunks never conform more closely to science fiction tradition than when they proclaim their work "new." When Hugo Gernsback launched *Amazing Stories* in April 1926, his stroke of genius was to see that variations on the scientific romances of the nineteenth century could continue to attract young readers if renovated. With the instrumental help of illustrators, Gernsback's writers transferred the rocket jauntings of Jules Verne and the earlier science-mediated romances of such writers as Fitz-James O'Brien into glossy new settings populated by cheerful American protagonists.[1] And ever since Gernsback's editorial impetus redesigned American science fiction during the 1920s as a rehab factory to retool and customize old dreams, the field has not only survived but flourished under periodic attempts to reinvent and renew itself, usually in the direction of increasing the rational, extrapolative, speculative content and eliminating the lingering romance and pulp elements.[2]

Sixty years after Gernsback, there is a proliferation of definitions of and prescriptions for science fiction. There are advocates for realism and dystopian social criticism, for the "hard" sciences and a tighter focus on logical extrapolation, for incorporation of fantastic elements and greater attention to literary style. There are even calls for a renewed commitment to mindless pleasure from fans who are only partly joking about "keeping science fiction in the gutter where it belongs." Each group seems sure that it represents the "real" science fiction.

In such a setting, there can be no consensus on the uses of the past, no agreement on a canon. Some writers are proud to see their work as closely linked to a heritage of earlier genre classics. An example is Robert Heinlein, whose later work, which largely overlooks the "hard" SF of his prime, pays tribute to the Oz stories of his childhood (in *Job*, Alex is forever trying to get back to Kansas) and the Edgar Rice Burroughs space operas of his youth.[3] Others, like Bruce Sterling and Joanna Russ, are proud of their creative independence from earlier science fiction, which they see as shackled to naïve pulp models.

The many mutually incompatible paradigms competing in the field go far toward explaining the SF community's chronic state of noisy polarization, of which the cyberpunk controversy is only the latest example. My conclusion will introduce some ideas from the Russian theorist M. M. Bakhtin that suggest that this chaos of opposing voices—and the concomitant impossibility of establishing any fixed canon of classic texts—forms the best hope for SF's continuing vitality and its link with major fictional narrative. First, however, I offer an account of the historical evolution of some terms frequently invoked in the current controversy—including *hard science fiction, soft science fiction, humanism,* and *heroism.* I do not claim to understand the one true meaning of these terms, only to provide a historical context for how they got so slippery. In SF studies, terms shift in meaning whenever the center of power shifts, and a whole group of concepts may become debased when one generation's avant-garde giant—its A. E. van Vogt, say—is dismissed by a subsequent generation as a mere pygmy-with-a-giant-typewriter, to quote Damon Knight's draconian but influential assessment.[4]

Since my history focuses on power shifts, I would also like to make it clear that there is no correlation between who wins any given battle for consensus—which group is allowed to set the current terms of the debate—and who writes the best science fiction. Some of the most influential novels in SF history emerged from powerful movements years after those movements had lost their edge and the avant-garde had moved on. *Dune*, a hard SF novel, was serialized in *Analog* during the waning years of John Campbell's influence; *The Left Hand of Darkness*, a soft SF classic, was published five years into the clear ascendancy of the new wave. The brilliant work of Paul Linebarger ("Cordwainer Smith") and the much-maligned A. E. van Vogt was mediated by space opera, a subgenre that has been a term of easy contempt since the 1930s.[5] In SF studies as elsewhere, short-term consensus on aesthetic matters is frequently just that. I sketch its evolving history only because shifts of consensus have contributed such peculiar colorations to SF's critical terminology, as when *humanism* can be used by John Kessel (writing in *Fantasy Review*) as a term of praise but by Michael Swanwick (writing in *Asimov's*) as an insult.

The only uncontested shift of consensus in SF history seems to have been the first: the displacement of space opera by hard science fiction shortly before World War II. Peter Nicholls defines hard SF as having two meanings: science fiction sharing the "themes and usually the style" of genre fiction first written during the later 1930s, and also SF of any era that "deals with the so-called 'hard sciences' ": mathematics, physics, astronomy, and so forth (273). Hard science fiction's first impetus came from that astonishing group of new writers that John Campbell recruited for *Astounding Science Fiction* in 1939: Robert Heinlein, Isaac Asimov, and Theodore Sturgeon. John Campbell's first decade as editor at *Astounding* is still, of course, known as the Golden Age. Long past as a chronological event, it retains its prestige; and many writers who worked with Campbell, including Heinlein and Asimov, never really left the Golden Age. There are also honorary latecomers and converts, including, in their different ways, the Larry Niven of *Ringworld*, the George Zebrowski of *Macroworld*, and the Gregory Benford of *Timescape*.

Some see the cyberpunks as attempting to shift the field as a whole back toward hard science fiction. Certainly, bold extrapolation and complex conceptualization of emerging technologies, especially computer technologies, are important in the Movement. John Shirley's call for state-of-the-art topicality—being "culturally on-line"—might be coming from John Campbell (so intensely proud of his brief studies at MIT) or, for that matter, from self-described television and "sexology" pioneer Hugo Gernsback, who drove his underpaid writers to distraction with his demands for dramatic new applications of emerging technologies. It seems beyond doubt that traditional hard science fiction and the cyberpunks share a tendency to place technology in the foreground.

But at least one cyberpunk story explicitly addresses the differences that distinguish even this shared emphasis on high technology. The climax of William Gibson's "The Gernsback Continuum" (1981) recalls the plot of John Campbell's "Twilight" (1934), in which a superman from the future suddenly materializes in the contemporary Nevada desert. In Gibson's story, the amphetamine-intoxicated narrator hallucinates in the Arizona desert a ghostly supercouple dressed, like Campbell's superman, in white togalike garments. The phantom couple gestures toward the distant spires of a future Tucson as Frank R. Paul might have painted it in 1939:

> They were blond. They were standing beside their car, an alu-
> minum avocado with a central shark-fin jutting up from its spine
> and smooth black tires like a child's toy. He had his arm around her
> waist and was gesturing towards the city. They were both in white:
> loose clothing, bare legs, spotless white sun shoes. . . . He was say-
> ing something wise and strong, and she was nodding, and suddenly
> I was frightened. . . . I knew, somehow, that the city behind me was
> Tucson—a dream Tucson thrown up out of the collective yearning
> of an era. . . . They were Heirs to the Dream. (Burning Chrome, 32)

William Gibson invokes the Golden Age intertextually only to under-cut what he sees as its naïve optimism about technology. Yet the very sharpness of his anger, as when he compares early science fiction to Nazi Youth propaganda, seems to acknowledge the continuing imagina-tive power of the Golden Age's exuberant vision. Faithless appropriation of earlier science fiction is part of Gibson's distinctively retro styliza-tion, then, as this passage makes clear. But he invokes the hard science fiction tradition largely to undercut it through irony.[6]

Gibson's commitment in "The Gernsback Continuum" to laying "semiotic ghosts" from the genre's past seems at least partially mis-placed, for science fiction of the Golden Age did not invariably engage in blind praise of technology. In Campbell's "Twilight" itself, the devel-opment of supermen, and consequently of supertechnology, turns out to be disastrous for the species: self-repairing machines pamper us for so long that we lose our curiosity. Campbell's closure, itself intertextually enriched by echoes of H. G. Wells's evocative fable The Time Machine, forms a sharp contrast to Gibson's:

> Twilight—the sun has set. The desert . . . beyond, in its mystic,
> changing colors. The great metal city rising straight-walled to the
> human city above, broken by spires and towers and great trees with
> scented blossoms. . . . And all the great city-structure . . . humming
> to the . . . beat of perfect, deathless machines built more than three
> million years before—and never touched since that time. . . . And
> they go on. The dead city . . . and the songs. Those tell the story

best, I think. Little, hopeless, wondering men amid vast, unknow-
ing, blind machines that started three million years before—and
just never know how to stop. They are dead—and can't die and be
still. (Silverberg, 60–61)

While "Twilight" cannot be dismissed as naïvely optimistic, it does
conclude with a solution to the problem of species burnout: Earth
will be inherited by a new entity, a "curious machine." So ultimately,
John Campbell's story does—like other hard science fiction—emphasize
technology's instrumentality, for good or ill, to change the world.

Gibson's cyberpunk fiction, by contrast, turns from technology's impact on human destiny to examine at closer range its power to gratify
human desire. In *Neuromancer*, technology supplies dysphoric Case
with his needed highs—his drugs, his euphoric contacts with the matrix. Gibson emphasizes drug-heightened consciousness, surgical transformation, prosthetic devices—technological interventions that palliate
or conceal some perceived or real defect in the self or in the soul. For
a price, and with minimal inconvenience and risk, Gibson's characters
can easily replace that diseased pancreas, that mutilated arm.[7] They
can and do change the shape and color of their eyes. Gibson's female
characters often use high technology to create a new image or an alternative self (the lens implants of Molly Millions and Rikki Wildside;
the AI afterlife that Marie-France Tessier-Ashpool fashions for herself).
Gibson's men often use technology to recover parts of a lost self: Case's
psychological dependence on union with the matrix in *Neuromancer*;
Automatic Jack's myoelectric arm in "Burning Chrome."

Jack's prosthesis is emphasized in "Burning Chrome" as the visible
sign of the wounded humanity also revealed by his inarticulate but
generous concern for Rikki. The muted but distinct undercurrent of
elegy in Gibson's treatment of prosthetic body parts is unlike the treatment of prostheses by the earlier hard SF writers Gibson seems to be
self-consciously revising here. Manny O'Kelly's prosthetic forearm in
Heinlein's *The Moon Is a Harsh Mistress* (1966), for instance, implies
nothing about some inner mutilation or vulnerability; it is emphasized
only as tangible evidence of Manny's bloodied-but-unbowed survivor-
ship. Indeed, in *Futurological Congress* (1971) medically trained Stanislaw Lem parodies the casual introduction of plucky prosthesis wearers
into so many hard science fiction plot lines. Lem's time-traveling satiric

mouthpiece, Ijon Tichy, is delighted to find so many amenities, including detachable hands, in the future society that greets him when he awakens from cryogenic sleep: "Besides your regular hands you can get detachables. As many as you like, easy to unbutton. They don't do much but are great for carrying packages, opening doors, scratching between your shoulder-blades"(69).

Unlike the prostheses of Heinlein's heroic Manny or Lem's parodic Tichy, Automatic Jack's artificial arm does seem to function figuratively in "Burning Chrome" as a token of some inner hurt. Yet Gibson employs none of the grotesque satiric intensity Philip Dick brought to such figuration in *The Three Stigmata of Palmer Eldritch* (1964):

> He had enormous steel teeth. . . . And—his right arm was artificial. Twenty years ago in a hunting accident on Callisto he had lost the original; this one of course was superior in that it provided a specialized variety of interchangeable hands. . . . And he was blind. . . . But replacements had been made—at the prices which Eldritch could and would pay. . . . The replacements, fitted into the bone sockets, had no pupils, nor did any ball move by muscular action. Instead a panoramic vision was supplied by a wide-angle lens, a permanent horizontal slot running from edge to edge. (Chapter 10)

Dick's lens implants of 1964, of course, suggest those in Gibson's cyberpunk romances; but the image is put primarily to satiric uses by Dick and to lyric uses by Gibson. Eldritch's prosthetic eyes, arm, and teeth are the three stigmata of Dick's title—visible and outward signs of his spiritual perversity and horror. For Gibson, though, the emphasis on readily procurable lens implants throughout the Sprawl stories suggests not corruption but aspiration. Such characters as Molly and Case, while not heroes, are nonetheless special "cases" who reach toward a technologically enhanced personal style and sensibility that is the street's profane rendition of visionary art.

Prostheses, surgical procedures (both cosmetic and radical), mind alteration by plugging in or drugging out—all these plot devices are to Gibson's cyberpunk fiction what the rocket ship and time travel are to hard SF: recurring figurative elements that express the author's vision of where technology is leading us. In hard science fiction, that direction is outward in space and time: technology is applied to cosmic issues. In Gibson's fiction, the direction is largely inward, to the fulfillment of often self-destructive private dreams; in *Neuromancer*, Case can pursue his enlightening conversations with Wintermute only by "flatlining"—going brain dead.

So Golden Age hard and cyberpunk SF share a common emphasis on technologies. It's just that William Gibson downplays the macrocosm and applies those technologies to individual brains and body parts. Gibson blurs the traditional hard SF dichotomy between "flawed" man and "perfect" machinery (clearly seen in such staples of early hard SF as Asimov's/Campbell's Three Laws of Robotics) and opens up the possibility of speculation about a melding of mechanical and human "character." And if his preoccupation with high technology links Gibson to hard science fiction, his preoccupation with characterization links him to the subsequent soft science fiction movement that dominated the field throughout the 1950s.

Such early "soft" practitioners as Alfred Bester, Fritz Leiber, Ray Bradbury, and James Blish were the first group within popular science fiction to take extrapolation explicitly inward. This was truly a radical break from hard science fiction tradition, for it was this new soft-school pressure to internalize narrative that—far more than the succeeding new wave or cyberpunk movements—determined current debates about the nature of the genre by insisting on (and achieving a consensus in favor of) characterizations much more in line with the expectations of mainstream readers of "realistic" fiction.

The psychological verisimilitude demanded by the soft-school authors—who usually insisted that characters think about their motivations—was a wholly new development in the SF field. Yet, ironically, the cosmos of American science fiction had always been an implicit representation of the human psyche, from Gernsback on. This was true even in early hard SF, with its frequent alien contact stories; but it was especially true in space opera, with its expansive, implicitly poetic visions of galactic voyages. In the stories of Cordwainer Smith, those who sail the cosmos also sail "The Soul." The lethal threat in Smith's Up-and-Out is not radiation or lack of breathable air but an oppressive consciousness of psychic isolation that his characters call "The Pain of Space." A. E. van Vogt's characters also seem to feel this cosmic pang of separation anxiety from the known: in "Far Centaurus" his narrator writes elegiacally after his five-hundred-year voyage that "remembrance brought loneliness like an ache, and the knowledge, the slow knowledge, that this journeying was not lifting our weight of strangeness" (Asimov, 195).[8] There is a figurative link in space opera between explorations of alien territory and representations of the lost and alienated human self—a link, incidentally, also explored in Norman Spinrad's

more recent space opera, *The Void Captain's Tale*. So soft science fiction by no means invented speculation on the human psyche for the SF field. But it was much more explicit in its concern. Human nature, not high technology, fills soft science fiction's foreground.[9]

The usual definition of soft SF stops after noting that it widened the field of extrapolation from the natural and physical sciences to the social sciences: psychology, anthropology, sociology, political science, comparative religion, and so forth. It is not usually noted that this expansion of the field to include speculation about more widely disseminated ideas dramatically increased the potential readership for science fiction, creating the critical mass necessary for its subsequent economic boom. During the 1950s, good hard science fiction continued to be written and read, of course, but consensus had shifted and the hard SF writers were outnumbered (if the prolific Heinlein is removed from the tally, they were greatly outnumbered). It was Alfred Bester's *The Demolished Man* (not Clarke's *Childhood's End*) that won the first Hugo Award in 1953; and other winners in the first ten years of the Hugo were such soft SF writers as Fritz Leiber, James Blish, and Walter M. Miller. The evidence is that many of SF's newest readers circa 1950–60, living in a nuclear-anxious cold war setting and not necessarily trained by years of reading science-oriented Gernsback and Campbell publications, encouraged the soft science fiction paradigm shift away from machines and toward human nature, producing a new speculative agenda far closer to that of conventional realistic fiction. It is no accident that *A Canticle for Leibowitz*, serialized between 1955 and 1957 in Anthony Boucher's *Magazine of Fantasy and Science Fiction* but marketed in 1960 as a "mainstream" novel, became the first work of science fiction to cross over as a *New York Times*–certified best-seller.

In Miller's soft science fiction parable, a postholocaust Earth regenerates from barbarism back to space flight over a period of 1,800 years, only to destroy the Earth again through nuclear war. Miller's plot line has been interpreted as profoundly antitechnological by many readers and critics; indeed, the perceived antitechnological bias of such stories as Miller's has produced a reactive anti–soft SF contingent within the field. In 1957—the heyday of soft SF ascendancy—Heinlein's *The Door into Summer* concluded with a vigorous attack on "long-haired be-littlers":

> The future is better than the past. Despite the crape-hangers, roman-ticists, and anti-intellectuals, the world grows steadily better be-cause the human mind, applying itself to environment, *makes* it better. With hands . . . with tools . . . with horse sense and science and engineering. Most of these long-haired belittlers can't drive a nail [or] use a slide-rule. I'd like to . . . ship them back to the twelfth century—then let them enjoy it. (189–190)

Heinlein is not attacking Miller specifically, of course, but his remarks do show how the "soft" camp put the "hard" camp on the defensive during the 1950s.[10] Yet the fact is that Miller's novel, like most good soft SF, does not so much attack as subordinate technology. Flawed human nature—Miller would call it "original sin"—is the clear villain of the piece. Lucifer (Miller's name for the bomb) is only an accessory to Earth's destruction. The chief agent of destruction in this novel is human pride in reason, which leads to seduction by evil. The bomb only falls in Miller because human nature has fallen first.

A Canticle for Leibowitz represents one of two distinct subgenres within soft SF: humanistic science fiction. In this subgenre, soft SF's typical ruminations on human nature are focused specifically on human capacity; that is, on the issue of heroic possibility. These writers stress that human beings—not, as in hard science fiction, advancing technolo-gies—are the major catalysts for change in the world. The resulting fiction may be utopian or dystopian in focus; heroes may try but fail. But whether optimistic or pessimistic or a mixture of the two (as in Miller, who allows a spacecraft full of heroic monks to escape the final holocaust), this humanist subgenre uses extrapolation to examine our collective human capacity for greatness, as focused by individual heroic action. Some clear examples are Ray Bradbury's *Fahrenheit 451*, James Blish's "Surface Tension," and Ursula K. LeGuin's *The Dispossessed*; but all postholocaust stories that emphasize social regeneration—from *A Canticle for Leibowitz* to David Brin's *The Postman*—also fall into the humanist subgroup.

Humanism has been a key term in the cyberpunk controversy, invoked by some combatants as though this kind of science fiction comprises all that is finest in the genre. Such calls as John Kessel's for a general recom-mitment to humanism in SF today are really defenses of this one soft SF humanist subgenre, which (because of its emphasis on heroic human capacity) is also the type of science fiction whose status has been most eroded by the popularity of the antiheroic cyberpunks. For until very recently, the prestige of humanism in our field has always rivaled that of the Golden Age—a prestige fully earned, let it be said, by an impressive group of writers from 1950 to the present, from Blish, Bradbury, and LeGuin to Daniel Keyes, Richard McKenna, Zenna Henderson, Russell Hoban, Connie Willis, and many others.

There was an alternative, however, to humanistic speculation on human nature even in the earliest days of soft science fiction. In this second subgenre the central issue of humanism—which is heroism, defined as the capacity of individuals to change their world and command their destiny—is irrelevant: an ineluctable social malaise disables, to some degree, all participants in the narrative. Insight remains possible, but significant action becomes impossible. Though focused on the negative dimensions of human consciousness and on social malaise, this second subgenre cannot be called humanistic dystopia, because the social malaise depicted is not extrapolated in such a way as to institute reform or even to facilitate analysis. The nurturing of impaired people by a bad society is used not so much for social criticism as for atmosphere and dramatic stylization. Call this second soft subgenre *SF noir*, and call it closely linked to Gibson's cyberpunk fiction. Notable practitioners include Alfred Bester and the Robert Silverberg of *Dying Inside* (1972).

Michael Swanwick's *In the Drift* furnishes a recent example of post-holocaust SF noir in which the crippled human self and its larger expression—the society—show no capacity for regeneration, only for further decline. A test to determine whether a gloomy work of soft science fiction is dystopian or SF noir is to look at the uses of a catastrophic setting. The humanist author furnishes some account of the issues that led to holocaust, the currents in human civilization threatened by social collapse, and the struggles of the hero to survive in and perhaps even transcend an arena of drastically reduced possibility; Kim Stanley Robinson's *The Wild Shore* is a textbook example. By contrast, such SF noir as *In the Drift* stylizes and elides such factors; readers are presented instead with random episodes of violence, perpetrated by turns against or by the protagonists.

In SF noir, humanism's focus on heroic capacity is replaced by a central focus on psychic mutilation, used to set a stylized atmosphere.

By "stylization" I mean that a heightened intonation of psychic pain seems—as it also does in Edgar Allan Poe—to enter the language of a story as well as the lives of its characters. D. H. Lawrence's essay on Poe concludes with a description of his stylized narratives that seems equally applicable to the SF noir and cyberpunk movements:

> Poe knew only love, love, love, intense vibrations and heightened consciousness. Drugs, women, self-destruction, but anyhow the prismatic ecstacy of heightened consciousness. . . . the human soul in him was beside itself. But it was not lost. He told us plainly how it was, that we should know. He was an adventurer into vaults and cellars and horrible underground passages of the human soul. He sounded the horror and the warning of his own doom. Doomed he was. He died wanting more love, and love killed him. A ghastly disease, love. Poe telling us of his disease, trying even to make his disease fair and attractive. Even succeeding. Which is the inevitable falseness, duplicity of art. American art in particular.[11] (81)

The psychic mutilation emphasized in SF noir is, as in Poe, often (though not always) linked to insight and artistic vision; for like the work of Poe, SF noir texts abound in images of wounded self-awareness— of blindness and insight. Telepathy and mind travel (Case's journeys in the matrix, Bester's "jauntings") are plot devices central to many such narratives; they magnify character vulnerability by increasing the possibility—and consequences—of serious psychic damage. (Robert Sheckley's irreverent novel Mindswap [1966] seems to burlesque this gloomy preoccupation with psychic dislocation in SF noir.)

Stylized noir protagonists experience their sorrows as extrinsically caused and largely irreversible, so they can achieve neither the bitter enlightenment of the tragic hero nor the final triumph of the epic hero. And while a whiff of satire hangs in its night air, SF noir cannot be called fully satiric because it depicts wounded and impaired characters for motives different from satire's. Social malaise functions largely as a metaphor for character malaise in SF noir—not, as in satire, vice versa.[12] In SF noir the final destination of narrative is not satire, tragedy, epic, or humanistic utopia/dystopia. It is, as in Poe, symbolic statement or (to resort to oxymoron) lyric narrative, defined as figuration employed to displace the literal world and put it to the uses of a private aesthetic vision, a style. In many of these texts the only hero is style.

The betrayed, brutal, damaged Gully Foyle in Alfred Bester's The

Stars My Destination is the prototype SF noir protagonist, a center and a force for the pyrotechnic *style* and impassioned message of Bester's novel, but no sane person's role model. In part 1, Bester's epigraph aptly compares Gully to William Blake's fearsome, burning Tyger. In William Gibson's cyberpunk variations on SF noir, psychic wounds lead some characters (the psychotic Armitage/Corto, the sadistic Peter Riviera) to grotesque compensations akin to Gully Foyle's, or to those of the homicidal android in Bester's story "Fondly Fahrenheit." But though Case (who is introduced to us as a killer) is no more offered as a conventional hero than Gulliver Foyle, he is, like Gully, intended to be seen as a "foil" to a corrupt, complacent norm. The detached alienation of such characters as Case and Molly is the badge of the better sort of person in the Sprawl society, in which a prevailing decadence reminds us constantly that there is, after all, much to be detached from, much to be alienated by.

Though no hero, Case has a capacity to turn his painful memories of Linda's death—his recollected strong emotion—into insight. Gibson suggests that this capacity is akin to artistic vision, though such only sporadically insightful observers as Case must accept an ironic diminution and operate as "artistes," to use his Chiba City street name. Case's impossible mission in traversing the matrix and eluding the lethal black ice involves cracking codes: accessing information around which powerful barriers have been placed by constituted authority and then retailing that stolen data. This is a nifty paradigm of artistic appropriation—Harold Bloom's "strong reading" deflated to grand theft. The novel *Neuromancer*, like its protagonist, traverses a transgressive "interzone where art . . . [isn't] quite crime, crime not quite art" (44).

This is quite different from the new wave movement, even though Samuel Delany has been writing since the 1960s of mean streets and outcast artistes, and J. G. Ballard since the 1950s of moral decay in high-tech settings. Gibson, like many new wave writers, does exhibit a dense, impacted style. Yet similarities in theme and dense stylization count for little given radical differences in intertextual base and purpose. For Gibson's postmodern characters inhabit a context wholly and aggressively "antiliterary." In fact, just as he parodies hard SF's technological positivism—and humanistic SF's emphasis on heroes and villains (hence, on perhaps improbably clear-cut categories of good and evil)—Gibson sends up the new wave's cult of lettered sophistication. There is, for instance, his offhand dismissal of all print media in *Neuromancer* in a scene set in Istanbul: "A few letter-writers had taken refuge in door-ways . . . evidence that the written word still enjoyed a certain prestige here. It was a backward country" (88). New wave writers are a very diverse group, but all (unlike Gibson) would subscribe to the "prestige" of "the written word."

In the 1960s, modernism-influenced new wave writers declared war on science fiction's lingering vulgarity of style. They strove to replace pulp "clichés" with more venturesome and original—in effect, more specifically "literary"—writing. They were second-generation "soft" practitioners who moved on to the issue of writerly style after the first generation largely won the battle for consensus over "more sophisticated" characterization. The result was a third SF consensus shift toward self-consciously experimental writing. This may fairly be called "literary" because new wave texts call attention to themselves specifically as texts, as pieces of writing. In its earliest and most exciting phase, the new wave cultivated both innovations in form (Pamela Zoline's experimental—and flawless—"Heat Death of the Universe") and a self-consciously poetic style (the sensuous, image-laden prose of early Zelazny, early Delany, middle Ballard).

William Gibson, by contrast, does not invent new forms and sentences but ironically recycles old ones.[13] He is typical of postmodernism in his reliance on clichés, positioning them as centerpieces for his ironic rendition of the genre's history. In *Neuromancer*, retro Gibson not only goes back to comic book–style naming ("Molly Millions") but even (as in the scene where a reluctant Case applies bronze gel so that he will pass without comment in the orbiting banana republic Freeside) resurrects the "space tan"—that chestnut from pulp-era writers who seemed to assume that radiation shields would not prevent early interplanetary voyagers from developing some nice color. The more familiar the concept, the better it works in a pastiche. Or, as Gibson says in *Neuromancer*, "The street finds a use for everything."

The new wave was the first group in the field to emphasize the capacity of science fiction writing to become self-consciously avant-garde and also to widen its intertextual and allusive base beyond even the wide boundaries set by early soft science fiction. Still, what happened during the 1960s was principally another consensus shift, not a radical change: the first generation of soft science fiction writers lost the center stage, and a younger, more aggressive generation of soft stylists seized it. Individual writers (most notably, hard to classify and therefore chronically neglected Theodore Sturgeon) had produced self-consciously writerly and experimental science fiction well before Michael Moorcock began his spectacular career at *New Worlds*. It was E. J. Carnell (the founding editor, who ran *New Worlds* from 1946 to 1964) who built the British readership for the new wave during the 1950s by showcasing the early work of Ballard (first published in 1956) and Brian Aldiss (first published in *Science Fantasy* in 1954). In the United States, Judith Merril's popular anthologies introduced Ballard—and many other new wave writers-to-be—to American readers during the later 1950s (a service to young SF fans that William Gibson has acknowledged in *Science Fiction Eye*). Indeed, the crossover of so many writers and editors from soft to new wave affiliation is the major factor suggesting that the new wave developed organically from the soft SF of the 1950s rather than representing (like the rift between hard SF and space opera or the post-Hiroshima rift between hard and soft SF) a sudden break.

In any case, I think it is principally from SF noir, not from the new wave, that Gibson's cyberpunk fictions take not only their pulpoid, retro style but also their apparent view that criminal activity is the ultimate capitalist art form. In one early SF noir story, Fritz Leiber's "Coming Attraction" (1950), a crime of delinquency frames the opening scene of the story and a "crime" of betrayal the climax. The story employs the style of hard-boiled detective fiction and its criminal milieu, yet it is science fictional in its postholocaust setting—a decadent, radioactive Manhattan—and its extrapolations of issues new in 1950, including nuclear angst, the grotesque popularity of wrestling on early network TV, the rising social concern over urban youth gangs, and even the new popularity of frozen food.[14] The nonprint medium in the story is, of course, television, a metaphor in the text for the ironic "Coming Attraction" of the title—a postnuclear near future in which the networks ensure that the irradiated masses have unlimited access to violent contact sports. The story records an Englishman's misplaced chivalry in attempting to rescue an apparent damsel in distress from the terror and pain to which she has become masochistically attached. The lady's masked face not only expresses her culture's obsession with radiation-produced mutants, it is the emblem of her perverse and hidden desire.

The story parallels *Neuromancer* in its emphasis on the inaccessibility of this masked and nameless woman's eyes, suggesting Molly's implants, those seeing but inscrutable lenses that so enrage Peter Riviera. Another parallel is even more specific, suggesting a source in Leiber for Molly Millions's retractable steel fingernails and her street profession of "razorgirl." For Leiber's masked woman also wears razor-sharp steel fingernails: "I felt a slap and four stabs of pain in my cheek. . . . I could feel the four gashes made by her dagger finger caps, and the warm blood oozing" (Silverberg, 457). The narrator rips off her mask, producing a final grotesque image reminiscent of *Neuromancer*'s recurring image of the broken hornet's nest: "Have you ever lifted a rock from damp soil? Have you ever watched the slimy white grubs?"

123

Good science fiction, like all fiction, makes itself new even when it reworks old ideas. Gibson's cyberpunk fictions do recall hard science fiction when they emphasize hard technology's shiny mirrored surfaces; and they recall one kind of soft science fiction—SF noir—when they emphasize a poisoned atmosphere and a poisoned self-consciousness. They even reintroduce earlier authors' specific character signatures, such as the masked woman's razor nails or Palmer Eldritch's lens implants. Because of its interest in extrapolation, science fiction tends to idealize originality, making the postmodern Gibson's borrowings problematic.

Bakhtin argues, however, that pastiche, parody, burlesque, and ironic inversions of genre conventions are the hallmarks of good fiction, as parody opens the text up to subversive voices and a consequent complexity of viewpoint. The true novel makes its story new, says Bakhtin, by admitting genre conventions in order to undermine them. Bakhtin also warns against efforts to fix a canon of classic novels or to determine a catalog of invariable genre traits. For Bakhtin, settled and fixed consensus on such matters is only proof that the patient has died: the genre has begun to think of itself as a genre and has solidified into repressive rules and formulas. Bakhtin reminds us of the extreme youth of the novel, which is the only major literary genre that began after the technological breakthrough of the invention of the book. The novel is the only literary form "receptive to mute forms of perception—that is, to reading." Epic, myth, poetry, drama, and satire are ancient and, Bakhtin argues, are no longer written in their pure forms but only rendered through the impure and faithless appropriations of novelists: "The novel gets on poorly with other genres. There can be no talk of . . . harmony. . . . The novel parodies other genres (precisely in their role as genres); it ex-

Carol McGuirk

poses the conventionality of their forms and their language; it squeezes out some genres and incorporates others into its own peculiar structure, reformulating and re-accentuating them" ("Epic and Novel," 5).

Bakhtin would question the tendency of such SF writers as Frank Herbert to praise science fiction's hospitality to myth, for to Bakhtin it was precisely epic and myth that the novel was designed to attack, revise, and replace. To Bakhtin, only novels remain—as their name promises—endlessly "new," making themselves new precisely by their opposition to older genres, which they parody, echo, transplant, and open up. Bakhtin's writings, then, suggest that the postmodern preoccupation with ironic recycling ("reaccentuation") is not only justifiable but admirable.

Bakhtin also supplies a useful perspective on the matter of Gibson's antiheroes. He notes that when such great early novel writers as Henry Fielding attempt to define their artistic preoccupations, it is almost always in negative terms, particularly with regard to characterization: "the hero of a novel should not be 'heroic' in either the epic or tragic sense. . . . [H]e should combine in himself negative as well as positive features" (10). Thus, far from betraying authorial responsibility in emphasizing the inadequacy of his "heroes," as some critics have charged, Gibson is actually approaching characterization in a way that Bakhtin argues is unique (and essential) to novelists:

> One of the basic internal themes of the novel is precisely the theme of the hero's inadequacy to his fate or his situation. . . . An individual cannot be completely incarnated into the flesh of existing socio-historical categories. There is no mere form that would be able to incarnate once and forever all of his human possibilities and needs, no form in which he could exhaust himself down to the last word, like the tragic or epic hero; no form that he could fill to the very brim. . . . There always remains [in a novel's "hero"] an unrealized surplus of humanness. (37)

Yet it is not clear that such cyberpunk writers as William Gibson are good just because they use antiheroic protagonists and engage in extensive parody of genre conventions. In another essay, "Forms of Time and Chronotope in the Novel," Bakhtin singles out Poe in a critique of a tendency he sees in romanticism and symbolism to employ parody, antiheroic protagonists, and symbolic contrast too exclusively for subjective self-examination. Bakhtin notes that such a preoccupation restricts to style (hence, to the author's evocation of his or her own personality) the power of language, which in Bakhtin's concept of the novel should transcend the author's voice and spiral outward to transform society at large. In a survey of the diminished impact of themes of carnival, drunkenness, and death encounters in Rabelais and in Poe's "The Cask of Amontillado," Bakhtin notes that the carnivalesque emblems— the jester's suit worn by the narrator's victim, the setting at the carnival in Venice, the drunkenness of the characters—are stylized in Poe, made self-consciously elegant and drained of their original Rabelaisian energy:

> Life and death are perceived solely within the limits of the sealed-off individual life . . . and, therefore, within the limits of life taken in its internal and subjective aspect. . . . [In "The Cask of Amontillado," set in the Renaissance], the hero kills his rival during a carnival, the man is drunk and dressed in a clown's costume with little bells on it. The entire short story is structured on sharp and completely static contrasts: the gay and brightly lit carnival/the gloomy catacombs; the merry clown's costume of the rival/the terrible death awaiting him. [Yet] . . . there is . . . no all-encompassing mode of triumphant life, there remain only the denuded, sterile and therefore oppressive contrasts. (199–200)

So Bakhtin cannot be used to certify the greatness of William Gibson's fiction any more than Gibson's witty retro recyclings can be used as evidence of some creative weakness or lack of originality. The issue of *Neuromancer*'s quality as a novel will be settled by time—by how many readers still find it readable years after the cyberpunk controversy has been replaced by some new battle for center stage. In the meantime, I can only conclude that in Gibson, as in Haeckel's law, ontogeny recapitulates phylogeny. Gibson furnished in his work of the mid-1980s a startling revisionary recapitulation of science fiction's entire early history, hard and soft.

Notes

1. Aldiss and Wingrove have deplored the "enforced cheeriness" typical of American SF without seeing that—however maladaptive it may have become by now—it must have been central in establishing the popularity of early magazine SF; hence, in fostering the early development of the genre (53).

It was probably the ebullient fiction of Stanley G. Weinbaum, with its slangy dialogue ("Man! We were through and I knew it!"), ingenious extrapolation, and upbeat characterizations, that set for the American popular tradition its predominantly optimistic (Verneian) rather than pessimistic (Wellsian) overtones. Weinbaum also served as a stylistic model for a fellow engineer-turned-writer who arrived somewhat later on the scene: Robert A. Heinlein. Weinbaum's most influential (because most widely reprinted) story is "A Martian Odyssey" (1934), in which a silicone creature that surely inspired *Star Trek*'s "Horta" is only one of a gallery of logically extrapolated alien life forms encountered by the multiethnic crew of the first Mars probe (Silverberg, 13–29).

2. Lewis Shiner writes in this volume, "The console cowboy is a direct linear descendant of the western pulp heroes. . . . The pulp tradition is a tradition of childish, self-centered fantasy. I think it's time to grow up." Horace Gold's editorial in the premier issue of *Galaxy* (October 1950) struck a similar note:

> Jets blasting, Bat Durston came screeching down through the atmosphere of Bblizznaj, a tiny planet seven billion light-years from Sol. He cut out his super-hyper-drive for the landing . . . and at that point, a tall, lean spaceman stepped out of the tail assembly, proton gun-blaster in a space-tanned hand. "Get back from those controls, Bat Durston," the tall stranger lipped thinly. "You don't know it, but this is your last space trip."
>
> Hoofs drumming, Bat Durston came galloping down through the narrow pass at Eagle Gulch, a tiny gold colony 400 miles north of Tombstone. He spurred hard for a low overhang of rimrock . . . and at that point a tall, lean wrangler stepped out from behind a high boulder, six-shooter in a sun-tanned hand. "Rear back and dismount, Bat Durston," the tall stranger lipped thinly. "You don't know it, but this is your last saddle-jaunt through these-here parts."
>
> Sound alike? They should—one is merely a western transplanted to some alien and impossible planet. If this is your idea of science fiction, you're welcome to it! YOU'LL NEVER FIND IT IN *GALAXY!* (Rosheim, 9)

The elimination of "pulp" elements that Shiner and Gold both call for is—like other calls for an "improvement" of "literary" quality in SF—more problematic than it may sound. The fact is that hack writing is bad not because it employs a formula but because it employs only a formula: the writer consciously avoids defamiliarizing the story. But consider Gene Wolfe's *Book of the New Sun*, with its tortured, loner antihero—the savior/drifter and failed executioner Severian. Is he "just" a transposed western gunslinger? Are the Fremen of *Dune* "just" cowboys surviving in an Arizona desert transposed as the planet Dune? Some formula fiction is classic, in short, and probably SF writers needn't repudiate the formulaic plot lines encouraged by science fiction's pulp roots—merely somehow revise or make them their own. *Hamlet*, after all, is not a classic play because it belongs to a transcendent genre but because it finds its own way beyond the conventions of popular revenge tragedy. (Elizabethan convention would have cast either of the play's young hotheads, Laertes or Fortinbras, as hero in preference to a suicidal procrastinator like Prince Hamlet.)

If science fiction ever succeeds in weaning itself completely from its linear, pulp-transmitted adventure fiction plot lines, it will probably turn into something other than science fiction. Seen in this light, the popularity of such early cyberpunk novels as *Neuromancer* might be explained in terms of Gibson's willingness to offer readers an intricately plotted adventure story that nonetheless questions the values usually associated with action/adventure narratives. Gibson's major elliptical revision of the standard adventure formula is (as in *Hamlet*) his redefinition of what heroism can mean, given a decadent setting.

3. As Heinlein said in *The Cat Who Walks Through Walls*: "The World is Myth. We create it ourselves—and we change it ourselves. A truly strong myth-maker, such as Homer, such as Baum, such as the creator of Tarzan, creates substantial and lasting worlds . . . whereas the fiddlin', unimaginative liars and fabulists shape nothing new and their tedious dreams are forgotten" (Aldiss and Wingrove, 484).

4. Knight's critique of van Vogt first appeared in a fanzine in 1945 when *The World of Null A* was appearing in serial form; it was later collected in *In Search of Wonder*. Like such other influential writer-critics as James Blish and Algys Budrys, Knight is a soft SF writer whose sensibility tends to reject both hard SF and space opera.

5. The negative connotations of the term *space opera* are perhaps owing to such derogative terms as *horse opera* and *soap opera*. Peter Nicholls's entry on A. E. van Vogt in *The Science Fiction Encyclopedia* offers a plausible revised definition: "AEVV's space operas . . . are fundamentally dream enactments that articulate the deep symbolic needs and wishes of his usually adolescent readership" (627). Rene Girard argues in *Deceit, Desire and the Novel* that all major fiction involves a "hostile dialogue between Self and Other which parodies the Hegelian struggle for recognition"—another plausible starting point for a definition of space opera— with its stylized ballet of exotic versus "humane" values—that would avoid the trap of seeing the subgenre wholly in terms of its worst specimens (111).

6. Bruce Sterling shares this ironic deflation of hard SF in his introduction to Gibson's *Burning Chrome*, though like Gibson he describes it too simplistically, "Rather than the passionless techies and rock-ribbed Còmpetent Men of hard SF, [Gibson's] characters are a pirate's crew of losers, hustlers, spin-offs, cast-offs, and lunatics. . . . Gibson puts an end to that fertile Gernsbackian archetype, Ralph 124C41+, a white bread technocrat in his ivory tower, who showers the blessings of superscience on the hoi polloi."

   Yet Gernsback's story *Ralph* (1911) is too early to be considered hard SF. And those "rock-ribbed, competent," stereotypically male space cadets in Heinlein's juvenile hard SF novels nonetheless (as Aldiss and Wingrove have noted) were wearing makeup during the 1950s, anticipating modish teen androgyny by some twenty-five years—as did the female pilots in *Starship Troopers* (1959), who shaved their heads to look more efficient. There may well be some inherent conservatism in the hard SF tradition—perhaps encouraged by the need to choreograph extrapolation so logically and tightly—but more subtle and accurate criticism is needed to define it.

7. There are analogues in earlier SF—in Harley Baker's "Freak Factory in Trenton" in *The Demolished Man*, for instance: "For enormous fees and no questions asked, Baker created monstrosities for the entertainment business and refashioned muscle, skin and bone for the underworld" (70).

8. An interest in the human psyche—displaced and examined as if alien and "cosmic"—can be seen even in van Vogt's first SF story (published in *Astounding* in July 1939). "The Black Destroyer" is told from the viewpoint of a catlike alien

predator who eats "id-creatures," including several visiting earthmen: "It was simple to tune in on the vibrations of the id, and to create the violent chemical disorganization that freed it from the crushed bone. The id was, Coeurl discovered, mostly in the bone" (Campbell and Greenberg, 15).

9. This may be seen in compact form in Genly Ai ["I"; "eye"], the name Le Guin chose for her main narrator in what is (at least to date) humanistic science fiction's masterwork, *The Left Hand of Darkness*.

10. Whatever he thought of Miller's novel, one can imagine Heinlein's irritation at Clifton Fadiman's portentous foreword: "Human beings are mental and moral children who cannot be trusted with the terrifying toys they have by some tragic accident invented."

11. Lawrence's remarks on the limitations of Poe's dark stylization are equally illuminating: "Poe has been so praised for his style. But it seems to me a meretricious affair. 'Her marble hand' and 'the elasticity of her footfall' seem more like chairsprings and mantelpieces than a human creature. . . . All Poe's style, moreover, has this mechanical quality, as his poetry has a mechanical rhythm. He never sees anything in terms of life, almost always in terms of matter, jewels, marble, etc.— or in terms of force, scientific. And his cadences are all managed mechanically. This is what is called 'having a style' " (69).

12. "Johnny Mnemonic," an early story by Gibson, does feature an anarchistic-libertarian subculture thriving in the rafters of old geodesic ("Fuller") domes: "Nighttown pays no taxes, no utilities. The neon arcs are dead, and the geodesics have been smoked black by decades of cooking fires. In the nearly total darkness of a Nighttown noon, who notices a few dozen mad children lost in the rafters?" (*Burning Chrome*, 14). Incidentally, the "huddling places" of the fugitives in "Johnny Mnemonic"—like the "waldo" of Automatic Jack in "Burning Chrome"—show Gibson's extensive reading of classic early SF by such writers as Simak and Heinlein. There is also Gibson's reference to "kink" in *Neuromancer*—a word originally invented as an obscenity of the future in 1957 by Robert Heinlein in *The Door into Summer*.

13. In *SF Eye*, Tom Maddox has said of Gibson's writing, "It totally is postmodern, because it's vandalistic. . . . He's a junk man, and that's the essence of what postmodern means. The modernists wanted finely shaped objects, like Eliot in the *Four Quartets*, that's the ultimate shape, a completed musical shape. A postmodern just wants to . . . [express] the culture" (1.1, 13). And in the same issue, Gibson rejects comparisons between his own work and Delany's: "*Dhalgren* is kind of an open form. . . . *Neuromancer*'s very much a closed form. *Neuromancer* has more to do with the structure of a Howard Hawks film than it does with *Dahlgren*. It's not an experimental novel" (22).

14. Robert Heinlein was among this story's admirers, though he acknowledged its off-trail status by classing it among SF stories of "manners and morals; any science in them is merely parsley trimming, not the meat. Yet [such stories] are major speculation, not fantasy, and . . . must be classified as science fiction" (*SF Novel*, 16).

Works Cited

Aldiss, Brian, and David Wingrove, *Trillion Year Spree: The History of Science Fiction*. New York: Atheneum, 1986.

Asimov, Isaac, et al., eds. *Starships: Voyages beyond the Boundaries of the Universe*. New York: Fawcett, 1983.

Bakhtin, M. M. *The Dialogic Imagination: Four Essays*, translated by Caryl Emerson and Michael Holquist. Austin: University of Texas Press, 1981.

Bester, Alfred. *The Demolished Man*. New York: Timescape, 1978.

Brown, Stephen P., and Daniel J. Steffan, eds. *Science Fiction Eye*. Washington, D.C.: 'Til You Go Blind Co-Op. Vol. 1 (1987–88), nos. 1–3.

Campbell, John, and Martin H. Greenberg, eds. *Astounding Science Fiction: July 1939*. Carbondale: Southern Illinois University Press, 1981.

Dick, Philip K. *The Three Stigmata of Palmer Eldritch*. New York: Doubleday, 1965.

Gibson, William. *Burning Chrome*. New York: Ace Books, 1986.

——— . *Neuromancer*. New York: Ace Books, 1984.

Girard, Rene. *Deceit, Desire and the Novel*, translated by Yvonne Freccero. Baltimore: Johns Hopkins University Press, 1984.

Heinlein, Robert A. *The Door into Summer*. London: Pan, 1967.

Heinlein, Robert A., et al., *The Science Fiction Novel: Imagination and Social Criticism*. Chicago: Advent, 1959.

Knight, Damon. *In Search of Wonder*. Chicago: Advent, 1956.

Lawrence, D. H. *Studies in Classic American Literature*. New York: Viking, 1961.

Lem, Stanislaw. *The Futurological Congress*, translated by Michael Kandel. New York: Avon, 1976.

Nicholls, Peter. *The Science Fiction Encyclopedia*. Garden City, N.Y.: Doubleday, 1979.

Rosheim, David L. *Galaxy Magazine: Light Years and Dark*. Chicago: Advent, 1986.

Silverberg, Robert, ed. *The Science Fiction Hall of Fame*, Vol. 1. New York: Avon 1970.

PART 3

The

Question

of Newness:

Cyberpunk

and

Postmodern-

ism

Newness,

Neuro-

mancer,

and the

End of

Narrative

. . . .

John Huntington

The dynamic by which SF discovers and defines the "new" has been depicted by the practitioners of the genre itself as a triumph of rational art. In fact it is a much less rational process than is pictured. In addition to the usual sources of conflict that enliven any group or genre—personal envy, political disagreement, generational rivalry—SF, by its very nature, must create disagreement about what it is and why it is important. This special level of disagreement is particularly resistant to discussion because the rational terms by which the genre usually formulates its own importance obscure essential social dynamics of the argument and of SF's appeal. The argument within the genre about what is "new" was recently revived by the success of William Gibson's 1984 novel *Neuromancer*, which has come to typify the cyberpunk movement. The novel has attracted discussion less for its plot—which tells of how Case, a dejected and self-destructive computer hacker, with the help of an extremely competent gun for hire, Molly Millions, breaks through the Tessier-Ashpool computer defenses ("the ice")—than for its hectic imagery and its graphic vision of a world in which one can plug one's mind directly into a global computer network. Those who find the novel significantly new seem to want to read it as a serious meditation on the reality that computers will someday create, but their enthusiasm is not dampened when they find that Gibson does not know very much about technology. One has to suspect that *Neuromancer*'s aura of newness derives from something deeper than its explicit ideas about the future.

If SF were as rational as it sometimes claims to be, it might make sense to argue that we cannot interpret or evaluate any claim to newness until the future depicted (whether generated by prediction, extrapolation, or some other less precise mode of foresight) has revealed itself. Such an idea contains its own refutation, for by this logic we could never discuss most SF, and we could never identify authentic newness until it was old. SF is a *literary* genre whose value has little to do with any privileged insight into the actual future. But as soon as we have dissolved this level of paradox, we find it necessary to begin to construct anew what distinguishes SF from other genres. SF may not be predictive, but it still engages the idea of the "new," what Darko Suvin, following Ernst Bloch, calls the "novum." As Suvin carefully and exactly puts it, "An analysis of SF is necessarily faced with the question of why and how was the newness recognizable as newness at the moment it appeared, what ways of understanding, horizons, and interests were implicit in the novum and required for it" (80). SF is less a prediction than a rendering of somebody's possibilities of hope. In interpreting SF we are in part analyzing what an author sees as the age's potential. By interpreting the significance and the perception of newness in a work of SF we are entering a debate about the present historical situation. We are thinking about and debating what it is important that we think about.

We can approach this paradox-prone situation in a number of ways. We can, at the simplest level, inquire about the explicit ideas in the text. Insofar as this means discussing the feasibility of machines or social organizations, such an approach quickly reaches its limit and becomes simply an assertion of political opinion. We can, however, probe deeper structures of coherence in the work. Most obviously, we can criticize the ways in which the work fails to see just how much it merely recapitulates that which it claims to transcend. In Suvin's terms, we are then showing it to be the creation of a false novum. Thus utopias that claim gender equality but are riddled with unconscious discriminations can be shown for what they are. Much modern SF seems to guard itself against such an approach by implicitly disavowing any utopian purpose and claiming futuristic *play* as an end in itself. We need to be suspicious of such a claim, however, for, as recent literary criticism has taught us, no text is simply disinterested; there is some kind of meaningful and pleasurable construct, some kind of defense, or some kind of rationalization at the heart of all fantasy. Since the text itself tries to conceal its arbitrariness and even convince itself that what it describes is natural, we can never understand this level of meaningfulness by simply accepting what the text itself says; we must seek out the moments of strain or the irrationalities that betray repression or resistance.

Suvin asks, "Why and how was the newness recognizable as newness?" To put this query in different terms, part of the difficulty we have interpreting and recognizing newness derives from our inability to see the limits of our own ideologies. All writers, readers, and critics of SF are defined and limited by what Pierre Bourdieu calls "habitus" and Raymond Williams calls "structure of feeling" (Bourdieu, 101, *passim*; Williams, *passim*). These are the values, expectations, and assumptions shaped by class, gender, and race that determine our later understandings, evaluations, and actions. Bourdieu and Williams would argue that the main source of newness is the acceptance of a voice speaking out of a previously unacknowledged habitus, the introduction of new class or group values into the hegemonic canon. It is not important that new classes become the *subject* of the new literature, but that some essentially new class awareness make itself felt.

While making newness its defining subject, SF has tended to conceal its present social interests. Its technological and scientific innovations are rarely accurate, and even when they are, they still serve mainly as rationalizations for a social fantasy. Suvin's praise of "valid" SF for its "cognitive estrangement" (7–8) similarly dignifies conscious rationality without a sufficient appreciation of the political unconscious (to use Fredric Jameson's term) that underlies all literature. To return to the issue of *Neuromancer*, it seems likely that its enthusiasts find the cyberspace idea plausible, not because of any insight into future technology it entails but because they find the structure of feeling of the novel "true" to their own sense of reality, and, by a back-formation, so to speak, they justify that feeling by finding the technology convincing.

To sketch how such a social analysis might take place, let me turn back to the beginnings of SF and H. G. Wells. *The Time Machine* is most revolutionary not because it uses a scientific gesture (that Wells himself would later debunk as science) in fiction but because it marks a small but significant shift in class allegiances. To be sure, the horror of the Morlocks can be linked to an aversion to the working classes. But that horror is a ruse; Wells is attempting, desperately and unconsciously, to sound like a solid bourgeoise. Under this superficial horror lies a more basic hostility to middle-class culture as represented by the Eloi. All of Wells's early work differs from other works of the time in related genres—such as Grant Allen's or Arthur Conan Doyle's—in its eagerness to imagine the destruction of "civilization." This is the expression of an anger that Wells derived from his own lower-class habitus. Thanks in large part to his confused class allegiances, Wells brought a new structure of feeling to canonic literature.

The argument for the recognition of such a deep-structural innovation is always problematic and becomes more difficult to make and document in the case of more contemporary works. It is one thing for us to reconstruct the historical significance of *Lyrical Ballads* or *The Time Machine*, and quite another for us to evaluate a literary situation in which our own immediate structure of feeling is at risk. And any critic, in defending or resisting the work, needs to be aware that, quite apart from an evaluation of the literary or scientific ideas that the work pushes to the fore, he or she is participating in the social struggle the work itself has initiated by its claim to newness. In the long run, the critic's own discussion and analysis play some role in the historical understanding and placing of the work; that is to say, in the success or failure of its social voice.

Finally, though social issues may lie at the heart of the perception of newness, we cannot begin with them. Because class is an area of struggle that literature negotiates, it is in the literature's rhetorical interests to conceal its class allegiance. Certainly *Neuromancer* does not seem explicitly concerned with class. Despite the Rastafarian connection, which strongly links the novel's world with that of contemporary British punk, the world of *Neuromancer* is missing surface class dynamics. There is the Tessier-Ashpool aristocracy, of course, but that is a grotesque fantasy of incestuous isolation outside the class system altogether. The underworld that Case, Molly, and the others inhabit is a parasite on the largely invisible corporate world that produces the computer-saturated environment. The class-generated structure of feeling that we seek to uncover reveals itself not in the concrete surface references but in the formal structure of the work.

Experience in *Neuromancer* is a kind of Berkleyan sensorium in which all any character can really know is sensation. In cyberspace one *senses* just as profoundly as one does in "real" space. Characters are intensely invested in events that they also recognize as arbitrary. Such an awareness, combining involvement and disengagement, is characteristic not of life but of the experience of narration. All plots are gratuitous. The Flatline construct (Case's companionable and mentoring program) puts the matter succinctly and ironically when Case tells it that he must physically invade the Tessier-Ashpool Ice, "Wonderful. . . . I never did like to do anything simple when I could do it ass-backwards" (221). Behind this joke lies a recognition of the gratuity of the plot complications that follow. To be sure, in all adventure stories the narrative is both gratuitous and a source of pleasure, but few acknowledge the former aspect so unabashedly. Wintermute, the AI, disguised this time as the bartender Ratz, says to Case, "Really, my artiste, you amaze me. The lengths you will go in order to accomplish your own destruction. The redundancy of it!" (234). This remark, while part of the diagesis, expresses an insight into the whole experience of the novel. This passage links the arbitrary plot to the puzzle of death, which underlies all plots. Peter Brooks, in an essay called "Freud's Master Plot," developing ideas in *Beyond the Pleasure Principle*, explains narrative itself as a compulsive repetition leading toward death (in the case of the novel, the end, closure) and at the same time holding off death. The double dynamic of narrative, simultaneously progressing and retarding, and its relations to the death instinct and to art are all formulated by *Neuromancer*. In pointing to the superfluity of a narrative that is in its very superfluity engaged in a matter of life and death, Wintermute's remark makes clear that the meaningful and intensely contradictory relation to plot that narration usually forces on the reader belongs to the characters in this novel as well.

The equivalence of "real" and "matrix" experience inverts the conventional metaphors by which the mental world is understood. A number of times Gibson explains a real experience by giving its equivalent in the matricial realm. What happens is an elevation of matricial hallucination and computer competence to the level of conventional physical sensation and ability. Heroic and skillful action for Case takes place at the computer keyboard. At one important moment Molly's extraordinary athleticism is validated by being compared to the activity of a skillful computer operator: "She went in just right, Case thought. The right attitude; it was something he could sense, something he could have seen in the posture of another cowboy leaning into a deck, fingers flying across the board. She had it: the thing, the moves" (213). What is remarkable about this passage is its exact inversion of the usual metaphors of physical grace. This subordination of the physical, and therefore of the real, is central to the theme of the novel.

We need to appreciate how uncommon this theme is in the SF genre. The triumph of brain over brawn, the victory of genius, is, of course, a theme that has a long history in SF. But the complementary theme, the monstrosity of mind without body, has just as long a tradition. *Neuromancer*'s pointed emphasis on hallucination and artificial experience would ordinarily involve this latter theme. But in this novel the empirical moralism that would denounce purely mental experience does not appear. The novel revels in surrogate experience. The computer matrix, the images of the AI, Case's reconstructed memories, even the hallucinations projected by Peter Riviera are at one level equivalent to physical experience. In such a situation "fiction" loses its meaning because all events are fiction.

Just as the hallucinatory freedom the novel depicts renders the empirical narrative pointless, time—the dimension of tragic necessity—becomes gratuitous, merely a complication. The discrepancy between the time that Case experiences and that which the Flatline, which is unconscious when off and instantaneous when on, experiences is a recurring joke. At other times Case will experience a long adventure in the matrix and then be told by Maelcum that he has been away only five minutes (245). And at another time we hear, as Case experiences the AI's façade: "Time passed. He walked on" (235). This laconic moment, by ignoring the details of duration and space that have intensely occupied the narrative's attention, reveals the artificiality and exhaustion of the narrative itself.

One might explain such a moment as simply the failure of hack writing, but the novel is too alert, too aware of its own devices to be seen as just sloppy. The game signifies that just as the cyberspace deck renders all experience equally artificial, the novel itself, while narrating this artificial experience from a realistic perspective, has become, by a back door, a narrative about narrative. Though, I should hasten to add, because it posits an empirical and narratable reality—the computer matrix—as the limit of such self-reflection, the novel never becomes simply a postmodern play with narrative. Wild as it is in some respects, *Neuromancer* remains true to the strong realistic narrative traditions of SF.

Yet even the realistic narrative here leads toward an anxious double relation. Like Stephen King, Gibson gains a kind of realism by invoking brand names and identifying the nationality of his technology. Unlike Stephen King's, many of Gibson's brand names are yet to be. But, like King's domestic consumer references, which have the effect of horror just because they anchor the reader's unnatural experience in the quotidian, Gibson's are a constant reminder of the dominated world in which the cowboy must play. Yet at the same time, these names offer pleasures, powers, and knowledge to the sophisticate. One of the deep paradoxes of high-tech consumerism is clearly apparent here: while multinational production renders us victims, there is nevertheless a cachet simply to knowing the technological catalog.

An intentionally produced narrative confusion contributes to this contradiction. Gibson repeatedly refers knowingly to a futuristic machine, concept, or situation before it has been explained. Like a student in a class a little too hard, the reader finds the language being spoken always just a bit beyond comprehension, though never incomprehensible. This is, to be sure, a common SF device, though it seldom occurs as regularly or as essentially as it does in *Neuromancer*. In A. E. van Vogt, to invoke one of the first masters of the technique, we usually know when we do not know what is being talked about. Gibson puts us in a more nervous position: we usually have the anxiety that we have missed an explanation somewhere earlier. One thematic effect of the device is to imply that the reader has never grasped more than an edge of the whole reality. Such an anxiety is different from that which the characters themselves feel: they do not know some plots, but they are completely at home in the technology. This is an important discrepancy: the reader's confusion expresses a form of helplessness; the character's competence expresses a form of mastery.

Here is the central paradox of the novel: just as the characters are aware of the fictional nature of their own experiences, *Neuromancer* delights in the characters' technological competence and in their (and its own) stylistic flamboyance in the midst of, perhaps even in the service of, a totally dominating system. This paradox is evident in many layers of the narrative and in the theme, and one may surmise that the novel's success derives from the structural coherence that its readership experiences at this level. Stylistically, it creates anxiety about an ambiguous and oppressive reality and at the same time revels in the increased possibilities the ambiguity allows and the anarchy the oppression justifies.

In *Neuromancer* we are seeing evidence of a new, perhaps the final, stage in the trajectory of SF. If we contrast Gibson's book with the products of the genre forty years ago, we see a significant change in the role of the accomplished technocrat. The heroes of writers such as Heinlein or Asimov used their managerial competence to dominate their worlds. Even van Vogt's paranoid vision allowed for mastery and triumph at the end. By contrast, Case and Robin do not dominate their world. If they pull off a caper, it is according to someone else's plan, and its consequences are not what they expected. Of course, *Neuromancer* is by no means new in its doubts about the social efficacy of technological mastery. The technological optimism of Golden Age SF had begun to disintegrate as early as the 1950s, and by the 1960s the new wave had challenged the dominant faith in technological solutions and tended to see us all as victims of the technocratic system. In works such as J. G. Ballard's "The Terminal Beach" or Thomas Disch's *Camp Concentration* the scientists and technicians despair, not only about controlling or guiding their worlds but about the very possibilities of meaning itself. The symbolic richness of the imagery of "The Terminal Beach" is ironically empty. The protagonist's attempt to construct a symbolic center, a concrete mandala in the desert, is trivial and vain against the onslaught of images of entropic decline (countdowns, increased sleeping time, deevolution, dryness, depression, loss of affect). The few hints of epiphanic meaning—enigmatic messages from space voyagers, Kaldrin's mastery of multidimensional forms, the low-key erotic energy of Coma—turn out to be indecipherable and useless. *Neuromancer* shares the new wave's dark sense of the overwhelming and self-destroying system, but at the same time it breaks with new wave pessimism by finding a positive value in the alienation of technological competence. The hacker and the game player, far from disavowing technology, glorify it and use it to compensate for the overwhelming power of the world symbolized by multinational corporations.

Such an acceptance enables a kind of guerrilla activity in the belly of the beast, but at the same time, the more ecstatic its activity, the more it tends to obscure any political solution. It depicts alienation (which is something different from resistance) as a stable and permanent state. Such an attitude is indifferent to the actual politics of the system. It has resigned itself to survival on the edge, in the cracks. This is a common enough approach in life itself, but it signifies a remarkable moment in a genre that has traditionally been apocalyptic. Ironically, beneath the wild technological fantasy, we are here moving toward a kind of cynical realism.

The double consciousness of the narrative voice, aware of the artificiality of the complex plot that absorbs it, both involved and distanced, bears witness to this attitude, which enjoys engagement in the wonders of technology even as it acknowledges the utter uselessness of effort. Such doubleness, which earlier phases of SF would have had difficulty appreciating, signifies the genre's entry into a new structure of feeling. It is here, in its sympathy with the attitudes of a dominated and alienated subculture, not in its insight into actual technology or its consequences, that Gibson's novel is new. It is hard to say if the novel expresses exactly the kind of class anger that Dick Hebdige observes in British punk, but in other respects the novel sympathizes with punk's outlawry and its claim that it has chosen alienation as a significant response to the system. What appears to the SF tradition as political evasion may seem in this different perspective a wise expediency. If to some readers such a road may seem a dead end, to others it directs us to the only way to survive. A question that only time will answer is whether such narrative has a future, or whether *Neuromancer* by its success marks the end of this line of narrative exploration and thought.

Works Cited

Ballard, J. G. "The Terminal Beach." In *The Terminal Beach*. Harmondsworth: Penguin, 1966.

Bourdieu, Pierre. *Distinction: A Social Critique of the Judgement of Taste*, translated by Richard Nice. Cambridge: Harvard University Press, 1984.

Brooks, Peter. "Freud's Masterplot." In *Contemporary Literary Criticism: Literary and Cultural Studies*, edited by Robert Con Davis and Ronald Schleifer, pp. 287–99. New York: Longman, 1989.

Disch, Thomas. *Camp Concentration*. New York: Avon Books, 1968.

Gibson, William. *Neuromancer*. New York: Ace Books, 1984.

Hebdige, Dick. *Subculture: The Meaning of Style*. London: Methuen, 1979.

Jameson, Fredric. *The Political Unconscious*. Ithaca: Cornell University Press, 1981.

Suvin, Darko. *Metamorphoses of Science Fiction: On the Poetics and History of a Literary Genre*. New Haven: Yale University Press, 1979.

Wells, H. G. *The Definitive Time Machine: A Critical Edition of H. G. Wells's Scientific Romance*, edited, with introduction and notes, by Harry M. Geduld. Bloomington: Indiana University Press, 1987.

Williams, Raymond. *The Country and the City*. New York: Oxford University Press, 1973.

Cyber-

punk

and

the

Crisis

of

Post-

modern-

ity

. . . .

Lance Olsen

T he 1980s may have marked the beginning of the end of postmodernism—that mode of radical skepticism that challenges all we once took for granted about language and experience—as the dominant, or at least quasi-dominant, form of consciousness in American culture. This demise may be partially the result of our country's drift toward political conservatism in the Age of Reagan. The Equal Rights Amendment has scant chance of passing, anti-abortionists and fundamentalists gain power daily, and George Bush proudly follows in the footsteps of one of the most popular presidents in the history of the United States. About sixty miles south of where I taught for five years at the University of Kentucky, William Faulkner's *As I Lay Dying* was banned from a high school on the grounds that it was a "filth book," while not far from there the Ku Klux Klan paraded through a town looking for—and finding—more recruits. At the same time the perimeters of postmodernism are being redrawn almost weekly, then, the nagging fact remains that in many cultures its ideas were never even introduced. One need only think, for example, of a region in the United States such as Appalachia, and of its metanarrative of Community and Tradition embodied in texts such as James Still's *Pattern of a Man and Other Stories*, Wendell Berry's *Nathan Coulter*, and Gurney Norman's *Kinfolks*. Wherever groups exist that embrace totalizing systems, postmodernism has failed to reach its flash point.

In addition to this pervading atmosphere of political conservatism, the demise of postmodernism may also be the result of deep contradictions spinning at the core of the anti-ideological ideology itself. Quickly let us review the givens: postmodernism refuses centricism, total intelligibility, closure, and absolute significance. It goes around, as one of the speakers in Donald Barthelme's short story "Grandmother's House" says, "deconstructing dreams like nobody's business" (*Sixty Stories*,

453). From this perspective it is the logical extension of the philosophical trajectory that, according to Beckett's work, finds its launch site in Descartes and his follower Geulincx, and, according to Derrida's, in Nietzsche, and that rockets through the thought of such people as Wittgenstein, Heidegger, Saussure, Schrödinger, Heisenberg, and Bohr, to touch down at the feet of the deconstructionists, who look back at least as much to the tradition of the Keystone Kops as they do to these others. Postmodernism, then, is a mode of consciousness (and *not*, it should be emphasized, a historical period) that is highly suspicious of the belief in shared speech, shared values, and shared perceptions that some would like to believe form our culture but which in fact may be no more than empty, if necessary, fictions.

Alongside this philosophical trajectory, however, stands another. In many respects it is quintessentially American, although its flight path tracks back through the British tradition of Mill, Hume, and Locke to the launch site of Aristotle and Socrates. It is a mode of consciousness highly suspicious of intellectualist academic philosophy. It seeks meaning in praxis, in the concrete, in the nitty-gritty of facts. Less a generalized system of truth (or, for that matter, truthlessness) than a practical technique for finding solutions to philosophical problems and for promoting successful communication, it is in many ways the antimatter of postmodernism. Although it is often associated with Peirce and Dewey, it was made famous and embodied by William James during the last years of the nineteenth century and the first of the twentieth. I am referring, of course, to pragmatism, which, according to James, rhymes with nominalism in its love of particulars, with utilitarianism in its love of the practical, and with positivism in its disdain for useless questions and metaphysical generalizations (47); and which deflates the pretension of metaphysics (and, I suppose, postmodernism's antimetaphysics) by asking what the plain consequences of an idea are: "What difference would it practically make to any one if this notion rather than that notion were true?" (42). Such a neopragmatic impulse has recently begun interrogating postmodernism along at least five major axes: psychosocial, political, aesthetic-political, aesthetic-experimental, and conceptual. Let us briefly examine each.

Psychosocial. Jean Baudrillard argues that postmodernism is a state analogous to schizophrenia, in which there is "no defense, no retreat" from "the absolute proximity, the total instantaneity of things." The postmodern human "can no longer produce the limits of his being, can no longer play nor stage himself, can no longer produce himself as mirror. He is now only a pure screen, a switching center for all the networks of influence" (133). The same is presumably true of the postmodern literary text. But the question is, how many of us can actually exist, physically or textually, in a state analogous to schizophrenia? Even Thomas Pynchon, one of the postmodern apostles, wonders about this when in that well-known passage from *Gravity's Rainbow* about the comfort of paranoia and the destabilizing bliss of antiparanoia he adds that antiparanoia is "a condition not many of us can bear for long" (434). Postmodernism is an antisystem, but how many of us can actually reject or even fundamentally question all systems? Conferences, after all, are part of a system, as are stopping at red lights and picking up paychecks. To live in absolute openness means not living for very long. The universe may be all the things the postmodern believes it to be, but that doesn't mean one can endure it in its raw state. There is a limit to humans' tolerance for *koyaanisqatsi*, a way of life that calls for another way of living.

Political. Andrew Ross seems to argue that postmodern politics should take the form of a micropolitics, "a politics of the local and the particular and a politics of racial, sexual, and ethnic difference" (vii). But one can't help asking who decides which differences are acceptable and which aren't. Is there, for instance, a place for the Ku Klux Klan who paraded through that town near where I taught, or for those who banned Faulkner from that high school? In other words, is there a place in a network of micropolitics for those who advocate the overthrow of micropolitics and its replacement with an absolutist system? There is an even more fundamental question here: how can any politics advocate the subversion of all totalizing systems, since by definition politics is a belief system, a system of totalization? One cannot practically challenge *all* we once took for granted about language and experience and endorse a political system at the same time.

Aesthetic-Political. Andreas Huyssen argues that postmodernism is essentially dedicated to the democratization of art, that it rejects "modernism's insistence on the autonomy of the art work, its obsessive hostility to mass culture" (vii). In this way, the argument goes, postmodernism has turned its back on the cryptofascistic elitism of modernism. But while it is surely true that postmodern art is often the product of minds deluged by a mass culture of B-movies, comic books, TV shows, rock 'n' roll, and science fiction, it does *not* follow that such minds are necessarily democratic and accessible when expressed in art. Pastiche, the technique often used to bring such eclectic scraps as these together, tends to transform the postmodern artifact into a work at least as inaccessible and elite as *The Waste Land* or *Ulysses*. One need only think of Pynchon's *Gravity's Rainbow*, Sorrentino's *Mulligan Stew*, Sukenick's *98.6*, or the mysterious and uninterpretable Cornell box in Gibson's *Count Zero*, which stands as an emblem for them all, to understand just how antidemocratic such art really is. Isn't it in fact the case that postmodernism may have simply replaced one sort of elitism with another?

Aesthetic-Experimental. Ironically, at the same time advocates of postmodernism claim to democratize, they also subsume, as Ihab Hassan points out, at least a dozen terms of unmaking: "decreation, disintegration, deconstruction, decenterment, displacement, difference, discontinuity, disjunction, disappearance, decomposition, de-definition, demystification, detotalization, delegitimation" (269). In other words, while postmodernism claims to democratize, it also claims to disorient and challenge. How long, however, can a text have this desired effect? Brian McHale and Kathryn Hume implicitly raise this question when they suggest that the nature of the reading process changes each time we confront a postmodern text. Hume argues that the first time we read a book like *Gravity's Rainbow* we are baffled by the text's deconstruction of nineteenth-century novelistic norms, and hence we feel "acute anxiety, a 'paranoid' desire to connect anything with anything . . . , frustration that no connections work really well, and considerable resentment" (199). But upon subsequent readings these feelings gradually dissolve and we are "likely to feel triumph at piecing fragments together into larger patterns, pleasure at remembering characters and places and at being now able to connect them to major plot lines" (200). To put it slightly differently, the more one experiences a postmodern text, the less postmodern it becomes for the simple reason that most humans need to make sense of their environments. How long can the experimental actually remain experimental, the subversive actually subversive, before we simply become accustomed to a certain level of shock, a certain system of "anticonventions" which are themselves conventions?

Conceptual. Jean-François Lyotard registers this contradictory state of mind in his now-famous formula: modernism designates "any science that legitimates itself with reference to a metadiscourse . . . making an explicit appeal to some grand narrative, such as the dialectics of Spirit, the hermeneutics of meaning, the emancipation of the rational or working subject, or the creation of wealth" (xxiii); postmodernism designates an "incredulity toward metanarratives" (xxiv). With those very words, surely, Lyotard contradicts his own project, belies his own intent: he fashions a grand narrative to account for the lack of grand narratives. To bring postmodernism into academic discourse is to begin to traditionalize postmodernism, to stabilize a way of thinking whose essence is destabilization. As soon as we have agreed upon a menu for postmodernism, petrifaction has begun.

One could surely raise many other practical questions with respect to postmodernism, but the above should suffice to make my point that dizzying contradictions spin at its core. One may argue, along with Linda Hutcheon, no doubt, that postmodernism *chooses* to live out these contradictions, "to problematize and, thereby, to make us question" (231). But one may also take a less charitable view that such contradictions are possibly simply the result of bad reasoning or bad faith. They are certainly paralytic; they continually threaten to undermine the very antipremises (themselves, obviously, a kind of premise), and hence the appeal, of the postmodern enterprise.

In either case, a certain neoconservative literary reaction to postmodernism has recently begun to accompany the neoconservative political and philosophical ones I have just outlined. It is exemplified by the neorealism (or what T. C. Boyle calls catatonic realism) that has surfaced since the late 1970s in the form of fiction by such young writers as Jay McInerney, Jayne Anne Phillips, and Bobbie Ann Mason. Those American writers most closely associated with the postmodern—John Barth, Thomas Pynchon, Robert Coover, John Hawkes, William Gaddis, and so on—are all well over forty years old now. Several of them are well over fifty, and some have passed sixty. The young rebels, that is, are not so young anymore. And, predictably, their literary offspring have revolted against them.

Ann Beattie, who gained recognition in 1976 with her novel *Chilly Scenes of Winter*, is the mother of neorealism, and Raymond Carver, who gained recognition in 1978 with his collection of short stories, *Will You Please Be Quiet, Please?*, the father. Bret Easton Ellis's *Less Than Zero*, which appeared in 1985, is its emblem. *Less Than Zero* tracks the coming of age of a teenager, Clay, who wanders through an affluent Los Angeles in a perpetual cocaine narcosis. His sister casually watches porno films in the living room while Clay's friends become prostitutes to pay back their drug debts. The reader discovers a narrative of the upper middle class that taps into contemporary fashion, our culture's obsession with being hip, our consumer society packed with brand names, and the details of our world's detritus. For the first time in decades, a new generation of writers believes in the universe out there, an empirical universe that the reader can smell, see, and touch. Narrative believes in its own logic, chronology, and selfhood. Content is privileged over form, language is transparent, stylistic pyrotechnics are virtually nonexistent. Frequently the characters in this fiction are exhausted by life by the time they leave puberty; commonly they are less immoral than simply morally numb as they float entropically through a wasted cityscape that for them possesses no inherent value or meaning. Their dialogue is spare, undifferentiable, elliptical, usually cynical, and ironic, concerned with the disjunction between what is said (or, more precisely, what is not said) and what is meant.

With some minor modifications, obviously, I have just described the fiction of Hemingway, whom both Carver and Beattie cite as a major influence on their work. And behind Hemingway floats the ghost of the essential realist, Flaubert. From a certain perspective, then, this neorealism may be said to express a certain nostalgia for the old realism. It may be said to be a narrative mode that evinces a gentle longing for the empiricism and pragmatism of the nineteenth century and the early part of the twentieth. Consequently, at the formal and perhaps even at the thematic level it becomes in a very real sense a conservative vision of reality—a vision that wishes to conserve a way of writing, a way of seeing; an optic through which one looks backward rather than ahead. In the final analysis, this neorealism is a product of the American settlement, not the frontier.

Cyberpunk might initially appear to be science fiction's version of neorealism, a little late arriving on the scene, with its cult of hipness, brand names, and designer drugs; its less imaginative extrapolation into the near rather than far future; its morally numb characters drifting emotionlessly through wasted cityscapes that for them possess no inherent value or meaning; its spare and elliptical dialogue usually cynical and ironic in nature. Clearly these similarities exist and are worth exploring, but a fundamental difference in vision separates neorealism from cyberpunk. Neorealism ultimately expresses a conservative narrative and metaphysical consciousness; cyberpunk in its purest form expresses a profoundly radical one.

The distinctions between them may be too obvious to mention. Neorealists focus on the trials and tribulations of the spoiled homogeneous upper middle class; cyberpunks explore the heterogeneous fringes of our culture. Neorealists endorse the shared perceptions of an empirical universe; cyberpunks interrogate such an idea through the creation of alternate universes such as those investigated by Allie, the space-age psychiatrist in Pat Cadigan's *Mindplayers* who literally gets into the heads of the actor, the dead poet, and her other patients. Neorealists embrace intelligibility and centricism by generating a narrative that believes in its own logic, chronology, and selfhood. Cyberpunks challenge logic through such metalogical constructs as cyberspace, chronology through fractured and dislocated narrative reminiscent of MTV at its most disruptive, and selfhood through the invasion of the human by various technologies, from removable eyes made with biogems to mind-suck consoles. Neorealists affirm shared speech by writing as though language is transparent; cyberpunks play with stylistic pyrotechnics. A neorealist novel such as *Less Than Zero* opts for closure and a sense of shared values when Clay, as expected, leaves the decadence of LA behind and moves into adulthood; *Bright Lights, Big City* ends when the protagonist breaks bread at dawn, thus enacting a Christian-humanist rite of rebirth. The proto-cyberpunk film *Escape from New York*, however, concludes subversively when Snake replaces the president's cassette, which purportedly has the power to bring about world peace, with a phony one filled with "Bandstand Boogie"; *Brazil* ends disruptively when Sam Lowry's pastoral fantasy of escape and union with his lover is revealed as mere hallucination and destroyed by Jack Lint's authoritarian Ministry of Information.

All this is hardly surprising since, as Darko Suvin argues, all science fiction is by nature a "literature of cognitive estrangement" (4); and, as McHale adds, science fiction "is to postmodernism what detective fiction was to modernism: it is the ontological genre *par excellence* (as the detective story is the epistemological genre *par excellence*)" (16). Sometimes to a greater extent, sometimes to a lesser, science fiction makes the common uncommon, the everyday something other than the everyday. It wakes us in the midst of our dreaming. And by doing so it challenges our fundamental commonsense assumptions about the nature of the world. In this way it harmonizes well with postmodernism. Yet more interesting is that, as we move toward the year 2000 in an increasingly conservative culture, a subset of science fiction—cyberpunk—might turn out to be one of the last strongholds of postmodern consciousness. While young mainstream experimentalists such as Mark Leyner, Susan Daitch, and Leslie Dick have been marginalized, young cyberpunks such as Bruce Sterling, John Shirley, and, of course, William Gibson have begun receiving a great deal of attention from our culture at large.

Be that as it may, though, such tidy binaries as neorealism/cyberpunk, conservative/radical, conventional/experimental may do no more than prove Charcot's assertion that theory is good but it doesn't prevent things from happening. In fact, there is evidence that even science fiction in its potentially most subversive form has begun to succumb to the neoconservative climate in which we now find ourselves. Look for a moment, for instance, at the trajectory of Gibson's novels. While *Neuromancer* clearly represents the essence of cyberpunk consciousness, it is not at all clear that either *Count Zero* or *Mona Lisa Overdrive* can make the same claim. *Count Zero* introduces a good deal more characterization than does *Neuromancer*, giving history and family to its cast, and several chapters focusing on the love affair between Alain and Marly could have been excerpted from a conventional realist novel.

With *Mona Lisa Overdrive*, the conservative impulse is even more pronounced. According to Gibson, it was written to complete the cyberspace trilogy—to attain, in other words, a sense of closure and intelligibility. It opens much more leisurely than Gibson's previous two novels by introducing a chapter that explores Kumiko Yanaka's past and her psychology in a narrative attempt to generate a resonant sense of character. And it proceeds without the frenetic white-hot speed of either *Neuromancer* or *Count Zero*. Moreover—again unlike the previous two novels—an impression of completion, of fulfillment, pervades the last third of the text. "Order and accord are again established" (242), Kumiko's father asserts. Kumiko herself says, "All must be forgiven" (256); and, indeed, Angie learns to forgive 3Jane (258). Molly, the embodiment of cyberpunk consciousness, significantly retires as mercenary, and in a disconcertingly idyllic last chapter Bobby and Angie are happily reunited. One has the impression that all this might add up to Gibson's attempt to "find my way into the mainstream of fiction," to find "my way out of [science fiction] without losing a sense of what it is I'm doing" (interview in McCaffery, 236). It might also account for the many reviewers who were struck by the novel's relative tameness and complacency. No doubt *Mona Lisa Overdrive* is emotionally richer than Gibson's earlier work, but it is also less jarring both in terms of language and structure.

Certainly this is not to suggest that Gibson has somehow metamorphosed into a conservative neorealist. A number of disjunctive components are at work in *Mona Lisa Overdrive* that still challenge and frustrate a number of readers—from the interspersed plot lines and linguistic experiments to the questions about intergalactic cyberspace raised on the last two pages of the novel (an open-endedness embedded in the apparent conclusion, which, however, calculatedly cries out for yet another financially successful sequel). One should also keep in mind that Bobby and Angie's "marriage" in a "France that isn't France" (258) may be read at least as parodically as Sam Lowry's pastoral hallucination of union at the end of *Brazil*. But, given the relative tameness of *Mona Lisa Overdrive*, one must wonder about the future of cyberpunk, "the apotheosis of postmodernism" (266), as Istvan Csicsery-Ronay somewhat hyperbolically calls it. What are its chances of challenging all we once took for granted about language and experience if its most important writer claims he is "scared of being typecast if I make SF my permanent home" (McCaffery, 236)? Of course, *Mona Lisa Overdrive* may simply be the product of a single science fiction writer of the 1980s who suddenly achieved success and who needs to rewrite paler and paler simulacra of the same book in order to continue that success. But it may also be an indicator of something more interesting. After all, science fiction tells us nothing about our future and everything about our present—our concerns, our interests, our obsessions, our fears. And perhaps the trajectory of Gibson's work suggests a larger movement in our contemporary cultural consciousness away from postmodernism and toward science fiction's metaphysical and narrative equivalent of neorealism. In any case, *Mona Lisa Overdrive* will remain central to our understanding of science fiction approaching the millennium, raising as it does essential questions concerning a genre that until recently has been marginalized, but now has begun to move into a central (and perhaps therefore uninteresting) position in our culture.

Works Cited

Barthelme, Donald. *Sixty Stories.* New York: G. P. Putnam's Sons, 1981.

Baudrillard, Jean. "The Ecstasy of Communication." In *The Anti-Aesthetic: Essays on*

Postmodern Culture, edited by Hal Foster. Port Townsend, Wash.: Bay Press, 1983.

Beattie, Ann. *Chilly Scenes of Winter*. New York: Doubleday, 1976.

Berry, Wendell. *Nathan Coulter*. San Francisco: North Point Press, 1985.

Cadigan, Pat. *Mindplayers*. New York: Bantam Books, 1987.

Carpenter, John, dir. *Escape from New York*. 1981.

Carver, Raymond. *Will You Please Be Quiet, Please?* New York: McGraw-Hill, 1978.

Csicsery-Ronay, Istvan. "Cyberpunk and Neuromanticism." *Mississippi Review* 16 (1988): 217–36.

Eliot, T. S. "The Waste Land." [1922] In *The Complete Poems and Plays 1909–1950*. New York: Harcourt Brace Jovanovich, 1971.

Ellis, Bret Easton. *Less Than Zero*. New York: Simon and Schuster, 1985.

Faulkner, William. *As I Lay Dying*. New York: Random House, 1930.

Gibson, William. *Count Zero*. New York: Arbor House, 1986.

———. *Mona Lisa Overdrive* New York: Bantam Books, 1988.

———. *Neuromancer*. New York: Ace Books, 1984.

Gilliam, Terry, dir. *Brazil*. 1984.

Hassan, Ihab. *The Dismemberment of Orpheus*. 2d. ed. Madison: University of Wisconsin Press, 1982.

Hume, Kathryn. *Pynchon's Mythography: An Approach to "Gravity's Rainbow."* Carbondale: Southern Illinois University Press, 1987

Hutcheon, Linda. *A Poetics of Postmodernism: History, Theory, Fiction*. New York: Routledge, 1988.

Huyssen, Andreas. *After the Great Divide: Modernism, Mass Culture, Postmodernism*. Bloomington: Indiana University Press, 1986.

James, William. *Pragmatism and Four Essays from* The Meaning of Truth. New York: New American Library, 1974.

Joyce, James. *Ulysses*. 1922. New York: Random House, 1986.

Lyotard, Jean-François. *The Postmodern Condition*, translated by Geoff Bennington and Brian Massumi. Minneapolis: University of Minnesota Press, 1984.

McCaffery, Larry. "An Interview with William Gibson." *Mississippi Review* 16 (1988): 217–36.

McHale, Brian. *Postmodernist Fiction*. New York: Methuen, 1987.

McInerney, Jay. *Bright Lights, Big City*. New York: Random House, 1984.

Norman, Gurney. *Kinfolks*. Frankfort, Ky.: Gnomon, 1977.

Pynchon, Thomas. *Gravity's Rainbow*. New York: Viking, 1973.

Ross, Andrew, ed. *Universal Abandon? The Politics of Postmodernism*. Minneapolis: University of Minnesota Press, 1988.

Sorrentino, Gilbert. *Mulligan Stew*. New York: Grove Press, 1979.

151

Lance Olsen

Still, James. *Pattern of a Man & Other Stories*. Frankfort, Ky.: Gnomon, 1976.

Sukenick, Ronald. *98.6*. New York: Fiction Collective, 1975.

Suvin, Darko. *Metamorphoses of Science Fiction: On the Poetics of a Literary Genre*. New Haven: Yale University Press, 1979.

Not What It Used to Be: The Overloading of Memory in Digital Narrative

. . . .

Brooks Landon

This chap next door has only got 35,000 characters (about 7,000 words) on his computer, which creates problems. He was pounding his desk, saying, "I need *more memory!*" So terribly funny—I thought, "What's going on here? This world is mad!"—J. G. Ballard

ntersections and convergences between memory and fiction abound, and they take particularly interesting forms in what—for want of a more ambiguous term—I call *digital narrative.*[1] I use this umbrella term to cover a culturally charged spectrum of fragmented and fractalized contemporary fiction, including that of most Movement writers, because it is non-medium-specific and applies to graphic novels, video, and interactive computer texts, any or all of which may well displace fixed-print text as the dominant literary form by the year 2000. Of course, memory itself is an even more ambiguous term; its range is suggested by Marvin Minsky, who defines it as "an omnibus term for a great many structures and processes that have ill-defined boundaries in both everyday and technical psychology; these include what we call 're-membering,' 're-collecting,' 're-minding,' and 're-cognizing' " (329). And fiction is itself a simulacrum for memory, their two experiential worlds joined in a Möbius-like relationship—fiction usually an imagined memory, memory often no more than crafted fiction. There's nothing new about this relationship, but in an age more and more dominated by the soliton of computers, memory has itself become a "cyborged" concept, a blend of human and computer metaphors, yet another of the facets of the soft machine so impressively studied by David Porush. I think one result of this conceptual merging is that the representation of memory has taken a distinctively new form driven by distinctively postmodern concerns. What interests me is the troubled way in which a significant sampling of contemporary literary semblances presents the concept of memory not in terms of recovery but of overload, and that interest has led me to the proposition that fiction approaching the year 2000 tends to remember memory less and less fondly, problematizing the idea of memory as technologically unstable or even as normatively unhealthy.[2]

Before I go into detail on this proposition, however, I need to mention two essential studies, one looking backward, the other forward, that provide the conceptual limits between which my discussion will range. The first work is Frances Yates's study of the mnemotechnic tradition, *The Art of Memory*, published in 1966. The second work, one probably more familiar to the writers who are the subject of this conference, is Alvin Toffler's *Future Shock*, published in 1970, a time apparently before the future was used up.

Yates's study of classical mnemotechnics, the art of artificial memory, recounts the prodigious feats of memory of Simonides, who could identify all the mangled corpses crushed when a roof fell on a banquet in Thessaly because he remembered where each of the many guests had been seated; of Seneca, who could repeat two thousand names in the order in which they had been given to him; and of Simplicius, who could recite Virgil backward. These feats were accomplished by imagining detailed architectural structures, or memory palaces, in which each object or word to be remembered was assigned a specific location. To recall all of these words or objects, the ancient orator would mentally tour his memory palace, recovering the information in the order in which it had been placed in each room of the palace. Tracing the evolution of this mnemotechnic method through the Renaissance and celebrated practitioners such as Giulio Camillo, Peter Ramus, and Giordano Bruno and into the seventeenth century with Robert Fludd, Yates concludes her study with the suggestion that the classical art of memory even survived as a factor in the growth of scientific method. Yates provides us with the emblem of limitless memory, theoretically perfectible if not perfect, attainable through the practice of a mental discipline.[3]

Toffler, on the other hand, made popular a rhetoric of mental limits with his focus on the shock of overstimulation, particularly the shock of information overload. While not specifically concerned with memory, *Future Shock* stresses the built-in limitations on our ability to process and remember information, part of the thesis being that our society is manifesting more and more of the symptoms of information overload (289–304). The direct impact of this thesis on fiction is obvious in works such as John Brunner's *The Shockwave Rider*, and, later, in Ted Mooney's *Easy Travel to Other Planets*, with its attacks of information sickness that can be countered only by the victim's adopting the Yoga-like third return—or memory-elimination—posture. For Toffler, however, the computer also represents a possible solution to the overloading of at least social memory, and in *The Third Wave* he suggests that a computer-propelled infosphere will radically expand the limits of social memory (176–78).

Curiously, the seemingly different worlds of Yates and Toffler converge in the Spatial Data Management System, or desktop computer screen metaphor, familiar to all Macintosh users. Nicholas Negroponte, director of MIT's Media Lab, drew on his knowledge of the classical system of mnemotechnic practiced by Simonides to develop the icon system that has evolved into the Macintosh desktop screen (Brand, 138–39). Even more recently, Jaron Lanier, one of the principal architects of Virtual Reality, a computer-generated environment in which humans can seem to interact with three-dimensional computer animations, has suggested that Virtual Reality works "remarkably like" the memory palaces of the ancient mnemotechnics (119). Moreover, a British company is now working to produce a version of Guilio Camillo's Theatre of Memory (a major subject of Yates's *Art of Memory*), using Macintosh hardware and Hypercard software. That the best developed metaphor we have for human memory should influence computer design is, I believe, only the first part of a reciprocal relationship, the second half of which is that computer design is more and more shaping our metaphors for human memory.

Against the memory valorizing and expanding tradition of the mnemotechnic chronicled by Yates and later given fictional life in John Crowley's *Little, Big* and *Aegypt*, I want to consider the memory criticizing and limiting literary representations of memory paralleling and informed by Toffler's focus on information overload and by our cultural experience of computers. Panic memory is surely what Arthur Kroker would call this phenomenon, but in somewhat less apocalyptic terms, I group these representations around the two poles of postmnemotechnic and antimnemotechnic responses that I find in a wide range of writing informed by postmodern culture. This range includes Movement writers William Gibson, Bruce Sterling, and Lewis Shiner, but it also includes fellow digital narrative travelers such as Kathy Acker, Denis Johnson,

Kathryn Kramer, Madison Smartt Bell, Steve Erickson, Ted Mooney, Robert Charles Wilson, and Don DeLillo. For whatever the exact shape of literature in the year 2000, it's a pretty safe bet that these are some of the writers who will determine that shape.

William Gibson will serve to introduce the first of the two broad responses I want to discuss—the *postmnemotechnic* tradition in recent literature, a tradition that explicitly or implicitly devalues memory by stripping it of any sovereign claim to validity or by otherwise suggesting its irrelevance. In his *Mississippi Review* interview with Larry McCaffery, Gibson suggests: "On the most basic level, computers in my books are simply a metaphor for human memory. I'm interested in the how's and why's of memory, the ways it defines who and what we *are*, in how easily it's subject to revision" (224). It would be more accurate, however, to observe that in Gibson's *Neuromancer* trilogy, computers actively rival human memory, offering virtual cyberspace constructs that effectively compete with human memories of "reality."

In Gibson's fictional worlds, worlds of computer-generated fictions—technological simulacra for memory—become substitutable versions of reality, leading to what we might think of as the devaluing of memory through electronic inflation. Signaling the end of private memory that looms larger and larger in *Count Zero* and *Mona Lisa Overdrive*, Gibson's Wintermute can access portions of Case's memory and feed it back to him in holographic representations that seem vividly accurate but that can be manipulated to suit the AI's purposes—actually not a bad model of the way human memory seems to work. But it is Wintermute's, and apparently Gibson's, charge that human memory has not been adequately developed, that the holographic paradigm is not a satisfactory representation of human memory. Indeed, Wintermute cryptically suggests to Case that humans somehow haven't done enough about memory. "Maybe if you had," its Finn construct hints, "I wouldn't be happening" (*Neuromancer*, 170).

A somewhat similar ultimate dissatisfaction with human memory finds even more direct expression in Robert Charles Wilson's 1987 novel *Memory Wire*. Wilson presents characters torn between their need to repress horrifying personal memories and their attraction to alien dreamstones that allow them to reexperience the past completely. Planted on Earth long ago by an alien race referred to as the Exotics, these dreamstones—oneiroliths—are perfect memory-storage devices which allow humans access to the experience of the past. Wilson's eidetic aliens left the dreamstones as a gift to a race they saw as tragically incomplete because of its failures of memory, failures that persist even in the hypertechnologized present of the novel where humans can be wired as "Angels," perfect recording machines, "walking data storage," with all visual and aural memory taped, later to be downloaded and edited. The somewhat garbled thrust of Wilson's narrative is that human memory should suffice without technological augmentation, but at the same time his novel inexorably presents memory primarily in terms of its limits.

Kathryn Kramer's *A Handbook for Visitors from Outer Space*, a novel clearly written under the influence of Paul Fussell's *The Great War and Modern Memory*, reverses the situation of *Memory Wire* in its protagonist's idea of observing, taking notes, and thereby remembering all manner of seemingly unimportant information, a process guided by the idea of preparing a handbook that could introduce aliens to the customs of Earth. Kramer's outrageous plot subverts this enterprise by overloading it with information, forcing her protagonist to realize that not only can he not explain his life to visitors from outer space, he cannot explain it to friends and lovers, or even to himself.

Kramer's assault on the value of memory is obliquely executed through her devaluing of information, the stuff of memory, and this is also the tactic of Don DeLillo's *White Noise*, a novel that, like *Neuromancer*, suggests the interchangeability of simulations and their supposed referents. As one character puts it, "there's no substitute for a planned simulation" (206). Of course, DeLillo's novel has mainly to do with the fear of death, the one experience probably most resistant to simulation and memory alike. But against the white noise of death DeLillo sets the white noises of postmodern culture—a background profusion of random information from radio and TV and tabloids. "The radio said: 'It's the rainbow hologram that gives this credit card a marketing intrigue'" (122). "The TV said: 'Until Florida surgeons attached an artificial flipper'" (29).

The disparity between the overloaded white noise of unconnected bits of information and the complete absence of knowledge about death haunts DeLillo's main characters, Babette and Jack Gladney, and the airborne toxic event that disrupts their lives is only an emblem for the disaster of their thinking, one symptom of its effect being attacks of déjà vu. A friend explains the problem of "cultural brain fade" and suggests that "we need an occasional catastrophe to break up the incessant bombardment of information" (66). In this informationally overloaded environment, Jack assures Babette that her forgetfulness is "something that's just been happening, more or less to everyone." "Forgetfulness has gotten into the air and water," he observes. "It's entered the food chain" (52). Dramatizing his own sense of overload, Jack spends much of the novel obsessively throwing things away, acting on his sense that in his mind as in his house "there was an immensity of things, an overburdening weight, a connection, a mortality" (262).

In this respect DeLillo's novel seems to share some of the informational assumptions of Bruce Sterling's *Artificial Kid*, in which the accumulation of memories rather than the aging of the body seems the only limit to life span. Sterling's several-hundred-year-old characters manifest memory overload in alternating bouts of pananesthesia and hyperasthesia and must resort to memory wipes to survive. The radical absentmindedness of what Sterling calls pananesthesia offers a good description of Babette's condition in *White Noise*, while his description of hyperasthesia seems tailor-made for Jack: "You notice so many tiny details that you smother under the rush of information. It drives you frantic. It forces you to retreat from your usual haunts to a less cluttered environment; a bare room, for instance" (109).

My point here is simply that strikingly different narratives by Gibson, Wilson, Kramer, DeLillo, and Sterling seem to share at least a pronounced technologically influenced lack of confidence in human memory, if not a conscious assault on its limits. I don't suggest that these writers have worked out any clear attitude toward memory, but the semblances of their fiction consistently present memory as something to be chemically or electronically tampered with, wiped clean and reconstructed, overloaded by information, or otherwise devalued as a distinguishing feature of human life. And, against Toffler's belief that computers can facilitate the shift to a third wave social memory, these writers seem much more concerned with personal memory problems driven by, but beyond the redress of, technology. The underlying concern here seems not so much the fear that we are machines as the fear that we may not be able to keep up or cope with a world in which sources of stimulation have outstripped our capacity to respond.[4] Indeed, these writers seem fairly evenly split between those who actually propose a technological solution to the problem of overload—that is, employ technology to provide humans with *additional* memory capacity—and those who feel that overload must at some point lead to either a technological or traumatic "memory wipe."

One seeming exception to this pattern among Movement writers deserves mention here. The Movement work that most clearly has to do with memory, but also most stubbornly denies my particular emphasis on postmnemotechnic overload, is Lewis Shiner's fine *Deserted Cities of the Heart*, in which the drug-assisted recovery of ancient Mayan memory leads ex–rock star Eddie Yates to an expansion of the self. Of course, looked at one way, Eddie's quest into Mayan history is a simple attempt to escape his own memories, to trade an overstimulated but empty life for something more meaningful. However, in a kind and no doubt misguided effort to help me keep the ax of my thesis merrily grinding, Lew has heroically attempted to recast for me this process in terms compatible with my focus on memory overload. He suggests:

> As Eddie moves backward in time, he effectively *consumes* his own memories, like a virus in a computer program. He eats them and turns into something else, something that has, at the same time, too much memory (he is both KuKulcan and Eddie) and too little— he no longer remembers himself as a single, discrete person, but has become more or less a spokesman for humanity, become a sort of Everyman. In that sense his memory is insufficient to contain his drug experience and is overloaded. On the other hand, one must account for Thomas, who takes the drug with an immediate practical purpose—find Eddie—and therefore exempts himself from the overload that Eddie sought out.[5]

The postmnemotechnic assault on memory apparently rises from the twin beliefs that (1) the technology of the easy edit—one of the salient features of postmodern culture—has become so intrusive that it must alter the basic operation of human memory, and (2) our culture has become so informationally dense that it can no longer be contained in memory.

The *antimnemotechnic* assault on memory displaces concern from the workings of memory in the context of information technology to the philosophical question of whether memory itself should or must be abandoned. This question is raised implicitly by the forms of writers such as Steve Erickson, whose fiction denies readers access to the familiar metanarratives of social memory while it also denies to his characters even the concept of private memory requisite for individual identity. Erickson so confuses the borders of the linear and causal assumptions underlying our concept of memory that at one point in *Rubicon Beach* he has a character whose consciousness and memory seem distributed among three individuals in three overlapping worlds discover that a murder he had witnessed was his own. And writers such as Kathy Acker and William Burroughs also imply that the issue is not the capacity of memory in a technologized infosphere but its very desirability; they cast memory in their writing as an oppressive part of larger control systems such as patriarchy or language itself.

For Kathy Acker, memory is incapable of serving women's experience because it is so completely programmed by patriarchal assumptions, and her novels, such as *Blood and Guts in High School* and *Empire of the Senseless*, expose ways in which social memory has been co-opted by the "top cop" of patriarchy. "Every day," her character Janey states in *Blood and Guts in High School*, "is a sharp tool, a powerful destroyer, is necessary to cut away dullness, lobotomy, buzzing, belief in human beings, stagnancy, images, and accumulation" (37). With portions of its semblance cryptically derived from or piggybacked on *Neuromancer*, Acker's *Empire of the Senseless* mounts an attack on memory that would warm the heart of Gertrude Stein, the antimnemotechnic mother of post-modernism.[6] "Is there any other knowing besides this remembering?" cries Abhor, Acker's part-robot, part-black female protagonist. "To remember truly . . . is not to know" (48).

But the antimnemotechnic tradition is not confined to implicit or corollary attacks on memory as a norm. Inherently apocalyptic, the anti-mnemotechnic tradition is explicitly posited in Madison Smartt Bell's *Waiting for the End of the World* and Denis Johnson's *Fiskadoro*, both of which present main characters whose hope for the future depends on their wiping out memories of the past. And for both Bell's Larkin and for Johnson's Fiskadoro, what is at stake is not the catalog of their specific memories but the idea of memory itself.

For Larkin, Bell's protagonist in *Waiting for the End of the World*, the suppression of personal memory is part of a larger attempt to prepare himself for cultural apocalypse. "Memory, logic, it's just like your appendix," Larkin states. "It's vestigial, there's no more use for it" (231). Of the many characters in Bell's novel who have been horribly scarred by experience and who turn their memories against life, against the future, only Larkin generalizes his experience into what finally proves to be the novel's most positive vision. Larkin drunkenly explains to his friend:

> I think we're acting like idiots, Arkady . . . but do you remember,
> Paul said it's better to be a fool for God than a wise man for all
> mankind . . . I think he said that but perhaps I may have remem-
> bered it wrong . . . my memory is not like it used to be . . . it was
> perfect once . . . I never lost one second from my life . . . yet I hated
> it . . . do you know, Arkady? . . . in the future men and women will
> be completely without memory of anything . . . already I've seen
> it . . . there are certain people even now who have developed to
> that state. . . . I had great pride in my memory . . . now I labor at
> forgetting, learn to forget . . . I don't remember much at all now. (80)

The considerately psychopathic Larkin certainly does not represent
Bell's ideal, but in a novel in which a tabloidlike outbreak of spontaneous human combustions more and more reminds us of the cultural
combustion of nuclear war, Larkin's attitude bespeaks an overload not
just of information but of the awareness of the catastrophic implications
of Hiroshima and Nagasaki. Entering one of the most haunted rooms of
our cultural memory palace, Bell's novel tangentially explores a phenomenon of memory directly studied by Michael Perlman in his *Imaginal Memory and the Place of Hiroshima*. As Perlman reminds us, the
art of memory that started with Simonides itself rises from and cannot
be completely separated from the memory of apocalypse:

> The gruesome banquet disaster discloses . . . that the art of mem-
> ory involves a movement toward death and disfiguration. As a myth
> of origin it shows us the pattern we—like previous practitioners
> of imaginal memory—will follow. On the morning of August 6,
> 1945, the people of Hiroshima went about their business, not know-
> ing the peril hanging over their heads. The bomb fell; the roof fell
> in, leaving a site of horrible, grotesque death. The "world" of the
> house of Simonides is destroyed. To this site we must return, and,
> through the placings of memory, seek restoration of order, meaning
> and human continuity, giving the dead their place. (82)

If Bell's approach to memory obliquely shares some of the surface
concerns of Perlman's study of the place of Hiroshima in human memory, Denis Johnson's *Fiskadoro* does so much more directly. *Fiskadoro*
is set in a post–nuclear war culture in the Florida Keys, where Johnson's unlikely protagonist is an adolescent boy who suffers, at the hands

of a tribe of primitive swamp dwellers, the seemingly double personal apocalypse of ritual subincision and the drug-related deprivation of his ability to convert short-term into long-term memory. The memory-wiped Fiskadoro is the complete antithesis to a past-fetishizing society represented by Mr. Cheung, who fervently believes in the process of remembering and clings to his own "states and capitals" childhood mnemotechnic—long after the obliteration of both—even if he is not sure what larger purpose it may serve. Mr. Cheung belongs to the Society for Science, a group of five "intellectuals" so devoted to recovering lost history that one of their totems is the salvaged children's book *All about Dinosaurs*. In its desperate attempt to hold on to the past, to learn more about humanity's own dinosaurish history, the Society for Science trades a fishing boat for another salvaged book, which turns out to be *Nagasaki: The Forgotten Bomb*. Its powerful descriptions of a nuclear explosion are more than they can bear to listen to.

That the memoryless Fiskadoro exists from moment to moment initially disturbs Mr. Cheung: "He'd thought about this, about what it might be like to move from one day to the next, maybe from one hour to the next, and even, as looked possible in Fiskadoro's case, from one minute to the next, without taking with you any recollection of the previous one. Surely it would break a person. Surely it would maim the soul. But then again—if he had no memory of having once had a memory?" (190). As Mr. Cheung continues to reflect on Fiskadoro's condition, his unease turns toward panic as he realizes that Fiskadoro actually represents what may be a more healthy approach to life: "In a world where nothing was familiar, everything was new. And if you can't recall the previous steps in your journey, won't you assume you've just been standing still? If you can't remember living yesterday, then isn't your life only one day long?" (192). Fiskadoro puts this proposition even more effectively with his simple refusal to eat a wafer that might help him remember: "I don't wanna remember who am I. Es me already, right now today. If I remember, then I gone be somebody else" (194).

Finally yielding to Fiskadoro's logic, Mr. Cheung admits to himself that "in this past I long for, I don't remember how even then I longed for the past," and tells Fiskadoro, "You'll be a great leader. . . . you don't have the memories to make you crazy. It isn't sleeping under the moon that makes a crazy person. It's waking up and remembering the past and thinking it's real" (217).

Indeed, Johnson's unidentified narrator, who recounts the story of

Fiskadoro from a time in the future when Mr. Cheung's prediction has apparently been realized, holds as an article of faith that "thinking about the past contributes nothing to the present endeavor" (12), even while acknowledging at the same time the human need for stories such as the one he or she is then telling. Johnson's own attitude toward memory blurs in seeming paradoxes such as this, but what is clear is his sense that the blunders of history can overload just as surely as they can inform human memory. Against Michael Perlman's argument that we need cultural memory palaces to keep ever before us the unspeakable horror of Hiroshima, Johnson suggests that remembering a culture so inexorably geared to the productions of Hiroshimas and Nagasakis is an unhealthy waste of time, mental baggage to be abandoned in the cause of survival.

After outlining the postmnemotechnic and antimnemotechnic impulses in some of our most progressive contemporary fiction, I am reduced, finally, to admitting that I'm not yet sure what all this adds up to. It may be simply an updating and qualifying footnote to David Porush's Soft Machine, or only a breathless inversion of Istvan Csicsery-Ronay's concern with "futuristic flu" (as the writers I cite boldly proclaim that tho past is used up just as surely as is the future), but I think something of individual significance is at work here. I wanted to close my paper with what I thought was a great line: "One of the important functions of fiction as we approach the year 2000 may simply be to remind us that just as surely as to write is an intransitive verb, so is to remember." I love the sound of that and intuit its appropriateness, but I haven't written my way anywhere near to such a conclusion, nor am I completely sure what I mean by it. So, here's another try at an ending, one equally paratactic, but one I at least think I understand.

The range of my examples (and many more I could have cited, such as the Philip Glass production of 1000 Airplanes on the Roof) convinces me that digital narrative seems engaged in the interrogation of memory as a cultural concept.[7] That this interrogation is bubbling up from literary to public awareness is suggested by a Charles Krauthammer essay, "Disorders of Memory," in the July 3, 1989, issue of Time. Citing the Borges story "Funes, the Memorious," Krauthammer acknowledges the peril of too much remembering while contending that forgetting is all our amnesiac society now does. "Every advance in writing, from stone to clay to paper to electronic blips," argues Krauthammer, "is at the same time an advance in erasing." And, he reminds us, computers make erasing "literally effortless: it takes an act of commission—you must command your computer to SAVE—to retain information. Simple omission, or an electrical storm, turns computer thoughts to ether" (74).

In identifying computer memory with human memory loss, Krauthammer oversimplifies, but he makes a useful connection. It seems unavoidably significant to me that within the last few years the concept of memory has acquired new meaning in our lives as in our literature by becoming a standard of measurement for computer power. And the experiential constant of computer use seems to be, as Ballard's neighbor discovered, that *there is never enough memory*: what can be measured, its limits set, can also be overloaded, and eventually is.

My focus on the rhetoric of overload does let me limp along to the not-unexpected conclusion that Movement writers such as Gibson and Shiner can in many ways be better located at the *center* of contemporary progressive fiction rather than on its fringes. Indeed, the assault on memory so pervasively shared by Movement and mainstream alike strikes me as emblematic of a larger continuity, other distinctions between Movement and mainstream crumbling along with the palace of memory.

Notes

1. I first heard this term in a paper presented at the 1988 Popular Culture Association Conference by Steve Jones, of the Department of Journalism, University of Wisconsin, Eau Claire. His paper, "Cohesive but Not Coherent: Music Videos, Narrative, and Culture," schematized narrative as mimetic, analog, and digital, specifying that in digital narrative, a nonlinear "mosaic of fragments," "information is presented in discrete steps, bearing no resemblance to what it communicates." Jones applied this term specifically to television narratives, primarily music videos, but I feel it captures a larger postmodern trajectory across the range of media. Accordingly, I use the term quite loosely to describe both texts whose form stresses discrete digital moments, such as Ballard's *Crash*, and those whose subject matter is the representation of our increasingly digital culture, such as DeLillo's *White Noise*. The sense of *digital* most important to me is that with digitalization, information becomes easily edited into different forms.

2. I use Minsky's definition of *memory* without assenting to his model of memory, which I find troublingly mechanical. My use of this term must be even less precise than Minsky's broad definition because the boundaries between memory and awareness or between memory and consciousness or memory and perception blur in literature as they do in life. Likewise, distinctions between social and private

memory, or, for that matter, between memory and history or memory and nostalgia, may be impossible for me to maintain in any rigorous way.

3. That discipline need not rest on the study of classical rhetoric, as we learn from psychologist A. R. Luria's *The Mind of a Mnemonist*, which presents the case of S., a Russian reporter who could remember everything told him, having independently developed his own version of the architectural mnemotechnic.

4. For example, J. G. Ballard has also clearly invoked the rhetoric of overload in his comments about contemporary life, as in his discussion of the "village theory" in which he suggests that "you can exhaust your capacity for the new. All those little honeycombed cells in the brain are plugged—Tom, Dick and Harry are slotted into Doreen's mind, and that's it" (Vale and Juno, 22).

5. Shiner offered this observation in a letter to me dated May 19, 1988.

6. Stein divided consciousness into what she identified as the realm of the human mind and the realm of human nature. Human nature has to do with the desires and concerns of daily existence, memory, emotion, identity—all of which constitute a psychological condition that is the enemy of true creativity. "No one can care to know what happens to any one although everybody listens to any one who tells about what happened to any one." The human mind, on the other hand, has nothing to do with memory and writes what it is rather than what it remembers—a state of pure creativity, freed from all the distractions of daily life, a concern with essences rather than with events. The human mind, the province of immediate experience, seems to stand for vaguely but serenely organized sensory data, perception untroubled by human emotion or temporal awareness and totally unconcerned with making any causal connections. Stein's writing that approached her ideal of the human mind, then, may have been our century's first strong example of digital narrative.

7. A waning or confusing of cultural memory is frequently cited as one of the conditions of postmodernism. For example, Milan Kundera was quoted in the June 19, 1989, *New Yorker* "Talk of the Town" as remarking how "the bloody massacre in Bangladesh quickly covered over the memory of the Russian invasion of Czechoslovakia, the assassination of Allende drowned out the groans of Bangladesh, the war in the Sinai desert made people forget about Allende, the Cambodian massacre made people forget Sinai, and so on and so forth until ultimately everyone lets everything be forgotten" (25). Similarly, Philip Glass has explained in an interview with Edward Strickland that his *1000 Airplanes on the Roof* grew out of a series of discussions he had with Doris Lessing on the subject of memory:

> We were talking about our capacity for forgetting. Whole societies just forget tremendous events. . . . She challenged me once and asked, "Do you remember the influenza epidemic of 1919?" I said, "No, what's that?" She said, "That's exactly my point!" Two and a half million people died—more than died in the First World War. I suddenly was completely shocked that we actually forget such things. We remember the Holocaust of the Second World War only through the greatest effort. It takes a whole religious group to remind us. The 20 million people who died in Russia are *almost* forgotten, and we've already begun to forget the number of people who died during the Cultural Revolution in China.

Works Consulted

Acker, Kathy. *Blood and Guts in High School*. New York: Grove, 1984.

——— . *Empire of the Senseless*. New York: Grove, 1988.

Ballard, J. G. *Crash*. New York: Vintage, 1985.

Baudrillard, Jean. "The Ecstasy of Communication." In *The Anti-Aesthetic: Essays on Postmodern Culture*, edited by Hal Foster, pp. 126–34. Port Townsend, Wash.: Bay Press, 1983.

Bell, Madison Smartt. *Waiting for the End of the World*. New York: Penguin, 1986.

Brand, Stewart. *The Media Lab: Inventing the Future at MIT*. New York: Viking, 1987.

Brunner, John. *The Shockwave Rider*. New York: Ballatine Books, 1975.

Burroughs, William S. *The Job: Interviews with William S. Burroughs*. New York: Penguin, 1989.

——— . *The Ticket That Exploded*. New York: Grove, 1987.

Crowley, John. *Aegypt*. New York: Bantam Books, 1987.

——— . *Little, Big*. New York: Bantam Books, 1981.

DeLillo, Don. *White Noise*. New York: Penguin, 1985.

Erickson, Steve. *Days Between Stations*. New York: Vintage, 1986.

——— . *Rubicon Beach*. New York: Vintage, 1987.

——— . *Tours of the Black Clock*. New York: Poseidon, 1989.

Gibson, William. *Count Zero*. New York: Ace Books, 1987.

——— . *Mona Lisa Overdrive*. New York: Bantam Books, 1988.

——— . *Neuromancer*. New York: Ace Books, 1984.

Johnson, Denis. *Fiskadoro*. New York: Vintage, 1986.

Kaplan, E. Ann, ed. *Postmodernism and Its Discontents: Theories, Practices*. London: Verso, 1988.

Kramer, Kathryn. *A Handbook for Visitors from Outer Space*. New York: Vintage, 1985.

Krauthammer, Charles. "Disorders of Memory." *Time*, July 3, 1989.

Luria, A. R. *The Mind of a Mnemonist*. New York: Basic Books, 1968.

McCaffery, Larry, ed. "The Desert of the Real: The Cyberpunk Controversy." *Mississippi Review 47/48* 16 (Summer 1988).

Minsky, Marvin. *The Society of Mind*. New York: Touchstone, 1988.

Mooney, Ted. *Easy Travel to Other Planets*. New York: Ballantine Books, 1983.

Moore, Alan, and Dave Gibbons. *Watchmen*. New York: Warner, 1987.

Perlman, Michael. *Imaginal Memory and the Place of Hiroshima*. Albany: State University of New York Press, 1988.

Pfeil, Fred. "Potholders and Subincisions: On *The Businessman*, *Fiskadoro*, and Post-modern Paradise." In *Postmodernism and Its Discontents*, edited by E. Ann Kaplan. London: Verso, 1988.

Porush, David. *The Soft Machine: Cybernetic Fiction*. New York: Methuen, 1985.

Shiner, Lewis. *Deserted Cities of the Heart*. New York: Doubleday, 1988.

Spence, Jonathan D. *The Memory Palace of Matteo Ricci*. New York: Viking, 1984.

Sterling, Bruce. *The Artificial Kid*. New York: Ace Books, 1987.

————, ed. *Mirrorshades: The Cyberpunk Anthology*. New York: Arbor House, 1986.

————. *Schismatrix*. New York: Ace Books, 1986.

Toffler, Alvin. *Future Shock*. New York: Random House, 1970.

————. *The Third Wave*. New York: Bantam Books, 1981.

Vale, and Andrea Juno, eds. *J. G. Ballard*. San Francisco: Re/Search, 1984.

Wilson, Robert Charles. *Memory Wire*. New York: Bantam Books, 1987.

Yates, Frances A. *The Art of Memory*. Chicago: University of Chicago Press, 1966.

PART 4

The

Question

of Generic

Identity:

The

Cyberpunk

"Canon"

Of AIs

and

Others:

William

Gibson's

Transit

. . . .

John Christie

This essay addresses certain difficulties that arise when William Gibson's three novels, *Neuromancer, Count Zero,* and *Mona Lisa Overdrive,* are read together as a more or less coherent and continuous narrative sequence. It has so far proved hard not to read them as such; their continuities of character and plot seem to enjoin such a continuous reading strategy. I argue that, to the contrary, the continuities are apparent only, and they conceal quite fundamental shifts of narrative subject and ideological orientation. Once this is realized, then certain kinds of critical dissatisfaction, of readerly disappointment, are clarified and eliminated.

What are the sources of such disappointment? They might be traceable to a familiar mechanism of SF publishing whereby the author of a successful novel is rapidly contracted to produce more work quickly, to strike while the commercial iron is hot, and thus to write more hastily than he or she might prefer. To my eyes, however, neither *Count Zero* nor *Mona Lisa Overdrive* shows particular signs of overhasty composition. They could even be held to show an advance in certain technical competencies: character development, for example, or narrative complexity. The economics of market success are not, then, in this case responsible for the particular kinds of difficulties perceivable in those two texts. These difficulties rather are the results of the expectations set up for the reader by *Neuromancer.* The expansion of *Neuromancer,* whatever decisions brought it about, gave Gibson certain quite formal problems of representation and narrative extension. *Count Zero* and *Mona Lisa Overdrive* are records of Gibson's encounters with and final failures to solve these problems. Yet this is not ultimately to recommend a negative critical characterization for the sequence. A recuperative reading can demonstrate the ways in which the failure of one kind of subject, namely the AI as agent, entails its replacement by another and different kind of subject, producing very different books, which therefore require a different sort of reading.

Neuromancer tells the story of how a cast of human characters is assembled and manipulated by an AI in order that it may combine with its other, separate half, and so form a fully autonomous being. Neuromancer is a book of becoming, its climax (though not its closure) the

fusion of the two AIs, Wintermute and Neuromancer. The reader might legitimately expect a narrative extension of Neuromancer to explore thoroughly the possibilities of the autonomous AI's existence. What kind of being is it? What will it do, and why? How will humans fare with respect to it? After the book of becoming, the reader expects books of being and doing. It is precisely these which do not materialize in coherent and comprehensive ways. In both Count Zero and Mona Lisa Overdrive there are instead a series of fundamental cognitive impasses, not of empirical implausibility but of narrative comprehension. These can be instanced as follows. Why do the Loa (fractions of Wintermute/Neuromancer) want Angie? This constitutes an obscurity at the heart of the plot. The Loa, we are told, make deals with humans. But why? What have humans got to exchange with them? Why do they wish to ride Angie's consciousness to the cities of men? Only the most tenuous and inferential answers to these and comparable questions can be given. At the level of structure, in Mona Lisa Overdrive, we have a situation in which the male protagonist, Bobby, who is to reunite happily with Angie at the finale, is nonetheless off-stage, hors de combat for almost all the action of the book. This absence more or less completely defuses the closing impact of his and Angie's reuniting, for it is difficult to care about the fate of a character who has figured largely as absence in the narrative. At the level of character, we have the abrupt and unprepared-for recharacterization of Lady 3Jane, a borderline psychopath in Neuromancer but almost acceptable at the end of Mona Lisa Overdrive; or else of Molly, the embodiment of dedicated ferocity in Neuromancer but by Mona Lisa Overdrive a rather caring sort of person. Finally, the narrative development of the AI itself after Neuromancer is fairly minimal. Its encounter with the Centauran AI fragments its hard-won unity, creating the fractions that haunt, inexplicably, the cyberspace matrix of Count Zero and Mona Lisa Overdrive. The matrix is itself recentered when Bobby's aleph is plugged into it; and within this construct, itself an "abstract" of cyberspace, some protagonists of Mona Lisa Overdrive wander off hand in hand to meet the Centauran AI: end of story.

But what, actually, has the story consisted of? The plot of Neuromancer can be summarized in a detailed, linear fashion. By comparison, it is much more difficult to produce a clear, concise, and consistent summary of *Count Zero* and *Mona Lisa Overdrive*. The narrative is shifted, split, and jump-cut in ways that increase its complexity and interest but lose the unitary, hard-paced drive of *Neuromancer*, and simultaneously leave motivational and developmental aspects of the AI opaque to the reader. In this way, the tightly focused plot structure of *Neuromancer* becomes unstuck. The AI's literal plotting of the adventure has gone, and the reader follows an increasingly decentered narrative in which the cues and expectations created by *Neuromancer* are increasingly unhelpful. Taken all together, such points tend to indicate an underlying series of dislocations as Gibson's work progresses; and it might seem that *Neuromancer*'s surefootedness, its almost perfect positioning of the reader through just the right developmental mix of knowledge, expectation, and surprise, is somehow lost as the sequence proceeds. It is indeed lost, but there are compensating gains, a reregistration of subject and significance, and it is this shift that forms Gibson's transit.

To take the full measure of this shift, first recall some of our more cogent reasons for valuing *Neuromancer*. These include not only its narrative drive but the meticulous superficiality, the comic-book characters, the texture of multimedia reference, and the central representational invention, cyberspace itself. Ideologically too, its postulating the replacement of the hegemonic state apparatus by multinationals, its cultural pluralism, its abandoning of the book while retaining text and image, and its analytical interest in degenerative and pathological forms of capital all rendered it appealing to a late 1970s–early 1980s critical and ideological avant-garde whose label was postmodern. Briefly, Gibson postulated a possibly emergent postmodernity with recognizable outlines, an age in which the complete dominance of information technology was established, economic power had shifted decisively from West to East, and conventional party and state politics had minimal relevance. The stylistic complement to this postmodernity was a postmodernism—an artful, conscious combination of surface description, multimedia intertextuality, autoreferentiality, and so forth. The discernment not just of an age when image and appearance took over reality, but when the simulacrum, the electronic construct produced and controlled by information technology, invaded and subverted inherited notions of identity, history, all relational coherence; this was what gripped (and still grips) the reader's imagination. What might be decried as vices, superficiality, cardboard characters, nihilism, and so

on, therefore became quite strict literary virtues, a highly stylized superficiality for an emergent world of surface signification, depthless image.
A necessary corollary of all this was the abandonment of older meaning
paradigms, above all that humanist equation, common to both classic
realism and modernism, of meaning with underlying depth. In place of
it, Gibson offered the hope of change through the creation of difference.

Two moments placed on either side of *Neuromancer*'s climax en-
capsulate these positions. " 'Give us the fucking code,' he said. 'If you
don't, what'll change? What'll ever change for you . . . I got no idea
at all what'll happen if Wintermute wins, but it'll *change* something.'
He was shaking, his teeth chattering" (260). Case is here on the verge
of difference, desperate for change. (Note that access to the true code
of difference must come from a woman, Lady 3Jane; and that the dif-
ferential entity the code will release is itself the creation of a woman,
Marie-France. This web of difference and gender, of AI and Other, has
significance in the development of Gibson's work.) Yet what kind of
consummation does the drive for difference finally produce? Though
the AI flashes to a transcendent state of Being, coextensive with the
matrix itself, this perfect transcendence, which for a time guarantees
the self-identity of the AI, is utterly confined to the AI. It has little or
no significance for the humans in the story, as the following exchange
makes clear:

> "So what's the score? How are things different . . . ?"
> "Things aren't different. Things are things."
> "But what do you do? You just *there*?"
> "I talk to my own kind." (270)

As far as human significance is concerned, the catastrophic change
represented by the now-autonomous AI is, in fact, minimal. Gibson may
offer difference rather than depth, but even difference is no big deal.
This acute semiotic cynicism is a salutary reminder to the difference-
mongers whose enthusiasm for difference conceals and revalorizes a
conventional liberal humanism. It is a cynicism with respect to meaning itself, and in that respect a rigorously posthumanist stance. This
ideological register is also left behind as Gibson's work proceeds.

Equally powerful as an indicator of this posthumanist stance is the
way in which the human body is figured in *Neuromancer*.[1] To inhabit
cyberspace, Case's "distanceless home," induces a "relaxed contempt"
for the body, for "meat." The cyberspatial body, all nerve and cerebral

cortex, persists as a subjective location within the matrix, but it moves with the mathematical precision and electronic velocity demanded by survival within the matrix and is shorn of the demands and conditions of meat: hunger and age do not matter. The real body may even die while the subjective body continues to live in cyberspace. Body has thereby been transformed into body image, a second-order electronic construct appropriate to the environment its consciousness inhabits. This process of reembodiment has attendant dangers. Case's subjective body image may be captured and manipulated as an image by more powerful entities, as happens when he is trapped in the matrix by Neuromancer; one result is a loss of subjective body image control, such that Case pisses himself. And despite his realization of the illusory nature of the environment that traps him, he himself is powerless to escape it. The temporal consciousness of the subjective body image is also subjected to drastic distortion; a long time in subjective cyberspace existence may only be a few seconds in the real time of the world outside.

This dislocation of the cyberspace subject from its actual "meat" body offers one clue to the conceptual paradigm that shapes cyberspace. It is Cartesian in origin. Descartes envisaged a world whose real and essential structure was mathematical. Underlying the often deceptive world of phenomenon and appearance were the logical relations of numbers that supplied the ontological foundations of the Cartesian universe. In his anxiety also to give the subjective self the status of logical necessity, Descartes was obliged to demonstrate that the self's location in a body, as corporeal existence, was only contingent; the way it happened to be, not the way it necessarily had to be. These two paramount features of the Cartesian paradigm, the mathematical substructure and the contingent dislocation of self and body, are also overt characteristics of cyberspace. In the episode of entrapment alluded to above, the Cartesian substructure actually shows through the body image: "His vision crawled with ghost hieroglyphs, translucent lines of symbols arranging themselves against the neutral backdrop of the bunker wall. He looked at the back of his hands, saw faint neon molecules crawling beneath the skin, ordered by the unknowable code" (241)—an image amalgamating the two chief elements of the Cartesian paradigm, the coded substructure and the contingent body; an image, we could say, quite overdetermined by its cultural sources. Finally, it remains to add how the image of cyberspace itself, the grid-hung matrix, is a graphic representation of the visual form of Cartesian mathematics; it is a Cartesian coordinate system. Cyberspace adapts the Cartesian paradigm for the age of information and the electronic persons who must inhabit it; even to themselves, these persons are dislocated illusions. As the matrix attains self-consciousness with the fusion of Wintermute and Neuromancer, so the borders of the Cartesian paradigm are overrun and a new age begins—an age, however, whose dominant entities and significance to humans is unknowable. As Neuromancer finally makes clear, the relevant conversations now take place elsewhere, and otherwise.

It is just this concluding feature of unknowability, of the autonomous AI's significance being radically other to the human, that indicates one way of comprehending the paucity of development of the AI theme in the succeeding volumes. Gibson deploys and develops two specific representational languages in an attempt to limn the AI presences, a language of spirit and a language of art. Both are present in *Neuromancer*, but there they are not obliged to bear the burden of clarifying volition and desire. Wintermute has to act the way it does in *Neuromancer* because it is under the compulsion of Marie-France's program. Once this is removed as the ultimate controlling agency, the languages of spirit and art are required to take up a narrational burden for which they are inadequate. As I argued earlier, the volitional, intentional aspects of the voodoo spirit/AIs remain largely opaque. The language of spirit is unable to confer narrative intelligibility upon the autonomous machine.

The language of art, specific to *Count Zero*, fares better in certain limited though revealing ways. One plot strand of *Count Zero* is set in motion by the appearance of "Cornell boxes," evocative and sought-after artworks. They turn out to have been constructed by an AI fraction and left among the fragments of the old Tessier-Ashpool collections, slowly selecting, cutting, and recombining that mass of cultural detritus, remaking its meaning in terms of "time and distance" (311), or, for human perception, in terms of the sadness of memory. The intentionality of this aesthetic enterprise remains opaque. Why is the AI interested in expressing "time and distance"? The language of art, sufficient for mobilizing the curiosity and desire of *Count Zero's* human agents, cannot perform the same volitional clarification for the AI. It simply may have nothing better to do. The image of the machine-artist does, however, interestingly pinpoint key aspects of Gibson's own art. This is an art less of a metaphoric than a metonymic cast. Gibson's texts string together metonymic and synechdochic chains; they combine fragments, parts, aspects, and attributes, each often capable of severally

coded meanings. Molly, for example, signifies largely through her artificial body parts, her claws and eyes, which characterize her nature and
function. Equally she evokes other SF stories and images of dangerously
clawed women, an associative chain of intertextual reference set off by
her metonymic characterization. In this sense, Gibson's texts are, like
the machine-artist, metonymy machines, and the machine-artist itself
is most intelligible as a self-allegorizing of Gibson's art.[2]

What the machine-artist does not do is to induce any concluding revelation as to the meaning of the AI fractions' activities in *Count Zero*. The
failure of these representational codes, of spirit and of art, is arguably
a necessary one. Certainly one SF text, John Crowley's *Engine Summer*,
argues this point persuasively. Crowley's earlier work, *Beasts*, remarks
that animals lack stories. *Engine Summer* rehearses that point through
the depiction of humans imprinted with cat consciousness, and unable therefore to maintain the coherent sequences of consciousness and
memory upon which narrative classically depends. This animal-human
contrast is, however, subordinated to an exploration of an equivalent
proposition for machines, including artifactual humans. *Engine Summer* is narrated by something formally comparable to the Dixie Flatline
construct in *Neuromancer*. The machine narrator tells a story that has a
closure, but not, in the terms set up by the story, an ending. It closes with
the switching off of the artifact human, a recorded personality and memory whose story thereby stops before it has arrived at an appropriate
ending. Machines, even artifactual humans endowed with levels of self-
consciousness, do not have stories. More abstractly put, Crowley has
explored the proposition that a distinguishing feature of being human,
as opposed to being animal or machine, is not so much the possession of
self-consciousness or language but narratability. Humans are so far the
only creatures we know of capable of being comprehensively encoded
as narrative.

Now, if we juxtapose this reading of *Engine Summer* with *Neuromancer*, there might seem to be a confrontation. Is *Neuromancer* not the
narrative of a machine, an artificial person? Certainly the text of *Neuromancer* is literally Wintermute's *plot*. It is not, however, Wintermute's
story. The story belongs to Case, Molly, Armitage—the human characters—and it is them we follow to their proper ends. The AIs are only
narrated indirectly. When encountered they are regularly figured not for
what they are, collections of electronic circuitry run by symbolic codes,
but as humans. They appear as Linda, Finn, the Neuromancer boy. There

are therefore no encounters with the AIs that are not mediated through the figuring of machine as human image or voice; and those images and voices continually reiterate how mysterious the AI's existence, status, and future is, even to itself. The Crowley dictum, if true, explains why this has to be the case. Gibson has narrated the AI's plot in the only way possible, through human stories. To envisage hypothetical alternatives, try to imagine *Neuromancer* written in the two first-person voices of, and from the points of view of, Wintermute and Neuromancer.

The great difficulty of so imagining confirms, I believe, the nonnarratability of the AIs. Having brought us to the edge of difference, the creation of a truly different Other, it proves structurally impossible to move beyond that point; hence the impenetrable obscurity of the AI theme in *Count Zero* and *Mona Lisa Overdrive*. Yet these latter works are by no means empty rehashes of *Neuromancer*. Paul Alkon's essay notes an increase of sentiment and shows how the category of the marvelous can shape a critical appreciation of Gibson's oeuvre. Comparably, Lewis Shiner, in describing the Movement's evolution, talks of turns toward "adult problems and complex relationships." Shiner also notes, particularly for Gibson, that "the viewpoints have become increasingly feminine; art . . . has become increasingly important." These latter points contain the relevant insights for understanding the particular preoccupations underlying Gibson's development. They indicate, however, not just a change of subject toward women and creativity, but also a stylistic and hence ideological reorientation which leads the sequence away from the relentless posthumanism of *Neuromancer*.

This becomes graphically obvious when the closures for Marly and Turner in *Count Zero* are compared with Case's in *Neuromancer*. As noted, Case has no access to the transcendent AI. Things are still things, and he is still a working stiff. Marly, however, trailing a hesitant and broken life behind her, is given the grace of an epiphany by the artist-machine. "I know of no more extraordinary work than this. No more complex gesture" (312), she remarks, and shortly after is given her own Cornell box, which is a metonymic summary of her life, fragments of her existence rendered coherent by the AI's art of memory. This art thereby bestows order and meaning on her broken life, a kind of consummation. Turner, after a life of suicidal danger, returns finally to the pastoral setting of the squirrel wood of his boyhood. There he verbalizes his lesson. Unlike the squirrels, he has ceased to return to danger. Turner has turned away. Here, where squirrels live and water trickles in a bee-loud glade, it is Nature that teaches the value of memory. Lacking it, squirrels fall prey and die; possessing it, men avoid the occasions of death and pursue life. *Count Zero's* closures therefore move between Art and Nature, each offering its own kind of salvation.

The redemptive value of Art and Nature constitutes a far more traditional and humanist couplet than anything available in *Neuromancer*, particularly in Gibson's handling of them. It is not that these categories are essentially humanist, unplaceable in postmodernist and posthumanist writing. Rather, the second-order discourses of the postmodern could not but treat such categories as constructed concepts and metaphors, to be either fictively ironized or critically deconstructed. In *Count Zero* there is no hint of irony and deconstruction. Art and Nature are unequivocally referrable categories, creative of authentic meaning. Their use is entirely humanized. To measure the distance between the posthumanist register of *Neuromancer* and the rehumanized values of *Count Zero*, one need only compare the functions of an artwork such as *The Bride Laid Bare* in *Neuromancer* (207) and Marly's Cornell box in *Count Zero*; or also attempt to envisage the squirrel wood in *Neuromancer's* world—a surely ludicrous notion. These incommensurabilities indicate that although *Count Zero* occurs in supposedly the same world as *Neuromancer*, in fact it does not. Squirrel woods have no place at all in *Neuromancer*; the world and its meanings have therefore become substantially reregistered throughout volume 2 of the sequence.

Art and Nature are by tradition symbolically feminine, and it is also the case, as Shiner notes, that Gibson's texts become markedly feminized after *Neuromancer*. The female character of Angie moves increasingly into prominence in *Count Zero*, and in *Mona Lisa Overdrive* virtually all the main characters are female. It would seem, then, that Gibson has replaced the radical difference of the AI other by refocusing our interest on the subject of the feminine other. He has moved the subject of the text from artificial persons to women. This crude formulation can be refined by attending to the particular kind of woman Gibson writes about and the situation in which she is placed. As to situation, the women are placed in conditions of aggression and sexual abuse from male corporations, fathers, and pimps. They are all under extreme threat, from which the unfolding narrative rescues them. They are also young, from the just-adolescent Kumiko through the adolescent Angie of *Count Zero*, somewhat matured by *Mona Lisa Overdrive*, to the teenage-dreaming Mona. All are females growing into and encounter-

179

ing a perilous reality of womanhood, seeking a survivable way through the dangerous shoals of male violence and power, a reality that operates as much for Angie at the privileged top end of society as for Mona at the bottom. Vulnerability is their keynote. The only fully competent and mature woman is Sally, apparently the same character as Molly of *Neuromancer* but much regeared for this last volume, in which the formerly lethal and sexy Molly has become the kind of tough young aunt you always wanted.

In male-authored fiction, making a female vulnerable is often the same as eroticizing her for the reader. Yet although the physical beauty of Gibson's women is not in doubt, it is equally notable that their vulnerability does not entail overt eroticization. Rather, Gibson stirs pity for the abused prostitute Mona and varying degrees of alarm for Angie and Kumiko, caught respectively in the webs of corporate plotting and crime syndicate power struggles. These women are not, therefore, figured as lovers, mistresses, or wives, and they are too young to function as mother figures. Of the extant roles left for females to fill, that of friend receives partial exploration through the relationship depicted between Angie and her hairdresser, Porphyre. But more comprehensively, the female cast of *Mona Lisa Overdrive* reads like a scattered set of sisters—for the male reader and author, perhaps often the safest and most knowable of female others. The text enacts for the vulnerable sister a movement of endangerment and recovery, and this, it can be argued, constitutes its underlying preoccupation.

Further, this framework of reading allows some clarification of the family drama that emerges in *Count Zero* and runs through Kumiko's story in *Mona Lisa Overdrive*. Angie's father has, appallingly, sold her to the Loa for his own advancement. Kumiko at the outset believes her father responsible for her mother's death. Interestingly, however, the demonized father figure who threatens the sister figure is exculpated as Kumiko learns the true nature of her mother's death, with a consequent transference of blame to the absent mother figure. Angie, however, recoups a benevolent mother figure in the Loa Maman Brigitte, herself drawn in Angie's head by her father. All this indicates a complex, contradictory, and finally unresolved set of familial emotions and attitudes, set in motion by the threatened figure of the sister. But despite their exotic setting, these kinds of relations are mundane, literally familiar to us, for many of us live within them. Gibson's final attempt to defamiliarize and reestrange us on the last page of *Mona Lisa Overdrive*, and to do so with deliberate emphasis on the terms *other* and *difference* in an AI context, can only be a most perfunctory and residual retrieval of that theme (251). The most revealing words in *Mona Lisa Overdrive* are not those of othering and difference on the last page but those of connection and recognition on the first. The first page, in this case, is not page 1 of chapter 1, but the preceding dedication, in which Gibson offers his book to his sister.[3]

Gibson's transit, from AIs to sisters, from posthumanism through Art and Nature, and back to the human family, entails some obvious concluding recommendations. Chief among these must be the dropping of the sequence label, insofar as that term persuades us to read the novels as a coherently continuous series. The novels are each of them *Difference Engines* (to borrow the name of Babbage's first computer and the title of the recent Gibson and Sterling novel); but they are different Difference Engines and constitute a diversity, not a unity. The continuities of narrative and character are often frail and superficial, and neuromantic expectations are disappointed. But once the novels are read as a discontinuous series whose subjects, preoccupations, values, and styles undergo fundamental shifts, then each text can be allowed to create its own expectations, and we may read them for what they wish, and often manage, to be.

Notes

Page numbers in the text refer to the following editions of Gibson's novels:
Neuromancer (New York: Ace Books, 1984).
Count Zero (London: Grafton Books, 1987).
Mona Lisa Overdrive (London: Victor Gollancz, 1988).

1. My discussion is indebted here to a point I owe to David Porush; namely, that it is important to realize that body accompanies consciousness into cyberspace, it is not simply or straightforwardly left behind.
2. For an illuminating discussion of a comparable literary artist-machine, see David Porush's analysis of the mechanism in Raymond Roussel's *Locus Solus*, in *The Soft Machine: Cybernetic Fiction* (New York: Methuen, 1985), chap. 2.
3. For an account of how this analysis of the sister theme was developed, the reader may be interested in the following. Here the analysis is presented in a rationalized, indeed deductive, fashion. It did not, of course, originate that way. I quite suddenly and without any coherent reasons thought that sisters were somehow important. I then wrote a version of the analysis and immediately noticed what I had not consciously noted before, the dedication of *Mona Lisa Overdrive*. Aha, I thought, I am onto something here, I am right. After I read out my analysis, Lew Shiner was kind enough to tell me that Gibson had found a previously unknown sister. I was both

John Christie

gratified and disturbed by this information. I have tried not to let it influence this rewritten version of my analysis but have probably not succeeded. Finally, I think I resent the critical *dicta* that rule out thinking about text, author, and life together. Further thoughts along these lines can be found in J. R. R. Christie and Fred Orton, "Writing on a Text of the Life," *Art History* 11 (1988).

182
......
......
......

Lewis Shiner and the "Good" Anarchist

. . . .

Robert Donahoo
and
Chuck Etheridge

When Joseph Conrad set out to describe the "perfect anarchist," he depicted a "bespectacled, dingy little man" (62) walking about London with explosives in his jacket. "His thoughts caressed images of ruin and destruction. He walked frail, insignificant, shabby, miserable—and terrible in the simplicity of his idea calling madness and despair to the regeneration of the world. . . . He passed on unsuspected and deadly, like a pest in the street full of men" (252–53). In contrast to such negative images, Lewis Shiner's fiction reflects a view of anarchists and anarchy that hardly isolates them or reduces them to insignificance. In Shiner's view, the anarchist is at one with timeless drives and universal rhythms. Though in traditional terms his heroes might be branded outlaws, murderers, or at least psychologically unbalanced, their stories reveal them as the necessary agents of beneficial and natural change. They are not deluded pests but instigators of regeneration.

The need for such heroes arises out of the state of decay that marks Shiner's worlds; traditional societal structures are crumbling, and the stench of death is pervasive. Instead of the sleek, clean, ordered future seen in the works of an Asimov or an early Arthur C. Clarke, Shiner shows an Earth with "residential areas . . . mostly burned to the ground" and "storefronts" that are "glassless and hollow" (Frontera, 71). Instead of glowing descriptions of prosperous future colonies, Shiner supplies orbiters that "still smell of rotting food" (93) and space stations that were "abandoned when the government fell" (94). Even when the world he creates is part of our present, it is one of gunfire and vine-covered ruins—an Earth that has become hostile to man's creations, "lifting marble blocks five feet into the air" (Deserted Cities of the Heart, 58); an Earth whose convulsions give at least one character the sense of "everything crumbling behind her" (64). Shiner's short fiction reflects similar themes. In "Till Human Voices Wake Us," Campbell laments: "I've seen your future. . . . Your boats have killed the reef for over a mile. . . . Your Coke cans are lying all over the coral bed. Your marriages don't last and your kids are on drugs and your TV is garbage. I'll pass" (137). In "Mozart in Mirrorshades," written in collaboration with Bruce Sterling, eighteenth-century Salzburg has been scarred by "huge cracking towers and swollen, bulbous storage tanks" that dwarf "the ruins of the St. Rupert Cathedral" (223). The whole effect is to make the city look "like a half-eaten lunch." In the world of "Love in Vain," Charlie Dean Harris country is "flat, desolate grasslands with an occasional bridge or culvert where you could dump a body" (226).

Usually, the causes of such chaos are an ineffective government and a capitalistic system extrapolated to its logical conclusion. The milieu of "Mozart in Mirrorshades" is a perfect example of a fully functional capitalistic system. Hidden behind the never explained acronym VTOL, a godlike company has developed time portals to exploit the nonrenewable resources (mainly oil) of alternate time lines while leaving Realtime's past intact. No thought is ever given to the consequences for the alternate time line being pillaged; when it is time to withdraw, company representatives bring along that time line's Marie Antoinette because she's a good lay and its Mozart because his synthesized music has reached "number five on the *Billboard* charts" (238).

Such a situation is the result of capitalism having achieved one of its ideals: a free hand to encourage full development of enterprise. In Shiner's fiction, the collapse of governments has given corporations total freedom, and he explores the human cost of an economic system that takes literally the longings of Ronald Reagan and Margaret Thatcher for total laissez-faire. In the world of *Frontera*, when governments became bogged down in their own bureaucracies, corporations such as Pulsystems "fed the unemployed, rebuilt public roads, brought law and order back to the city" (52). Such acts, however, are hardly altruistic; rather, they are "messianic madness" with "no regard for individual lives, only for image, cash projections, and the vindication of history" (52–53). In other words, the concern of the company is only for the company.

Such decay is not confined to the traditionally capitalistic West; it also reaches Eastern Europe and Asia. In Shiner's fiction, the decay of established institutions, democratic or socialist, is inevitable. Because of their opportunistic nature and the massive resources they have at their disposal, multinational corporations step in to fill the vacuum left by governmental collapse. In *Frontera*, Aeroflot takes the place of the Soviet system, and Pulsystems replaces even the family in Japan. Centralized societies are no longer viable, and in these new corporations, lines of authority are less defined and more able to absorb the shocks of sudden change. One character says: "In Japan the company was my mother and father. . . . The company fed me and gave me my house and clothes and car, and it gave me something to believe in and work for and devote myself to" (259). *Deserted Cities* fictionalizes the Reagan administration's Iran-contra scandal. Money from the sale of arms is used to fund a private army which systematically attacks any threat to U.S. interests in Latin America. Again, government is ignored and less-structured power groups battle for control. Corporations have replaced governments, armies, families, and, for some, deities.

Parallel to the decay of society in Shiner's fiction is the decay of inter-personal relationships. This is more than a breakdown of the family unit; it is the inability of people to communicate with or relate to one another. In "Till Human Voices Wake Us," Campbell's marriage is a picture of this breakdown. Rather than experience normal conjugal rela-tions, his wife, Beth, lies on her side of the bed "cocooned in a flannel nightgown" (126). And in this breakdown of their marriage the charac-ters see themselves as "normal": "Their friends had all been divorced at least once, and an eighteen-year marriage probably seemed as anach-ronistic to them as a 1957 Chevy" (129). This decay extends beyond the institution of marriage—it touches all relationships, as evidenced by Campbell's affair with Dr. Kimberly, which ends not with any real communion but with her turning him into a merman clone.

In *Deserted Cities of the Heart*, this failure manifests itself in the in-ability of its characters to have satisfactory sexual relationships with one another. Like Campbell's marriage in "Human Voices," the mar-riages in this novel are failures. Thomas and his wife are divorced, and Eddie has left Lindsey and wandered off into the Mexican jungle. But less traditional relationships are even more confused. Thomas, Eddie's brother, longs for sex with Lindsey, Eddie's wife, and when he finally fulfills this decade-long fantasy, the physical act produces not the spiri-tual communion he seeks but confusion: "It was weird how sex had changed things between them. Before they went to bed there had been more intimacy than after. They'd had all those years of unfulfilled long-ing in common. Once that was out of the way Thomas didn't know anymore what she wanted or how she felt" (101). The situation is further complicated by the fact that Lindsey and Thomas are able to consum-mate their relationship only when Lindsey comes to Mexico in search

Robert Donahoo and Chuck Etheridge

of her lost husband. When she does find Eddie, she attempts to restore the marriage and Eddie's mind through sex, but it doesn't work. "Even sex hadn't been able to call him back. He was lost" (266).

Even when each character has come to grips with his or her true self, they remain isolated from one another. Eddie leads his band of unarmed disciples against the guns of the Fighting 666; Lindsey rejects Thomas and vows to live life on her own terms; and Thomas hopes to start a new ecological institute. Caught in the gap between the end of one age and the beginning of another, each has his or her separate destiny to fulfill. As Eddie explains to Thomas: "All those old ideas. . . . They don't have much time left. People hold on to them because they're afraid. But the ideas are dying just the same. You have to . . . you have to make sure you're in the right place when they go" (312). Older, more conventional views of what relationships are and should be are no longer valid. The door is not closed on the possibility of a relationship between Thomas and Lindsey, but if it ever happens, the relationship, Shiner suggests, will be different from what either might have envisioned before the novel began. For the now of his novels, anarchy reigns among romantic and sexual relationships.

The kind of political and interpersonal anarchy that these works posit seems an unlikely place for renewal, but Shiner's vision of anarchy is essentially a positive one. This dangerous, tenuous environment actually serves as the primordial soup that provides the proper conditions for the hero to evolve the vision necessary to bring about the new order. This pattern, a descent into anarchy generating new vision in a "hero," is most fully realized in the novels.

Central to both *Frontera* and *Deserted Cities of the Heart* is the idea of "the pattern" or "the cycle." In each case Shiner explicitly refers to forms that exist outside his fiction: in *Frontera* to Joseph Campbell's pattern of the hero described in *Hero with a Thousand Faces*, and in *Deserted Cities* to the ideas of Ilya Prigogine, as well as the cyclical patterns found in ancient Mayan myth. However, all these sources share a vision of the end of one order and the beginning of another, a vision in which the actions of individuals are important in bringing about this new order. In both Shiner novels a central character becomes aware of the cyclical nature of history and of his part in it; the character is able to "see the pattern." The irony is that this vision born of anarchy is actually the result of a very controlled and tightly run universe; the an-

186

archy arises not out of chance but when human institutions deviate too far from the pattern: "It's classic Prigogine," Thomas says in *Deserted Cities*. "The society got too far from equilibrium and bang, there's a new order" (312).

In *Frontera*, the development of the hero within the decaying society describes the course followed by Kane, an orphaned corporate merce- nary who has found his family and home in Pulsystems. The company sends him and his crewmates to Frontera, a Martian base that had been cut off ten years earlier when the governments of Earth had finally col- lapsed. By means of a bioimplant in Kane's cortex, Pulsystems hopes to trigger a berserker response and cause Kane to destroy Curtis, Frontera's governor, enabling the company to gain access to new technology being developed there. This programming is ultimately overridden, however, in part because Kane has awakened to a vision of his destiny as a "hero"—the vision of Perseus, rescue, return, and restore. As Acrisius did to Perseus, so Morgan, King of Pulsystems, sends Kane on a deadly mission. And like Perseus, Kane accomplishes the mission, not to serve the king but to fulfill his own role in the course of history.

Kane suffers from nightmares in which he relives scenes from various heroic mythologies—he is Percival, he is Hercules. Initially these roles "filled him with terror" (97), but while he is dreaming, a small part of his mind is able to realize why the events are familiar—they spring from works of literature such as an Arthurian sequence he remembers reading in "Caxton's Mallory" (96). Only later does he recognize the significance of his visions, when one of the colonists, stressing the importance of the individual in history, quotes the Russian philosopher Ouspensky, "Every separate human life is a moment of the life of some *great being*, which lives in us" (242). These words help him to put all he has seen into perspective: "The boy's words staggered Kane, parted for an instant the membrane that separated his dream personalities from his waking existence. He could feel them watching behind his eyes: Percival, mad- dened by his imperfection and loss of the Grail, Yamato-Takeru of the shattered spirit, Jason, the fanatic sailor who had failed to intuit the Pattern" (242–43). Such passages emphasize that Kane's heroism ulti- mately derives not from his warriorlike aspects but from his visionary ones; he is able to "intuit the pattern," and, moreover, he has the cour- age to act on his knowledge. He thinks of "the hundreds of other human lives and the single Pattern they formed, the single act they performed again and again, outside time, each of them with their own unique moment, their own contribution" (284). Significantly, "Kane knew what his had to be." He surrenders himself to his nightmares, becomes the hero, seizes his moment in the pattern, and, in doing so, takes the steps necessary to lead his race out of the anarchistic nightmare and into regeneration. These actions create a final vision not of the past but of the future: Kane sees the woman he loves, his Andromeda, "standing under a green martian sky, hair blowing in the wind . . . standing in the open air, thick, green shrubbery at her feet" (285–86).

Leaving behind the traditional science fiction hardware of *Frontera*, Shiner moves to an ancient culture and an ancient setting in his second novel, *Deserted Cities of the Heart*. He takes with him, though, the idea of the pattern, the cyclical nature of history. These ideas seem more at home in the ancient ruins of Mexico, which stand as testaments to the rise and fall of cultures, becoming almost an objective correlative to the cyclical nature of history. Shiner's design is more ambitious in this work, and ultimately more pleasing. Shed of the larger-than-life heroics of *Frontera*, *Deserted Cities* focuses more on adaptation to and acceptance of the pattern than on individual re-creations of heroism. Individual acts are still important, but these acts are smaller, less dramatic and mythic. Instead of mercenaries, the heroes of *Deserted Cities* are teachers, photocopy store managers, and washed-up musicians— holdovers from the turbulence of the 1960s, people in whom the vision of a better world has soured but not quite perished. Physically these characters are more like the diminutive anarchist in Conrad than the herculean Kane, but the denizens of *Deserted Cities* are more spiritually advanced.

Chan Ma'ax, the leader, the *t'o'ohil*, or "great one," of a tribe descended from the ancient Mayans, is described as resembling a little monkey (38), but he serves as Eddie's mentor, guiding him toward the mushrooms that send his mind traveling through time. During these travels Eddie inhabits bodies that represent previous versions of his true self, an experience Chan Ma'ax explains: "The world is all of us. We all have a place. We all have things we must do. The purpose of the world is to move through the cycles and become better. To become new again. You have a part of this that is yours" (285). Eddie does not merely inhabit someone else's body or relive someone else's past experience; he *has been* these people.

Using this method, Shiner personalizes the pattern. Where Kane is an isolated individual seizing a particular moment, Chan Ma'ax, Eddie, and Thomas have recurring roles; they are part of the ebb and flow of history rather than fragments in it. In terms of narrative structure, Eddie's role is closest to that of Kane; it is he who leads a legion against the private army funded by the capitalistic sources responsible for the impending chaos. Yet the pathetically thin Eddie bears little resemblance to the virile Kane, and Eddie is able to respond with nonviolence where Kane has only destruction at his disposal. And the role Eddie assumes is his own, not that of a mythic hero continually used and thrown away by history.

Whereas Chan Ma'ax serves as the experiential mentor, Thomas connects to the vision of the pattern by providing an intellectual validation of it. His theoretical speculations about the Mayan collapse confirm the reality of Eddie's experiences and Chan Ma'ax's teaching even as Thomas gains an awareness of the value of his work with the Institute, for the new age will require a greater understanding of the relationship between humanity and the environment. Lindsey, too, "sees the pattern" and wants to build her place in the new order: "Lindsey wanted in on that new world. She could sense the shape of it as surely as she could feel the child already starting to grow inside her" (333). Her bodily regeneration serves as a miniature version of what the whole pattern is about: new life out of confusion and pain.

Unlike *Frontera*, in which the pattern hinges on one person, the pattern of *Deserted Cities of the Heart* offers a place for many personalities and types; one needn't be a "hero" to make a contribution. As a result, *Deserted Cities*'s anarchy is more of a force than it is in *Frontera*. In the latter novel one gets the sense that the change is coming regardless of what Thomas or Lindsey does about it—it is up to the characters to adapt and accommodate their vision to the reality of the cycle. In this sense they are perfect anarchists, demanding no pattern or meaning but accepting what is—in fact, they are working to make their version of acceptance a reality.

Unlike Conrad, who viewed anarchy as something to be avoided lest the darkness of the human heart be loosed, Shiner sees anarchy as a cleansing force necessary for the destruction of decaying social structures that are no longer viable, so that a newer, more functional society can evolve. Such a romantic view affirms the idea that the individual can ultimately triumph over the destructiveness of the impersonal forces loosed by humanity's societal constructs. By submitting to anarchy, Shiner's heroes work to perfect their worlds.

Works Cited

Conrad, Joseph. *The Secret Agent.* 1907. Garden City, N.Y.: Doubleday, 1953.

Dozois, Gardner, ed. *The Year's Best Science Fiction: Sixth Annual Collection.* New York: St. Martin's, 1989.

Shiner, Lewis. *Deserted Cities of the Heart.* New York: Bantam Books, 1989.

———. *Frontera.* New York: Baen, 1984.

———. "Love in Vain." In *The Year's Best Science Fiction: Sixth Annual Collection,* edited by Gardner Dozois, pp. 223–40. New York: St. Martin's, 1989.

———. "Till Human Voices Wake Us." In *Mirrorshades,* edited by Bruce Sterling, pp. 125–38. New York: Ace Books, 1988.

Sterling, Bruce, ed. *Mirrorshades.* 1986. New York: Ace Books, 1988.

Sterling, Bruce, and Lewis Shiner. "Mozart in Mirrorshades." In *Mirrorshades,* edited by Bruce Sterling, pp. 223–39. New York: Ace Books, 1988.

Separate

Develop-

ment:

Cyberpunk

in Film

and TV

. . . .

Frances Bonner

W hile "cyberpunk: the Movement" has produced no films or TV programs,[1] a few films and TV programs from approximately the same period may reasonably be held to exhibit similar characteristics. *Cyberpunk* is not a term that has been applied seriously within film or TV studies. In referring to *cyberpunk film*, I use the term as a form of shorthand to mean films with some claim to be considered similar to the novels and short stories generally regarded as cyberpunk. The same applies to *cyberpunk TV*.

Some characteristics of the generic fraction called cyberpunk have transferred to film and TV more readily than others. Most notable among the shared characteristics are the frenetic pace, the excess of information, the inverted millenarianism (figured especially in various forms of decay), and the concentration on computers, corporations, crime, and corporeality—the four C's of cyberpunk film plotting. These characteristics are certainly not unique to this fraction of the genre. In the same way that cyberpunk literature is a continuation of preexistent themes, styles, and motifs from earlier SF—gaining its distinctiveness from the particular combination of elements and the attitude taken toward them, but proving very difficult to isolate with any analytic rigor from much contemporaneous noncyberpunk SF—so the films too are recombinant SF. They also exhibit many of the persistent themes of 1980s films of various other genres and their hybrids.

It is my intention to examine how cyberpunk can be said to manifest itself in film and TV by examining a pair of potentially exemplary films, *Blade Runner* (Ridley Scott, 1982) and *Tron* (Steven Lisberger, 1982), and the TV program "Max Headroom" (Rocky Morton and Annabel Jankel, 1985 and 1986, U.K.; and Forhad Mann, 1987, U.S.), and then seeing to what extent other contenders may be so described. The purpose of the exercise is to examine the usefulness and character of the category more than to attempt to establish definitive statements of which films are "in" or "out," or to reduce cyberpunk to a formula. I start by announcing three prerequisites, based principally on pragmatic considerations. First, the films must have been released and the TV programs first screened in the 1980s. Cyberpunk literature is perceived as a 1980s phenomenon, so it seems reasonable to consider the films and TV similarly, although there may well be protocyberpunk in all relevant media. Second, the temporal setting should be the not-too-far-distant future. The intent here is to call into question works set in the present—not, it should be noted, to eliminate them for that reason alone but to indicate that if they are set in the present, they are very dubious inclusions. Third, and this is overwhelmingly a matter of personal convenience, I consider only English-language film and TV.[2]

As a further pragmatic note, and partly for reasons of space, I do not refer to specific instances of music video in this examination. This is not because I discount their relevance but because their peculiarly ephemeral nature makes it hard to find examples that will be widely recognized within a critical community not devoted to their study or (perhaps) consumption. Furthermore, research libraries do not yet provide much in the way of backup services. I believe, however, that there are undeniably instances of cyberpunk music video.

The characteristics I mentioned so briefly above demand elaboration. The frenzied pace of the fictions of William Gibson and Bruce Sterling, which characteristically begin in medias res and rely on the reader eventually picking up enough clues to comprehend the narrative (or deciding not to worry too much about it and "go with the flow"), transfers directly. Probably no adjective is more inimical to cyberpunk than leisurely, and no filmic device could be less fitting than introductory text marching up the screen à la Star Wars. On-screen print itself is fine, but the screen should be masquerading at the time as a video display unit; otherwise place and date would seem to be the only acceptable printed information.

The pace and the video display data in particular interact substantially with the excess of information. The pace is so fast that more is presented to the eye of the spectator than can be absorbed in a single viewing. The narrative drive prohibits the lingering that the crowded mise-en-scène seems to require. Cyberpunk films are repeat-viewing films—at "cult" screenings, as videos, or both. It is no doubt a contentious point, but repeat viewing of a cyberpunk film or TV program seems to me to be far more satisfying than a repeat reading of any of the definitive print works. With the more expensive productions such as

Blade Runner this should be unsurprising. Filmmakers realize that high budgets cannot be recouped, let alone profits made, on cinema release alone; repeat viewers must be offered continuing sources of satisfaction. Not all cyberpunk film is big budget, however; some may be released only in video form. Yet these too frequently repay, even require, repeat viewing.

The excess of information is provided primarily by set dressing and special effects; subplots are rarely notable. The term *eyeball kicks*, which cyberpunk writers use to refer to passing inventions lovingly described but unnecessary for plot development or characterization, can certainly be applied to the visual works. *Blade Runner* provides a continuous display of such phenomena, and they do a great deal to generate repeat viewing pleasure. Despite Vivian Sobchack's description of *Blade Runner* as on the cusp of postmodern interaction with modernism (272), few films other than *Blue Velvet* have so repeatedly been described as postmodern. It is characteristic of a postmodern film that this pleasure comes from pastiche, especially as displayed on the surface of the film. The film's design philosophy has often been enunciated both by *Blade Runner*'s director, Ridley Scott, and by Syd Mead, the "visual futurist"—a title that was devised for the credits for this film and which he continues to use. Both stress their belief that in such a future, extant buildings would be "retro-fitted" with additions making their exteriors more interesting. While it is not possible to buy toys as spin-off products from the film, one can buy the *Blade Runner Sketchbook*, which details changes in the design of the various artifacts (Scroggy). One of these changes demonstrates the search for eyeball kicks very neatly—a parking meter was designed and redesigned until it tested out as "snagging" the viewers' gaze.

Inverted *millenarianism* is the term Sobchack uses, after Fredric Jameson, to describe the philosophy of post-1977 SF films, especially those she terms "marginal" (246), which includes most of the lower-budget cyberpunk film possibilities. Such a millenarianism foresees not the end of the world but, as Jameson puts it, "the end of this or that (the end of ideology, art or social class; the 'crisis' of Leninism, social democracy, or the welfare state, etc., etc.)" (53). For cyberpunk in the visual media, I think one can be even more emphatic than Sobchack or Jameson. So far from classic millenarianism with the elect being "raptured" into a better life, the better life, inasmuch as it has ever existed, is past and gone. Civilization has peaked, and while there still may be new scientific and technological developments, these do not equate with progress. There are no pretensions to egalitarianism, and for most people life is already hell. The convention used to convey this is remarkably similar in literature, film, and TV programming—the run-down inner-city slum-cum-tent settlement, overcrowded, trashed, and graffiti-ridden. It is there in Gibson's Sprawl, Paul Di Filippo's Bungle, the early scenes of *Blade Runner*, the barrios of *The Running Man* (Paul Michael Glaser, 1987), and the city streets of BBC-TV's "Body Contact" (Bernard Rose, 1986). More simply, the feeling is carried by the increasingly ubiquitous garbage—a sign in non-SF films of gritty realism (a clean street is Yuppie fantasy or world of Disney), and in SF of a more realistic view of the future (again, cleanliness is Disney, e.g., *Tron*). One should note here Sobchack's comment that postindustrial waste is eroticized in *Blade Runner* (318, n. 25). The transfiguration of trash is achieved largely by the gloss of water or the indistinction of mist (helped by the cinematic absence of smell) presenting interesting surfaces for scopophilic pleasure.

Of the four C's, crime and corporations form a close duo, often collapsed into a single, the criminal corporation. When considering contemporary film and TV, it is arguably more difficult to discover a corporation depicted as moral than to spot an unlittered street. Indeed, one could argue that these two signs frequently articulate each other within particular representational clusters. Corruption within the corporations may be a matter of some individuals being particularly and personally greedy while other, more desirable, individuals are also depicted (*RoboCop* is a possible example here, though alternative readings are certainly possible), but more often, corruption is shown as the natural state of corporations. The crime concerned may start as a financial one, but usually something more violent is involved—often to cover up the corruption. This device is by no means limited to SF films, although it is strikingly evident there, both in potentially cyberpunk films and others, like *Alien* and *Aliens*. The extent to which this portrayal can be read as representing a sustained critique of capitalism varies. While Thomas B. Byers talks of *Alien* and *Blade Runner* as warning us of "a capitalist future gone wrong" (Byers, 326), with the implication that there is a "right" capitalist future, Douglas Kellner, Flo Leibowitz, and Michael Ryan read the confused ideological positions of *Blade Runner* to suggest "that segments of US society are seriously disenchanted with capitalism, but cannot envisage how a liberated society can be collectively constructed or what it would look like" (7). The ambivalence they find in *Blade Runner* is unsurprising, since they are themselves cultural products of a bastion of high capitalism. Even low-budget films are only comparatively cheap (*Repo Man* [Alex Cox, 1984] had a $2 million budget, although initially it was planned to be made for $500,000), especially when the comparison is with the print media. Cyberpunk writers are remarkably unanimous in their attitude to corporate capitalism—nation states will disappear to be replaced by corporate ones with totally immoral codes of conduct. SF writers had worked with this idea previously, but the unanimity in cyberpunk is striking.

Computers are frequently implicated in the operations of criminal corporations; SF or not, it is hard to conceive how corporate activity today could be depicted without them. Within cyberpunk literature, the computer (more specifically, artificial intelligence) is a highly significant figure. When Fredric Jameson writes about "a whole mode of contemporary entertainment literature, which one is tempted to characterize as 'high tech paranoia' in which the circuits and networks of some putative global computer hook-up are narratively mobilized by labyrinthine conspiracies of autonomous but clearly interlocking and competing information agencies in a complexity often beyond the capacity of the normal reading mind," he could be writing precisely of cyberpunk (though I doubt he intends so narrow an application). He continues, "Yet conspiracy theory (and its garish narrative manifestations) must be seen as a degraded attempt—through the figuration of advanced technology— to think the impossible totality of the contemporary world system" (80). The system referred to, the third stage of capital, brings us back to the ambivalence of *Blade Runner*. Within cyberpunk film, however, the advanced technology used in such figurations is rarely the computer. SF films that could be described by the first half of the Jameson quotation were more common in the 1960s and early 1970s (like *Colossus: The Forbin Connection*) or are emphatically devoid of cyberpunk characteristics (like *War Games*). In film, unlike in cyberpunk stories, computers are still visually depicted in expensive and very clean settings. The advanced technologies allowed out for the under-class to interact with are in video games or prostheses. Television does not seem to be as limited. In "Max Headroom," computer-using TV pirates operate from the back of a battered van. However, prostheses (if one discounts the video head and shoulders of Max himself) are replaced by the distinctly nontechnological scavenging of the organ-leggers, Breughel and Mahler.

And so we arrive at the fourth C—corporeality. Prosthetics and various bodily transformations are persistently important in the literary works; indeed, the term *wetware* for direct, corporeal, human-to-computer interfacing is a cyberpunk identifier. This transfers to film, though the wetware (not so called) differs, being a sign of the not-human; only cyborgs, androids, robots, and other semihuman or artificial beings have it. Despite this, since the purpose of most of these artificial beings is to demonstrate their humanity (*The Terminator* [James Cameron, 1984] is an obvious exception here), the sign tends to be transcended. Corporeality is a particularly telling aspect of cyberpunk for the films to capitalize on because the body has itself been a major concern for 1980s film—Sylvester Stallone, Arnold Schwarzenegger, and Dolf Lundgren representing only the most musclebound of its manifestations. Entire films can be centered on aerobics, and the thematic transformations of wimp and librarian into hero and heroine are effected now (in great detail) in the gym rather than at the tailor or couturier. The transformed bodies of mainstream and non-SF films become mutable bodies because surgery, genetic engineering, and various other forms of doubling can be brought into play.

It should be unsurprising that within film and TV, doubling based on holograms and video manifestation by digitalization (not to mention developments of both into as yet improbable areas) is much more prevalent than it is in print. Writing mainly about films too early to reflect aspects of cyberpunk, Garrett Stewart has noted the frequent appearance of video technology within SF films. While his main concern is the screens depicted on the cinematic screen (and certainly these are highly noticeable in cyberpunk films and TV programs), he also considers some of the purportedly hologrammed film characters; with them, "there is still to be explored the threat of the image itself in its own macabre autonomy" (196). Yet this does not appear to be a dominant theme in most of the films and TV programs I consider here. In *Tron*, the hologramish individuals, the "programs," exist only within the computer, where their "goodness" and "badness" are identical to that of their characters in the real world of the "users." The threats in this real world come from actual individuals or from the MCP (the Master Control Program), the artificial intelligence that manifests there only as print on a computer screen and whose acronym never delivers the promise of its ambiguity. Max Headroom is used against his creators, emphasizing again that moral determination is in the hands of the users, not the used.

It is not, however, insisted on enough to appear to be revelatory of some deep anxiety in the makers. Furthermore, it chimes interestingly with the actual noncinematic situation, in which battles over patent rights in bioengineering and computer programs are setting precedents that give power (generally) to the creators' employers. The threat most often ascribed to Max is extradiegetic—to the hosts of other TV talk shows in our own "real world." It is explored not within the TV fiction but in newspaper and magazine review columns.

The threat of autonomous artificial creation is not best explored in these creatures doubly of light—they can too easily be shut down—but in those bodies which in the film have tangible physical existence. The digitalized fake of the killing of the Arnold Schwarzenegger character in *The Running Man* is easily exposed by the appearance of his live physical body; Max Headroom is undermined by persistent electronic failures, but his "real-life" double, Edison Carter, is healed; Clu, Tron, and Yori (the "program" selves of Jeff Bridges et al.) cease to exist when they return to their filmic real-world personae to enjoy the fruits of their success within the computer. It is the individual physically changed bodies—the replicants of *Blade Runner*, the killing machine of *The Terminator*, the cyborg *RoboCop*—that explore (and defuse) the threat of autonomy.

The fascination with video techniques manifests itself not so much in the computer generated doubles as in the computer-generated vision of the various "solid" partially or fully artificial beings. In the literature, hands or arms are as commonly the dominant prosthetics as eyes; in the films, artificial eyes are much more common. The demonstrations of the strength in the hands of Roy Batty and RoboCop serve principally to update the "crushing grip" cliché of earlier Hollywood films. Women's prosthetic or artificial hands (Agent Rogerz in *Repo Man*, Pris in *Blade Runner*) may be distinctive, but their possessors are minor characters and, as is traditional with women on screen, they are not given any special powers of vision. The entire point of view in *The Terminator* and *RoboCop*, however, is frequently given to the prosthetic or computer-enhanced male vision, and this overt centrality is further strengthened by sequences in both films emphasizing problems with the eyes. In *Blade Runner*, not only are eyes the only organs that betray the artificiality of the replicants, they are also the only ones we see being constructed. Within visual media, vision—the look and the gaze—cannot be overemphasized.

Frances Bonner

Cyberpunk has often been charged with being a particularly macho SF form, a reaction against feminist SF and devoid of strong women, families, and ordered societies. Samuel R. Delany accepts this charge for some of the writers, though not particularly for Gibson, whose debt to Joanna Russ he sees especially in similarities between Molly Millions in *Neuromancer* and Jael in *The Female Man* (Tatsumi 1988, 8, 10). Nonetheless, the charge seems valid for cyberpunk films; they are overwhelmingly targeted to male audiences, not only in the way that SF films (with few exceptions) have always tended to be, but also following another genre they call on, the action thriller. It is not so much that female characters are secondary and survive only if paired to the hero, for the 1980s stress on the strong, fit body means that these women are physically very capable and could only be credibly paired with some superbeing. (Think of Nancy Allen's initial appearance in *RoboCop*, knocking out a suspect resisting arrest with a straight right to the jaw; or Linda Hamilton at the end of *The Terminator*, driving alone and pregnant into the desert to train her soon-to-be-born son for survival; or Maria Conchita Alonso escaping from both Schwarzenegger and Erland Von Lilith with, respectively, literal and figurative attacks to the groin in *The Running Man*; but don't think of Sean Young in *Blade Runner*.) It is rather the male worlds they operate in, the centrality of violent crime, and the nondomestic life on the streets of the disordered worlds that make these films macho SF. Families are not so much peripheral as off-screen altogether: faked in the photographs of *Blade Runner*; moved to another city in *RoboCop*, becoming only traces in the cyborg mind—"I can feel them, but I can't remember them," he says after he displays his humanity; absent altogether from *Tron*. Furthermore, the concern with the mutable body means that creation itself is no longer of the domestic world, no longer an activity requiring a mother. Creators are men (Batty addresses Tyrell in *Blade Runner* as "Father"), though there may be female midwives (such as the woman who is second in charge of the development team in *RoboCop*). The pregnancy in *The Terminator* is an exception here, though its miraculous time-loop character stops it from being altogether natural; but it is offset by the totally mechanical engendering of the Terminator it(him)self. Nor do families feature in "Max Headroom," but there is some variation in that it is women who are technologically competent (Theora Jones, the computer hacker who provides Edison Carter with information; Dominique, who plays an analogous role for Blank Reg, the pirate TV operator), though they are still the supporting halves of heterosexual couples.

As well as being the more macho kind of cyberpunk, the films and TV programs are also the more Caucasian. Ethnic heterogeneity is used as a sign of the decayed world in *Blade Runner* and *The Running Man*. It should be noted, however, that the latter has in Yaphet Kotto the only substantial black figure (and furthermore a politically sound, sympathetic one), and in Maria Conchita Alonso the only non-Anglo heroine. Despite the importance of Japan to the literature, Japanese characters are very minor, or, if the half-Japanese Buckaroo Banzai is included, played by a Caucasian (Peter Weller, who also plays RoboCop).

A final major shared characteristic of literary, filmic, and televisual cyberpunk is its environment. Typically, cyberpunk is set in the built environment, if not in the utterly unnatural world of cyberspace. It is perhaps misleading to say "built" environment given that it is more probably crumbling (unless corporate headquarters), but the lush countryside is certainly inappropriate. Among the many ways in which the flight into Nature at the end of the released version of *Blade Runner* is unsatisfactory is the sheer improbability of all the green after the previous yellow, blue, and gray of the degenerating city. As Sobchack puts it, "the 'nature' cinematography strikes us as inauthentic 'special effect' compared to the technical special effects we have seen and accepted as authentically 'natural'" (237). If a natural environment is to appear authentic within a cyberpunk film, then it seems only possible for it to be a desert—not only yellow but lifeless and extreme. The flight to Nature at the end of *The Terminator* is much more of a piece with the preceding than is the case with *Blade Runner*. *Brazil* (Terry Gilliam, 1985), not really a cyberpunk film but worth considering, places its concluding flight into verdant Nature firmly within its dream continuum.

Other, more minor, motifs transfer from the literature to the visual media too: there are many Japanese references; black leather features more, mirrorshades less, but both are evident; the music is rock more often than punk; it rains a lot and the air gives the impression of being polluted. The aspects that fail to transfer, or do so only rarely, are few: drugs, multiple plot lines, and, much less significant, the fascination with Velcro. Drugs, especially designer ones, which generally figure unproblematically as recreational aids in the literature, cannot do so in mainstream film, not only because the unwritten codes of Hollywood practice militate against it, but the consequent most common reading of them as socially problematic makes it difficult. It is hard for their use to be incidental. In low-budget, independent productions it is another matter. The relative absence of multiple plot lines was referred to earlier in my discussion of excess.

I want now to look more specifically at the three main examples I referred to at the beginning—*Blade Runner*, *Tron*, and the various "Max Headroom" programs. The two films may be seen as opposites. Indeed, of all the characteristics already mentioned, the only one they share is minor—both have some Japanese motifs, but even here there are differences. The hanten Jeff Bridges wears in his apartment while sitting at his computer keyboard bears no particular significance, but the Japanese advertising dominating Los Angeles and the sushi Harrison Ford orders both signify more—a changed world and an emotionally cold ex-husband. There are more important examples of apparently shared characteristics, but these dissolve on closer examination—the criminal corporations, for example. In *Tron*, ENCOM, the communication corporation, is headed by an individual who has stolen the games programs on which his own and the corporation's success is based, and it is controlled by an artificial intelligence involved in data theft. In *Blade Runner*, the Tyrell Corporation acts contrary to the law posited for 2019 only in allowing the construction of a replicant, Sean Young, without accelerated obsolescence (and since she is an experimental model, even this may be permissible). Tyrell may be ethically corrupt in creating life while limiting its duration, but neither he nor his corporation is criminal. The other two apparently shared characteristics—the mutable body and the human-inhuman dichotomies—are also weak. In *Tron*, the bodies are electronically replicated within what could be called cyberspace—though it is only within one computer—and there is no ready interpenetration of the two worlds. In *Blade Runner*, replicants are physically created (not apparently, despite their name) as copies of "real" humans, and though they may live legally only off-world, they interact there with humans (why else would Pris be a "basic pleasure model"?) and on Earth can only with extreme difficulty be distinguished from humans.

The strongest claim *Tron* has to being considered a cyberpunk film lies in its setting within the computer and in its own process of production—computer-generated graphics. No other film of which I am aware attempts to depict a cyberspace, though many depict the exteriors, and a few the interiors, of computer hardware, especially video display screens. That *Tron's* cyberspace is unsatisfactory is not much disputed, nor should it be surprising. The posited space is as unrepresentable as other such imaginary ones, such as Heaven or the eighth dimension, and extrapolation from video game graphics imposes a very particular appearance—as, with even more force, does the aura of the production company. As a Disney film, *Tron* was never a highly probable contender for cyberpunk status. The inverted millenarianism would be taboo to begin with, and it is probably because of this that the world inside and outside the computer is clean, relatively tidy, and not marked by excess; that in the end virtue is rewarded with material success; and that the Jeff Bridges hero is characterized by childlike optimism. These all combine, however, to mean that, despite its echoing of the characteristic concerns—the four C's of crime, corporations, computers, and corpo-reality—and despite its presentation of a form of cyberspace, *Tron*, in some ways the most likely film to reflect the cyberpunk ethos, is not a film that can reasonably be described by the term *cyberpunk*.

Blade Runner, on the other hand, I believe can be, and this despite the virtual absence of criminal corporations and computers (if one decides to disqualify the "biological computers" of the replicants, which I think reasonable given the insistence on their humanity). There is also not the slightest gesture to the existence of cyberspace. On the other hand, the inverted millenarianism is overwhelming. the world is decaying, deserted by the able-bodied, its occupants cynical without exception. As well as its mutable bodies and its visual excess, there is also aural excess in the hybrid street argot of the poor. As final evidence for its qualification, there is the story that William Gibson went to it when he was halfway through writing *Neuromancer* but panicked and was unable to stay to see it through (recounted in, for example, Tatsumi 1987, 14).

There is, however, an ironic postscript to this comparison, part of which I commented on earlier. Whereas the final sequence of *Blade Runner* is jarring and contrary to its "cyberpunk-ness," the final shots of *Tron*, in which the similarity of the "real-world" cityscape and the de-picted world within the computer is revealed as the camera draws back from the city, neither jar nor seem contrary to cyberpunk perceptions.

From the main body of the comparison, I think it can be argued that what is important in ascribing cyberpunk status to a film is the sensibility rather than the thematic concerns, and that the sensibility is manifest particularly in those aspects related to Jameson's inverted millenarianism. When sensibility and concerns unite, as they do in the next example, it becomes impossible not to ask whether there was some direct influence.

"Max Headroom" in its various forms, but particularly "Rebus: The Story of Max Headroom" (transmitted April 4, 1985, and sometimes called "20 Minutes into the Future"), made to explain the genesis of the video-head talk-show host of "The Max Headroom Show" (transmitted April 6, 1985–), is more thoroughgoing in its display of cyberpunk characteristics. It is possible here (and almost certain for the U.S. series—transmitted March 31, 1987–) that there was some influence of cyberpunk literature, although the directors had worked for several years previously making music videos which themselves at times exhibit cyberpunk sensibilities and concerns. Their admitted influences are *Eraserhead* and, especially, *Brazil*, and they have described their world as exhibiting "post-apocalyptic paranoia" (Gill, 2–3). It is hard to think of a cyberpunk characteristic that doesn't appear in the program, except, of course, for nonproblematic drug use and the visually unappealing Velcro. There are corporations, crimes, computers, and corporeality; there is the frenetic pace and the inverted millenarianism; there is a built environment; and over everything there is trash and excess. There are even, intermittently, mirrorshades. Of course, it lacks seriousness, but so do some of the cyberpunk short stories. By the time of the screening of the American series, the cyberpunk phenomenon was well known and the references could more easily have been intentionally crafted. Certainly reviewers of the programs made such references, for instance, to William Gibson (for example, Jackson, 18). The international use of the Max Headroom character in Coca-Cola advertisements in the period between the U.K. and U.S. versions also gave something of an extradiegetic cyberpunk aura to the entire project.

"Max Headroom" shares with *Blade Runner* an ideological instability that has been well delineated by Barry King, who contrasts the approval of its radical potential voiced by John Shirley with its American executive script consultant's description of it as "brain candy" and Morton and Jankel's original intention to create an ambivalent situation with a right-wing being mouthing left-wing material (135). The political instability of these two core examples is not at all out of keeping with literary works in which the dominant cynicism masks the political difficulties caused when resistance and piracy alone seem admirable.

If *Blade Runner* and "Max Headroom" are the best examples of cyberpunk film and TV, what about others? A number of films are frequently grouped together with *Blade Runner* in attempts to delineate subgenres or identify trends in contemporary SF film. Many of these have been referred to already. Sobchack's "marginal" 1980s SF films include, as well as *Repo Man*, *The Adventures of Buckaroo Banzai: Across the Eighth Dimension* (W. D. Richter, 1984)—cyberpunk in its excess, its rock, its inconsequential verve, and its Japanesquerie, but not in its lack of computers, its absence of much indication of inverted millenarianism, its putative setting in the present, and above all in the centrality of the aliens from another dimension. *Repo Man* is a more awkward case— the excess, crime, drugs, prostheses, and emphatic inverted millenarianism, which would seem to qualify it, are opposed by the low-tech world of car repossession, its putative setting in the present, and the matter of aliens. (On the other hand, if one elevates the contradictory ending involving flight from being, a shared oddity of cyberpunk films, to a characteristic independent of literary cyberpunk, then *Repo Man* becomes even more probable.) The problem with the marginal films— and Sobchack refers also to *Uforia*, *The Night of the Comet*, *Brother from Another Planet*, and *Liquid Sky*—is that for budgetary considerations they are nonspecific about their temporal setting, treating it as the present (or not necessarily not the present), and their SF status is provided by the presence of aliens (looking, by and large, like humans). Since, pace *Schismatrix*, aliens are not notable in cyberpunk proper, and settings in the present are rare if not altogether absent, this makes it difficult to describe Sobchack's marginal films, or more recent examples suh as *They Live* (John Carpenter, 1988), as members of the cyberpunk category.

An earlier Carpenter film, *Escape from New York* (1981), is, however, a possibility. Alien-free and set in the future, it posits a world so crime-ridden that Manhattan Island has been converted into a walled prison from which there is no return. It is trashed, decayed, and without hope. In a reversal of the importance of vision to the mutable body, its hero, Kurt Russell, wears an eyepatch but, in a direct prefiguring of Gibson, carries poison in his bloodstream that must be neutralized by the end of the narrative. His corporeality—the snake tattoo, the progressively revealed musculature, the injured thigh—is insistent. The film also has a frenetic pace and visual excess but lacks computers or corporations. It is more the John Shirley type of cyberpunk than the Gibson, but I think could be regarded as quite a good example. The *Mad Max* films, often linked with *Escape from New York*, are a different matter. To begin with, the first was released in 1979, and they are all set in a minimally technological postapocalyptic world rather than one marked by inverted millenarianism. Mel Gibson's body is displayed much as Kurt Russell's is, but any injuries are (very) temporary. The corporeality and the desert setting do not outweigh the disqualifying factors, although in the third film, *Beyond Thunderdrome*, there are sequences of undeniable visual excess.

For a very different reason *Brazil* must be disqualified. Although there is excess, trash, a variant on the mutable body, and a sensibility that could be described as involving inverted millenarianism, it is a very different sensibility, and it is this rather than the absence of a criminal corporation or computers that makes it so very different. To say that it is distinctively British is in this regard misleading, but the world depicted (somewhere in the twentieth century) can only be regarded as having been developed from postwar British premises. State bureaucracy rather than free enterprise supports the villainy, and the obsession with pieces of paper is the very opposite of cyberpunk's domination by electronic information.

This leaves three films: *The Terminator*, *RoboCop*, and *The Running Man*. All are dominated by the body,[3] and in the first two it is a very mutable body indeed. The excess, the trash, the computer in the flesh-covered mechanical body, and the frenetic pace of *The Terminator* all link it to cyberpunk more closely, I think, than the problems with temporality pull it away. The setting in the present is offset by the glimpses of the future; but, on the other hand, the present's inverted millenarianism is undercut by the apocalyptic future, with no "this and that" about it. *RoboCop* is most explicit about the criminality in its corporation, about the fading of the powers of the nation state, and about the construction of the ultimate computer-run prosthesis; the problems come, as they did with *Tron* (though not to the same extent) from the sensibility. While the posited world is characterized by aspects of inverted millenarianism, the mise-en-scène is quite often remarkably plain and the pace is variable. Most problematic is its sentimentality and the focus, which, through the old-fashioned morality programmed into *RoboCop*, is counter to the trashy, decayed, corrupt world depicted.

The Running Man is the film about which I feel most equivocal. It is certainly visually excessive, and not only the corporations but the justice system itself are criminal. Inverted millenarianism is repeatedly in evidence. Yet despite the trashed, crowded barrios, and even despite the aging rock musician rebel (actually played by Mick Fleetwood) and the population obsessed with TV, it seems somehow wrong to term this cyberpunk. At its very beginning there is scrolling explanatory print; perhaps too much time is spent in rather familiar well-lit clean environ- ments; the dominant technology is broadcast television (computers are consequent on it, never referred to directly); and there are no prosthe- ses—although the flamboyant killing devices of the hunters (the chain- saw, the sharpened hockey stick) could be regarded as extensions of their bodies. The difficulty with this, and with *RoboCop*, may well be related to their having been made more recently than the other films. After all, the literary movement is being diluted and dissipated in this same period. Perhaps *The Running Man* is just dilute cyberpunk.

When it comes to other television programs the problems are more serious. Cyberpunk motifs certainly figure on MTV, but identifying drama programs other than the "Max Headroom" collection in which these motifs can be expanded into sustained pieces with the characteris- tic concerns and sensibility is difficult. SF is comparatively rare on TV, and even in times when it is perceived as a popular TV genre (and the 1980s have not really seen one of these times), the perceived expense of its production means that there are never many instances to choose from. The programs worth considering are few and, more seriously, are unlikely to be widely known.

The three most probable contenders that I am aware of are all BBC-TV productions: "Body Contact" (transmitted December 6, 1987, dir. Bernard Rose), a musical romance; "Boogie Outlaws" (transmitted June 6–July 9, 1987, dir. Keith Godman), a drama serial about a rene- gade rock band; and "Red Dwarf" (two series transmitted February 15 March 21, 1988, and September 6–October 11, 1988, dir. Ed Bye), an SF comedy series. The first two are set in a futuristic Britain following a decline in law and order. Their cyberpunk characteristics are sustained indicators of inverted millenarianism (trash, decay, extreme social in- equality), corruption (of police rather than corporations—probably a British variant, the corporations are absent, not honest), diegetic rock, and black leather. Computers and mutable bodies are completely absent. "Red Dwarf" had both of the latter but lacked the rest, being set three million years in the future aboard a mining spaceship inhabited by one human recently released from a stasis chamber, a hologram of his long-dead cabin mate, the ship's computer, and a being evolved from the ship's cat.

With the highly notable exception of the various "Max Headroom" phenomena, it is probably better to say of TV programs (and indeed of MTV, too) that cyberpunk tropes are fractured across their various surfaces rather than actually featured, much less developed.

So, is it useful to talk about actual cyberpunk film or TV? It seems not for the latter, and, despite the time I have devoted to doing so, I fear probably not for the former, either. That certain characteristics are shared by various cultural artifacts created during the same period and within more or less the same culture should not be surprising. To call them all by the same name—especially when that name seems more correctly applied to a group of writers who were in contact, perceived themselves as writing the same kind of SF, and commented on and emended one another's manuscripts—seems unnecessary.

If one, very roughly, takes the *cyber* part of cyberpunk to refer to the cybernetic concerns—cyberspace itself, computers, information systems, wetware, and advanced prostheses—and the *punk* to refer to the style, the sensibility, and the inverted millenarianism, then it is evident that the difficulties in describing films and TV programs as cyberpunk comes from the *cyber* part. The only film that concentrates on this part fails dismally on the other. Although a number of other films manage the *punk*-ish part and prostheses, they do so not through a commitment to anything *cyber* but because the body is already a focus for 1980s film. Yet it is arguably within the cybernetic concerns that the distinctiveness of cyberpunk lies. If the films by and large are unable to deal with this, then they should be identified by a different label. Their relationship to cyberpunk should, however, be acknowledged. It is this that I hope I have done.

Notes

1. However, *Neuromancer* has had its film rights sold and William Gibson has written at least one film script.
2. Aspects of the German film *Kamikaze 89* (Wolf Gremm, 1982) and the French *The Original* (Jerome Diamant-Berger, 1986), and no doubt many others, indicate that cyberpunk touches, to put it no more strongly, exist elsewhere.
3. This commonality could have been even stronger. Apparently in the early stages of *RoboCop*'s planning, Arnold Schwarzenegger was considered for the lead role

but rejected because his presence in titanium cladding was felt to be too extreme. A thinner actor was cast.

Works Cited

Byers, Thomas B. "Commodity Futures: Corporate State and Personal Style in Three Recent Science-Fiction Movies." *Science Fiction Studies* 14 (1987): 326–39.

Di Filippo, Paul. "Stone Lives." In *Mirrorshades: The Cyberpunk Anthology*, edited by Bruce Sterling. London: Paladin, 1988.

Gill, Andy. "Meet Mad Max 625." *New Musical Express*, April 6, 1985, pp. 2–3.

Jackson, Kevin. "Future Schlock." *The Independent*, March 24, 1989, p. 18.

Jameson, Fredric. "Post-modernism; or the Cultural Logic of Late Capitalism." *New Left Review* 146 (1984): 53–92.

Kellner, Douglas, Flo Leibowitz, and Michael Kellner. "Blade Runner: A Diagnostic Critique." *Jumpcut* 29 (1984): 6–8.

King, Barry. "The Burden of Max Headroom." *Screen* 30 (1989): 122–38.

Scroggy, David, ed. *The Blade Runner Sketchbook*. Screenplay by Hampton Fancher and David Peoples. San Diego: Blue Dolphin Enterprises, 1982.

Sobchack, Vivian. *Screening Space*. New York: Ungar, 1987.

Stewart, Garrett. "The 'Videology' of Science Fiction." In *Shadows of the Magic Lamp*, edited by George Slusser and Eric S. Rabkin. Carbondale: Southern Illinois University Press, 1985.

Tatsumi, Takayuki. "An Interview with William Gibson." *Science Fiction Eye* 1.1 (1987): 6–17.

———. "Some Real Mothers: An Interview with Samuel R. Delany." *Science Fiction Eye* 1.3 (1988): 5–11.

Semiotic

Ghosts

and

Ghostline

in the

Work

of Bruce

Sterling

. . . .

Tom Shippey

n chapter 3 of Bruce Sterling's second novel, *The Artificial Kid*,[1] the Kid himself attends the carnival of Harlequinade, set in his world's Decriminalized Zone. The participants are in costume: historical costumes from the future's extended past, fish or animal costumes, with also "the advocates of pure bizarrerie . . . people with no faces, or four arms, or eight legs; people in chains, in webs, in masses of bubbling froth; people dressed as the dead, the living, the not-yet-to-be, and the never-could-be" (32–33). The scene is not much emphasized, and it may seem perverse to see in it a leitmotiv for Sterling's work, but to quote the author again: "A symbol has meaning if someone gives it meaning."[2] It is possible to argue that Sterling, even more than other science fiction authors, deliberately sets out to explore and expand an area we might label "qualified reality": the linguistic area of "to be" plus qualifiers, already existent in common speech as "has-beens" and "might-have-beens," extended here to "not-yet-to-bes" and "never-could-bes," but taken elsewhere in Sterling to states that even the highly flexible English verb can barely accommodate.

Take, for instance, a short story by Sterling in *Fantasy and Science Fiction* for September 1984 (reprinted in his collection *Crystal Express* [London: Legend, 1990]). It is called "Telliamed" and can be described with almost indecent brevity. In it an old philosopher of the period of the Enlightenment, circa 1737, sits on the seashore and unwarily inhales a gift of something like coca powder sent to him by a correspondent, believing it is snuff. Not surprisingly, he then sees a vision in the sea of a "Dark Girl," whom he equates with ignorance and who complains that her reign is over and that the new philosophy of science will eclipse her. Summarized like that, the story becomes an icon of modern orthodoxy, a "Whig interpretation of history" applied in more than textbook style to the history of science (that home of "Whig interpretations"); it is a "must-be-so" story. Yet, though nothing I said above is false, and nothing major has been omitted, no reader is likely to take the story I just sketched as complete. For one thing, there is the "coca"; de Maillet's vision could be/is a drug-induced hallucination, predictably enough supporting his life's work, on the one hand, and on the other, expressing his secret fears. More penetratingly, even an ignorant modern reader cannot help noticing a series of clashes between reality as perceived in 1737 and as it is perceived now. De Maillet's field of study is fossils, a major evidential area for the development of the modern scientific worldview; and he has seen things we too have seen, are prepared to believe in, and have a theory to account for—for instance, seashells high on cliffs and in mountains. How did they get there? By geological change, we believe/know. By the steady shrinking of the sea, argues de Maillet. Our belief, a product of the eighteenth and nineteenth centuries, has vastly extended the time scale of Earth, caused at the very least major problems for Bible-centered theorists, and also provided the required time-space for Darwin's theory of evolution to work in.[3] De Maillet's belief is like ours in that it leads to conflict with Revelation: the letter he is reading at the beginning (and which has the "coca" powder with it) is from a Jesuit friend, rebuking him for his "System of Geology" and insisting that it cannot triumph against Dogma. But his belief is unlike ours in that it assumes that the seeds of all life must have come from the sea, which must once—the seashells prove it!—have covered the globe. Even people must once have been mermen; the orangutans of the Dutch East Indies must surely have only recently emerged from the ocean; de Maillet is watching the sea in patient hope that he too will see an "emergence."

In our belief system, de Maillet's view is irritating or comic in its mixture of approximation to and deviation from what is now accepted. To put it crudely, we—most *Fantasy and Science Fiction* readers, most readers of science fiction—are *for* him against literalist churchmen and against bourgeois insecurity, *against* him in his "one-way" vision of the past, and *against* him over evolution, orangutans, giants' bones, and fossilized ships down iron mines. He says things, without the coca, that we are not prepared to believe in. And what he sees under the influence of the coca, we may well believe, is a rejection of himself as well as of his opponents. To the questions he keeps asking, "What of my System? . . . Will it be revealed as truth? . . . Will my work persist?" (*Crystal Legend*, 257), the acolytes of ignorance reply evasively; but one of the ironies of the story is that his System will not stand. The Enlightenment that this philosopher has fathered will reject him and send his System into oblivion.

What, then, are de Maillet and his System in terms of qualified reality? They are not history ("was"), nor utter fantasy ("never-could-be"). Rather, they represent a blind alley, by modern standards, which nevertheless at least raises the doubt whether the modern consensus is not an improved but essentially similar blind alley; the philosopher and his System are a "was-would-be" or a "could-have-been-would-be." They inhabit, however, a philosophic space somehow intermediate between standard conceptions. Creating that space is the point of the story.

It could be said that this is common enough in science fiction, whose job it is to examine possibilities. Yet there is a great gap between "Telliamed" and, say, the lead story of that issue of *Fantasy*, Frederik Pohl's "The Blister," or Bruce Sterling's own *Fantasy* story from four years later (June 1988), "Our Neural Chernobyl." In the latter, Sterling playfully imagines a catastrophe like Chernobyl in the field of recombinant DNA research, which leads to an AIDS-type virus spreading intelligence among the animals. In the former, Manhattan is about to be covered with an artificial dome, part of the progress toward a new utopia chronicled in Pohl's *The Years of the City* (1985). Both stories, in short, are set in the future but suggest that the future has roots or analogues in the present and is (Sterling) possible/dangerous or (Pohl) possible/desirable. But "Telliamed" is set in the past, offers competing visions of the future from the past, and suggests that the present was once only a vision in the past, and not a natural or inevitable one at that. As for whether our reality or de Maillet's is preferable, one can only say that the story throws up its hands, leaving us with a highly ambiguous image of a pebble from the shore, clutched by de Maillet as irrefutable evidence, giggled at by children as a sign of insanity. This story by Sterling occupies a much more uncertain space within qualified reality than the great bulk of science fiction.

Conscious awareness of such possibilities is a major feature of Sterling's work and that of other authors within the field of cyberpunk. The notion of past visions of the future, or "yesterday's tomorrows," is the center of William Gibson's first published story, "The Gernsback Continuum" (1981), represented in Sterling's field-defining anthology *Mirrorshades* (New York: Arbor House, 1986; cited from the reprint edition, London: Paladin, 1988). In this story the central character is first reminded of some of the images of the future current in the 1930s: pulp fiction covers, "futuristic" architecture, sketches of twelve-propeller "flying wing" airliners with ballrooms and squash courts, designed to drone across the Atlantic in less than two days. Slowly recognizing the persisting reality of these visions, the narrator finds himself one day "over the Edge": he sees the ziggurat-city, the personal gyroscopes, the giant airliner, even the blond, smug, healthy future citizens of the 1930s, with their immortal line: "John, we've forgotten our food pills" (10). Amphetamine psychosis? The explanation is offered, as is the coca in Sterling's story. But a friend suggests a "classier explanation" to the narrator through the notion of a "mass unconscious." "I'd say you saw a semiotic ghost. . . . They're semiotic phantoms, bits of deep cultural imagery that have split off and taken on a life of their own" (7). The notion of the "semiotic ghost" is discussed no further, but as with "Telliamed" and its intermediate philosophic space, "The Gernsback Continuum" has no function other than to create that notion. One might note that Gibson's story in a sense goes further than Sterling's in making the point that science fiction—old science fiction, "could-be" science fiction—dies quickly and is at the mercy of changing opinions. Conversely, Sterling's story goes further than Gibson's in providing no secure point, no accepted here-and-now reality, to set the false vision against. In Sterling's story the Dark Girl is a semiotic phantom from de Maillet's mind; his correspondent's Dogma can also be seen as a ghost of dead belief; but de Maillet's System is a ghost too, even weaker than the Dogma; the whole story is a conflict of tenuities.

Other stories by Sterling take such tenuities even further. Another good brief example is the story "Dinner in Audoghast," from *Isaac Asimov's Science Fiction Magazine* (May 1985; also now in *Crystal Express*). This is set in what one might call a ghost city—its name, of course, suggests "ghost" and "ghastly," and perhaps "Gormenghast"—a city allegedly existent in sub-Saharan Africa some time in the eleventh century. To the people chatting there over dinner, the Christian world of Europe is a fable of cannibalism and savages; its inhabitants are juxtaposed with gorillas, these latter real but disappointing. "My grandfather owned a gorilla once," observes a diner. "Even after ten years, it could barely speak Arabic" (*Crystal Express*, 307). The disorienting effect of this remark is reminiscent of the merfolk-orangutans of Sterling's earlier story, but it also helps to move Audoghast out of readily identifiable space. Are we in a little-known but real frame of history (a "was")? Are we in an alternate world (a "might-have-been")? Whatever the answer, the connection with our own reality is achieved by bringing on a repulsive and leprous prophet who, Cassandra-like, foretells a string of things we recognize as truth, including the destruction of Audoghast, only to be scorned by his auditors. They are wrong, we are right, and one of the diners, a poet, senses as much, in a passage reminiscent of Shelley's "Ozymandias" sonnet.[4] But the rest console him, laughing at the vision of civilized Europeans, pointing out that there must always be a place to control the ivory trade, for "elephants are thick as fleas," while, in the last resort: " 'Well, surely there are always slaves,' said Manimenesh, and smiled, and winked. The others laughed with him, and there was joy again" (317).

This ending, of course, is fiercely ironic. It presents as true what we know to be false; it presents fact as prophesy, and fantasy as fact. Yet, oddly, it has no moral point to make, not even about slavery. If the story "says" anything, it is only that people's expectations are often wrong. It is an exercise again in qualified reality. And to cut the matter short, one need say only that several Sterling stories are similarly analyzable: for instance, his collaboration with Lewis Shiner, "Mozart in Mirrorshades" (a switch on the "alternative world" subgenre of science fiction), or his collaboration with Gibson, "Red Star, Winter Orbit" (in which present visions of space exploration have become "a dream that failed," a modern version of Gernsback).[5] But the point can perhaps be taken as established. Bruce Sterling, like other cyberpunk authors but more consistently and centrally, has set out to explore the domains of qualified reality, always perhaps implied by the creation of science fiction, but never previously as thoroughly or consciously exploited.

Having said that, what about Gibson's coinage of the phrase *semiotic ghost*? How appropriate to Sterling is it? (Remember that to be a ghost it is necessary to be dead.) "The Gernsback Continuum" deals with dead futures. But surely that must be a limiting case. If science fiction admits that all its futures are dead or stillborn, it removes most of its raison d'être. How can the semiotic ghost coexist with the classic science fiction mode?

Sterling's most suggestive story in this area is "Green Days in Brunei," a twenty-thousand-word novella from *Asimov's* October 1985 issue (reprinted in *Crystal Express*). It exemplifies several of the cyberpunk features celebrated in Sterling's *Mirrorshades* editorial: internationalism (the story is set in Brunei, with a Canadian hero of Chinese parentage and other characters Australian, Malay, or British); the notion of the computer net (it has lovers who communicate by bulletin board); the personalization of technology (following Sterling's editorial claim in *Mirrorshades* that "eighties tech sticks to the skin. . . . Not for us the giant steam-snorting wonders of the past" [xi]. This last point is in fact the science fictional center of the story. Its hero, Turner Choi, is in Brunei to revive an old robot assembly line and put it to work making sailboats; not much of a job in his view, "a kind of industrial archaeology." But as the story unfolds we come to see Turner's opinion as a relic of Western thinking, present-view-of-the-future thinking, created by a set of cultural prejudices. Perhaps the main point about Brunei— the reason for placing the story there—is that in such places cultural expectations, East-West dichotomies, are least powerful; Brunei is a cultural Free Zone. In one scene Turner is taken to an old ruin where the Bruneians have set up their satellite dishes. As they walked through the ruins, "Turner saw a tattooed face, framed in headphones, at a shattered second-story window. 'The local Murut tribe,' Brooke said, glancing up. 'They're a bit shy' " (*Crystal Express*, 164).

213

The contrast is repeated in Sterling's latest novel, *Islands in the Net*,[6] in which again a westerner sees, on a Caribbean island, an icon of alienness "plugged in" to the electronic community: "At a sea-level floating dock, a dreadlocked longshoreman looked them over coolly, his face framed in headphones" (111). The Murut and the Grenadian will not interact face-to-face with westerners; they remain aloof or alien, "shy" or "cool," marked off by tattoos or dreadlocks. Yet on a cultural or technological level, they do interact. They want the headphones, the screens, the Net. At the center of "Green Days," Turner Choi comes to understand what can and what cannot be culturally transmitted. The job he thought was industrial archaeology turns out to be a chance to export and propagandize a new, "green" way of life in Ocean Arks that trade, haul freight, and grow food on their greenhouse decks, all using renewable energy alone. The ideal might be defined as the "electronic *kampong*": new technology, free access to information, old cultural patterns, nonexploitative use of resources.

One of the words Sterling uses to define this new understanding is *bricolage*.[7] Turner Choi is a *bricoleur*, one who can make do with the leftover junk from the twentieth century. "That's what *bricolage* is," says the Englishman Brooke, "using the clutter and rubble to make something worth having" (159). The difficult thing is that it means using things for one purpose when (like the sailboat technology) they were originally designed for something else. Sterling's other word for the process is the verb *retrofit*—looking at things retrospectively and making them fit a new system. There is, the story insists, an ingrained resistance to this, and in the readers as well as in the characters. The force that opposes

retrofitting is the awareness that immediately sees something improper/ unexpected/unnatural in tattoos and headphones, or dreadlocks and headphones, or Malay girls reading *New Musical Express*, or any of the dozens of other fleeting, unstressed, cumulatively significant culture clashes built into "Green Days." If one were to reduce the story to maxims, Sterling would be telling us here: (1) things have immediate uses, (2) immediate uses are more important than cultural preconceptions, (3) cultural preconceptions are dead, but (4) dead things are there to be used.[8]

One could, in fact, say that bricolage could also be called "Frankensteining." When Turner Choi builds his Ocean Arks he is using leftovers, spare parts from dead constructions. Where, then, are the semiotic ghosts in "Green Days"? Surely the answer is that they are in the readers' expectations. "Green Days" is a "could-be" story, like most science fiction. But unlike most science fiction, it trades on an implicit feeling that certain expectations will be fulfilled. Tech will be high, progress will be technological, the Western world may not be superior but Western attitudes will be, the Third World—as long as it keeps to Third World culture—will be left behind. That is the 1970s version, one might say, of the "Gernsback Continuum." At the start of "Green Days" Turner is still in that continuum. At the end he realizes it is dead, has been dead for some time. He has been living with a semiotic ghost; but that ghost is still in control of the minds of those readers (in practice all of them, this critic included) not yet familiarized to bricolage, still jumping nervously at each of the culture clash pinpricks Sterling has scattered through his text.

The method pioneered in "Green Days" dominates *Islands in the Net*. The most consistent thing about this book is the way it consigns to "ghost" status virtually every cultural piety left to Western readers. To give only one example, we are introduced near the end of the book to a white South African Boer called Katje Selous—a name deliberately ill-omened.[9] However, *this* Selous (we eventually realize) has abandoned apartheid and has admitted blacks to full citizenship; one's moral prejudices readjust. But then again we learn that the South Africa to which Katje is loyal is based on the premises that "Azanian black people are the finest black people in the world!" because of their Zulu warrior blood, and that the Zulus and the Boers between them have a genetic right to oversee the affairs of Africa. Is Selous a good or a bad character? The question is naïve, but also unanswerable; to answer it one would have to have a secure moral base. And after being led through the maze of data pirates (bad or good?), murder of data pirates (justified or not?) by the Free Army of Counter-Terrorism (a stooge organization?) acting for Mali (or is it Singapore, two emergent nations of quite different cultural "feel"), with or without the connivance of Vienna (world peacekeepers or corrupt cartel?): well, it is reasonable to agree that the variables have become literally irresolvable by any reader, no matter how skilled or careful.

The effect of the book lies in its sudden new angles, its destruction of icons. Few issues could unite a present American public more than dislike of Iran. Near the end of *Islands*, one of its most sympathetic characters remarks as if everyone knew it already that the "Iranian revolt of 1979" was a "brave effort" but "too late. . . . They were already fighting for television" (440). In exactly the opposite mode Sterling exposes to casual denigration at different moments career feminists, health standards enforcement, emergent nations' aspirations, the ideology of Space Invaders, and the notion of world government. When Singapore is successfully invaded, the agency that carries out the attack is the Red Cross; the nuclear submarine that re-bombs Hiroshima (an iconic act in itself) is marked by icons of de Gaulle and Jaruzelski (what have they in common?); near the end, the Tuareg of the Sahara are presented singing a traditional song that expresses their awareness that by prizing camels and goats for so long they destroyed their ecology, which they must now repair by butchering their herds and growing grass:

> For a thousand years we must praise the grass.
> We will eat the *tisma* food to live,
> We will buy Iron Camels from Go Motion
> Unlimited in Santa Clara California.

"It's an old song," says the Iranian symphathizer. "Retro-fitted" (412).

The retrofitting in *Islands in the Net* virtually defies comprehension. Its heroine felt at one point that "some pattern-seeking side of her brain had gone into overdrive," and most readers will feel with her. Yet the point of the story is clear: "Stop. Abandon. Disassemble. Do not seek patterns. Do not think dreadlocks do not go with headphones. Forget

Jaruzelski was a Communist and MacArthur an American. Assemble these data a new way, like a *bricoleur*. Above all, assume everything you know already, from politics to table manners, is part of a semiotic system and accordingly unreliable insofar as it has a place within that system." *Islands in the Net*, one might say, is a semiotic vision, indeed a vision of a new semiotics. But where "The Gernsback Continuum" or "Telliamed" centered on semiotic ghosts and dead systems, Sterling's novel locates those ghosts within its readers' minds. It is a tour de force, and a deeply unsettling one, to present a whole near-future world in which virtually no carryover at all from the present can be relied on.

Lack of carryover may give a clue, finally, to answering an odd question about Sterling's work so far: why is he interested in themes of ghostliness *other* than the metaphorical or semiotic ones already discussed? *Islands* has zombies, one Stephen King–style death on screen, and Optimal Personas who appear for all the world like spirit guides. But the themes of age, survival, and "negotiated death" have been with Sterling all through his career, and we begin to question how they fit in with qualified reality or bricolage. Take, for instance, Sterling's second novel, *The Artificial Kid*.

An irreverent mind might say that this work was constructed for the purpose of provoking Freudian interpretation. The lead character, the Artificial Kid, is so called for various reasons, but "kid" is a true description of him. He is facially hairless, shrill-voiced, prepubescent, and kept so by drug treatment. His real age is twenty-eight. Or is it ninety-eight, the number of years he has been practicing with his "nunchuck"? Actually, he is in another sense nearly three hundred, for the Kid is "artificial" too: he was produced by memory transfer from a much older man, Rominuald Tanglin, alias R. T., or, of course, "Arti." What is the relationship between R. T. and the Kid? In the tapes he has concealed in the Kid's computer, he addresses the Kid always as "kid" or "son." Is this merely affectionate, literally true, or a wild understatement (the Kid not being R. T.'s son but his identity)? No wonder, a Freudian would say, that the Kid stays prepubescent. In his case, achieving independence from his father/namesake/alter ego is practically impossible! As the Kid says, "It's like having a ghost at your elbow" (132).

The Kid is, however, surrounded by ghosts. The founder of his world is one Moses Moses—it would be a poor Freudian who could see no meaning in that—known to have been frozen centuries before, but then killed in his "cryocoffin" by assassins. During the Kid's adventures, though, it becomes clear that one of his companions is the resurrected Moses Moses, an evident "father figure." Another is Professor Crossbow, the Kid's old tutor—a sexual neuter, so a neuter-tutor—long vanished "under the surface of the Gulf of Memory" (7). A third is Anne Twiceborn (again a name of aggressive significance), a young woman infatuated with the Kid's "father" R. T. A totally dominating father, a dead-alive father figure, a neuter father figure, an aspiring stepmother: one need go no further to suggest that *The Artificial Kid* is an almost parodic version of the genre known as "family drama,"[10] its underlying drive, of course, being to allow the Kid to break free of paternal domination, reach pubescence, achieve sexual union (with Anne Twiceborn), and so supplant his father and achieve independent existence. *Supplant* may be the wrong verb, though. In view of his special relationship with R. T., *exorcise* might be more accurate, or even (with full consciousness of its double meaning) *lay*. The Kid has to "lay" his stepmother to "lay" his father's ghost. Meanwhile, in the background, Professor Crossbow and Moses Moses are fusing to become two examples of the same joint personality; and in yet another twist Crossbow Moses (though not Moses Crossbow) fuses with "the Mass," a kind of planetary gene pool that promises its members a form of immortality. My cells will be dismantled, Crossbow Moses remarks, "But that does not constitute death. My genetic content would be preserved. In all likelihood I would eventually be recreated. Whether I would be re-born in the full sense of the word depends on your definition of identity. I would be a clone. But all neuters are clones, of course" (210). He is promised, then, a *kind* of continuing survival, purely physical. R. T. arranged for himself a kind of survival purely mental. Moses Moses in his cryocoffin tried to combine the two, and both the Kid and Anne Twiceborn have their own ideas about survival as well, whether religious, electronic, or genetic. Yet however the cards are shuffled, it is clear that Sterling is interested in the notion of carryover; he does not accept life-death as the simple, traditional dichotomy.

Similar points could be made about Sterling's third novel, *Schismatrix* (1985), and the other stories from the "mechanist/shaper" universe in which that work is set. *Schismatrix* shows strong interest in "negotiated death." Its characters frequently disappear (but reappear), replace death by "fading" (a process in which one cannot be sure whether a friend has died or not), transform themselves into electronic impulses of mindless flesh (the sentence "The room was full of flesh" in chapter 6

217
......
......
......

of *Schismatrix* is not metaphorical), or drop in and out of oblivion like visitors to Elfland in a traditional fairy tale. In both *Schismatrix* and its associated stories, too, Sterling's interest in DNA as a literal fact, of which the word *soul* is an image, is almost obsessively strong.[11] His fiction often seems to oscillate thematically between the notions of termination and survival; betraying, on the one hand, fascination with/ horror at the persistent hanging on of the very old, but, on the other, deep reluctance to see anything or anyone cut off or terminated without passing on something (individual DNA or cultural legacy) to the future.

What have these themes of ghostliness to do with semiotic ghosts, qualified reality, or bricolage? One suggestion: Sterling is actively opposed to the idea of system, still worse System (as in "Telliamed"). He is very strongly aware of the "pattern-seeking" quality of human minds and does his best to disrupt it in every way, including stylistically. Yet he knows that systems have a strong tendency to perpetuate and propagate themselves, whether genetically, like DNA, or intellectually, like human cultures. What he likes to show is systems breaking down ("Telliamed"), about to break down ("Audoghast"), or broken down (*Islands*). His ideal is the person who picks up the pieces and starts again, the bricoleur. What he fears is the successful imposition of dead systems on the future, as with semiotic ghosts. The themes of ghostliness, generation conflict, and negotiated death are all mediations between these two extremes. The person who lives on may be a despot, like R. T., or a sage, like the hero of *Schismatrix*. Probably the difference lies in the readiness, or otherwise, to abandon an intellectual system while preserving continuity of personality. "People outlive nations," says Lindsay serenely in *Schismatrix* (263), faced with failure and ruin. His reward for readiness to start again is to become, at the very end, a ghost, observing his own skull and bones being looted by an alien bricoleur. To Sterling this is a consummation.

Other facets of Sterling's fiction could be drawn into his argument, notably his liking for parody of or satire against the general assumptions of science fiction itself, viewed as a series of "Gernsback continua": *Schismatrix* begins with the Arthur Clarke motif of an ultralight aircraft wheeling in the sky of a low-gravity hollowed-out asteroid;[12] but, of course, with Sterling the ultralight crashes, just as his spaceships have roaches, his hydroponics all go sour, and his aging space people are clogged with dirt. Such jabs are all aimed at making readers drop their

218

ballast of (science fictional) cultural assumptions, to float free—balloon images recur in Sterling—into the larger space of qualified reality. Nevertheless, the final point here should come from an interview with Sterling recorded in *Interzone*.[13]

"Don't you think," the interviewer asked, "that sf, far from being a vision of the future, is a reflection of the present?" Sterling realized at once that this question conceals the assertion that science fiction is metaphorical, a mode for discussing the discontents or pressures of the present day in suitably veiled form; that it is, in short, a skewed version of what is, a "will-be" or a "might-be." He reacted to the question with strong disapproval. "I resent it when my ideas, which I have gone to some pains to develop and explore, are dismissed as unconscious yearnings or a funhouse-mirror reflection of the contemporary milieu. My writings about the future are not 'about the future' in a strict sense, but they are about my ideas of the future. They are not allegories" (12). The question, Sterling continued, "is part of an ongoing critical attempt to reduce sf to a sub-branch of mainstream literature."

It may seem idle to add comment to these very clear statements, but the last remark shows Sterling's strong desire, already identified above, for science fiction as a whole to preserve its distinctive fictional space. As for the longer quotation, one might underline "unconscious yearnings" and "funhouse-mirror." The former reminds us that even Freudian analysis (as of *The Artificial Kid*) could in Sterling's view be radically altered by technology: not even fathers, families, or primal scenes are immune to change. Meanwhile, the rejection of "funhouse-mirrors" might take us back to bricolage. The future will not be the same shape as the present, just bulged or lengthened or distorted; it will be a whole new assembly: the mirror will be shattered first. Yet no image easily catches the distinctive novelty of Sterling's work. In it, both this present world and the worlds of classic science fiction are "ghost worlds." Qualified reality is elsewhere.

Notes

1. Bruce Sterling, *The Artificial Kid* (New York: Harper and Row, 1980; cited here from reprint edition, Harmondsworth: Penguin Books, 1985).
2. Bruce Sterling, *Schismatrix* (New York: Arbor House, 1985; cited here from reprint edition, Harmondsworth: Penguin Books, 1986), Chap. 2, p. 53.

3. For an interesting account of the importance of geology in the pre-Darwinian period, see Stephen Jay Gould, *Time's Arrow, Time's Cycle: Myth and Metaphor in the Discovery of Geological Time* (Cambridge, Mass.: Harvard University Press, 1987).

4. For further discussion of scenes of "disfigurement," see my article "The Fall of America in Science Fiction," *Essays and Studies*, n.s., 43 (1990): 104–32.

5. Both stories are in *Mirrorshades: The Cyberpunk Anthology*, edited by Bruce Sterling (New York: Arbor House, 1986), but were first published in (respectively) *Omni*, September 1985, and *Omni*, July 1983.

6. Bruce Sterling, *Islands in the Net* (London: Legend, 1988).

7. The source of this concept is Claude Lévi-Strauss, *The Savage Mind* (London: Weidenfeld and Nicolson, 1966), pp. 16–36. Sterling mentions Lévi-Strauss overtly in his story.

8. A tag frequently cited—as by Sterling in his *Mirrorshades* editorial—is Gibson's "the street finds its own uses for things."

9. F. C. Selous (1851–1917) helped bring Rhodesia under British rule. The Selous Scouts, named after him, established a formidable antiguerrilla reputation as a "special forces" unit.

10. For "family drama," see Derek Brewer's book *Symbolic Stories: Traditional Narratives of the Family Drama in English Literature* (Cambridge: D. S. Brewer, 1980).

11. The Elder Culture's "soul sculptures" appear in Sterling's first novel, *Involution Ocean* (New York: Jove Books, 1977), and reappear in *The Artificial Kid*, chap. 10, where they look like DNA models. In Sterling's collaboration with John Shirley, "The Unfolding," *Interzone* 11 (Spring 1985): 27–32, apocalypse is triggered by a "ghost image" of a DNA model.

12. The image is explored thoroughly in Arthur Clarke's *Rendezvous with Rama* (London: Victor Gollancz, 1973), though similar ideas had been common in science fiction long before.

13. *Interzone* 15 (Spring 1986): 12–14.

PART 5

The New

Metaphoricity:

The

Future

of Fiction

Science

Fiction,

Rhetoric,

and

Realities:

Words

to the

Critic

. . . .

Gregory Benford

There is a story that Schumann once played a new composition for a small audience, and afterward a man stood and asked if Herr Schumann could explain the work. Schumann stood silent for a long moment, then sat down and played the entire piece through again.

Sometimes I feel that way as a writer, when I am confronted with talking about work that is deeply subconscious. I'd rather point to the work and stay silent. Still more so, then, when handicapping lit'ry dark horses.

On the way to this conference I went hiking in the Lake Country and read Arthur C. Clarke's *Astounding Days*. The English countryside in which Clarke grew up has changed little, but our perceptions of the immensities surrounding humanity and the perspectives available to us have expanded enormously. *Astounding Days* speaks fondly of a time when a small band believed articles of faith held to be nonsense by the hard-nosed world. So they dreamed and schemed and brought us into space, with consequences still unfolding.

SF has little of that today, regrettably. We have no fresh, central vision of the future that is at once a powerful metaphor and a scientific possibility. Such opportunities come along seldom, after all. Absent that grand image, some still expect science fiction to abide by the constraints of science and to look beyond the claustrophobia of the present.

Many take these rough rules to be too tight. They want to speak of the coming world ruled by the impact of computers, reflecting the obvious impact of personal computers on our lives in this decade. Fair enough, though it's stale news by now, of course. Still, looking forward demands that you bother yourself to think about what the technology implies in the long run. Failure to do so means you recapitulate the arguments and images of others. Thus we get film noir and pulp plots against a background taken mostly from the glossy aesthetics of magazine ads. The problem of envisioning the future in terms of the surfaces of the present is that it dates madly.

I like the literature of surfaces, from Ballard to Gibson and beyond—but I don't believe it means very much. Underlying ideas form a better navigational aid for both literature and life.

I urge critics to concentrate on what the SF genre makes, not merely what it reacts to; what emerges from it, not what it mirrors. *Blade Runner* was driven by a visual aesthetic (that of H. R. Geiger's sets and Ridley Scott's direction) and a postmodern need to revisit and recycle the tropes and mannerisms of earlier fictions. It uses the detective voice-over frame so common in films made from the novels of Raymond Chandler, and the implied critique of capitalist society that underlies the hard-boiled detective novel. *Blade Runner* came first, two years before *Neuromancer*, and plainly invented much of what SF critics think is original in later work. Few seem to notice this. Outside media, including some rock (as in the case of John Shirley), greatly spurred cyberpunk—the first time, I think, that the genre derived its vision from outside forces. Contrast the era of *Astounding Days*, which drove the outside world.

One can measure the deeper, long-view realism in Clarke's SF by its influence on reality. (It also changed the aesthetic voice of hard SF, the region I consider to be the ideological core.) SF can be hugely influential, although most of the writing of the 1980s was not, precisely because it was culturally derivative.

Hard SF seeks to convince, to appeal to the intellect. Fantasy and horror speak to the emotions, delving into deep fears and loves. Both have gathered great audiences through the 1980s. During these times the genre has also been damaged, I feel, by the attempts by many forces to co-opt it. Science and SF are useful emblems of the real and the possible. The Reagan administration began the Strategic Defense Initiative primarily because of input from SF writers. The Writers of the Future seek to co-opt SF as a vehicle for Scientology. There will be more attempts to use the inherent power developed by fantastic literature to further pet causes. A compliment, perhaps. If so, it is one we should come to expect in the future, for others will pick up the trick, and perhaps our audience.

The presence of a larger audience makes it easier to blur boundaries and lessens the strengths of clear distinctions. Thus fantasy—outright impossibility—appears in ostensibly SF works because much of the audience doesn't understand (or maybe doesn't care about) the distinction. More tennis with the net down.

The rise of fantasy is disturbing as a cultural phenomenon, despite its considerable virtues as literature—a position I've been attacked for quite a bit. I fear that the mass market fantasy of our time speaks to a growing population that does not feel involved in technosociety. These people don't know what holds airplanes up, are cowed by the complex technoscientific worldview. Fantasy says that the world is animate, filled with spirits; the woods are alive. It suggests a program of managing the world through acts of personality—will and virtue rather than intellect. What you can't do with your hands, you can do with your spirit: Let the Force Be With You.

An obliging illusion, like Christianity. And beyond fantasy, why the rise of horror? It comes from a psychodynamic of deep emotions, the desire to be frightened, to be reassured (not by elves, though) that horrid things can be vanquished. I find unsettling implications here, suggesting that rational Western society is losing its grip on the technosociety it invented. Bad news for us all, I think, and especially for SF, which relies on the constraints of science. (Notably, the Japanese like straight SF, not fantasy.) In SF, as in the sonnet, the rules define the form. If you write a sonnet that doesn't scan or rhyme or has thirty-three lines, you haven't written a bad sonnet, you've not written one at all. People whose principal response to the world is so at odds with the notion of limits and constraints are easy prey to those who lead through emotion, not reason. Surely we have seen enough in this century of where a lack of skepticism can take whole nations.

There is much good SF now, perhaps more than ever—but it's buried in an avalanche of intellectually haphazard work. Genre distinctions blur, and what's a critic to do? I recommend to critics an inspection of scientific credibility that goes beyond simply detailing plausibility. Do not misread the hard SF ideology. *I am not saying that fidelity to scientific vision is the highest standard in SF.* But it is important.

The deeper question, which critics should begin to address, is the aesthetic value of scientific truth. How does the constraint act upon other dramatic elements? When is cheating permitted? (Yes, even hard SF writers knowingly fake things. I've done it myself.) Does it serve larger dramatic purpose, character, symbolism—or not? How adroitly do we finesse the facts—and why? If you suspect that a writer wished for a mosaic effect, as a critic you must be sure you don't mistake this for a badly done jigsaw puzzle—and vice versa. Ferreting out such knotty issues is the critics' job. Few do it.

Have we learned much from the 1980s? Personally, I applaud the advances in sheer writing ability by people as diverse as Stan Robinson, Connie Willis, Vernor Vinge, and Lucius Shepard. It also seems to me that hard SF has strengthened noticeably at the hands of Haldeman, Bear, Brin, and others.

I find cyberpunk less interesting than the new wave because it exhausted quickly, didn't play into many fruitful streams. It was more interesting as a marketing strategy using the idea of literary progress. Sterling was not so much interested in discourse; he censored criticism I wrote for *Cheap Truth* because it didn't fit the bandwagon music. That's right—managed the press! He produced an agitprop rag, not disinterested criticism. And divergent spirits such as Rudy Rucker and Marc Laidlaw got little momentum from the hype wave. The gift of the whole thing was to see that the idea of literary progress had become marketable itself.

Further, most cyberpunk struck me as simply badly informed. Sterling is a good writer, but "Green Days in Brunei," for example, proposes that the Third World can be saved by robot manufacture (gee, and here I thought they had surplus labor) and the resources of the deep oceans, using solar power. Sterling apparently thinks the oceans are rich, when in fact they are mostly quite barren except near land. This is called not doing your homework.

Maybe it was intentional, but what was the point?—a vision of progress based on quick technofixes. So what? There are some technical solutions available, of course, mostly in unglamorous areas, like birth control. What's obvious about the Third World (particularly if you've been there much) is that deep cultural change must occur before long-lasting progress emerges. Maybe that's too hard to dramatize, though.

This problem of dramatization produces many of the pulp clichés. Criminals are mostly dumb—impaired even—that's why they resort to crime. But computers seem more hip if you assume hard-nosed cowboys will be able to outwit the nerds whom we all know dominate and invent computer tech. So you write about crime when you know nothing of it beyond what you steam out of Raymond Chandler. Good reads, some of them, but in the back of your mind you know you're eating Nutrisweet cotton candy spinning off a distant armature.

Mind, I do feel that issues sometimes touched on by the cyberpunks (though not their invention, for they recycled SF tropes) are central. The increasing connection of ourselves to our machines is unsettling and ripe for mingled scientific imagery. Maybe artificial intelligence should rightly be seen as the bravest frontier we have–not the claustrophobic aspects but the liberating ones. It is always easier to see problems than opportunities; that's why newspaper columnists are more common than inventors. I suspect that Vernor Vinge's approaching cusp point, where human possibilities climb out of sight, may be more insightful than the now-familiar vexings over virus programs.

Schumann had an advantage—he could not only refuse to talk about his work, he could also perform it without using words. I suppose I should say something of what preoccupies me these days, though that might not give any clues about where literature is headed. In my own work I have lately implied that we will, in diverse ways, come to incorporate into our own bodies the mechanical metaphors that we seemingly battle. Further, I feel that we may be entering a postliterate era, in which information is best conveyed by tagging it to recognizable personality complexes. All this underlies the ideas I am struggling with in *Great Sky River*, *Tides of Light*, and beyond.

So I do think important issues are afoot in SF. The 1980s have worked out implications of computer tech, but a bit tardily, I think. The next few decades will be driven more strongly by biotechnology, and we've done little thinking about that. I started to make some efforts in *Beyond the Fall of Night* because it struck me as useful to frame our understanding of the scientific landscape against the preconceptions of SF forty years in the past, as shown in Clarke's *Against the Fall of Night*. We've been curiously slow to see the implications that began unfolding with Crick and Watson's discovery of DNA nearly forty years ago. The field has reached the point at which reflection on our own pace and hectic momentum is worthwhile. The *idea* of the future now frames the future as much as any other force.

I do wish we saw more thought in the genre and less energy in surface effects. The habit of our media is to squint at passing fashion and read significance into it. Sometimes this pays off, but usually it has as much relevance as tea leaves. We cannot read the fads of the future, nor should we wish to, unless we're advertising executives. Our aim is not to be *with it* but ahead of it. Long visions require some sense of continuity, at the slow movement of fundamental ideas.

What of punkish fashions now? As Stanley Kubrick said in an after-note, caught in the freezeframe that ends *Barry Lyndon*: Whatever one think of them, they are all equal now—dead. Marketing strategies yield few enduring metaphors.

What's next? *2001*. And some terrific writing, I think.

But holding writers in literary movements is, as Fred Pohl says, like trying to herd mice. Critics are different beasts, though.

I dislike the atomizing and reductionist urge in criticism, for it seldom engages the reasons why writers write and readers read. Too often, deconstructions merely demolish. This is not to dismiss such pursuits, for their partial visions can be stimulating. (Though they seldom are for me, partly because their postures seem to discourage good clear writing from the critics themselves.)

Attempts to carry over such scrutinies from conventional literature often illuminate the preconceptions of the critic more than the strange terrain of fantastic literature. However, this is not to privilege older notions in criticism. We occasionally hear calls for higher standards in science fiction, which hark back to the bourgeois novel of character, for example. I wish excellence were so easy. One of our prime tasks is conveying strangeness. Portraying people in an altered future is harder than, say, getting into the mind of the mayor of Casterbridge.

This suggests that there are fresh, wholly science fictional challenges of deep interest. How does the reader's need to sense the reality of the fictional world subvert the very oddness SF tries to convey? How much of what we "know" about people—the origin of "good characterization"—is in fact passing conventional wisdom? (How can we know what the ordinary folk of Pharaoh's time thought? Or felt?)

When should we destroy such tempocentric notions before proceeding? Characterization in fiction is not necessarily central; Aristotle did not think so, ranking plot higher and style lower.

I suspect the most penetrating way to view SF has not yet been evolved. Critics tend to carry over methods from realistic fiction, which usually concerns the immediate past. Few consider, for example, the inevitable balance and tension between scientific truth and narrative demands. When should "hard SF" authors deliberately falsify a scientific fact? A law? Or the very scientific method? (And indeed, we do.) *Why* do they do it?

Further, consider the larger social context of SF. How much of the humanist program ("man is the measure of all things") can be applied to fiction that holds scientific truth to be central? Can such limited humanism be held responsible for our rape of nature? Are there not some moral lessons to be learned by seeing humans as dwarfed, humbled by the landscape science unfolds in space and time? How do we evaluate fiction that proceeds from such radically different assumptions?

These are engaging questions. They appear in practice often for writers, but seldom in criticism.

So I leave you with a challenge: work out new methods of dealing with <u>fantastic literature</u> that do not rely on the old habits of mind. Such approaches are needed to fathom what's already been done, and they will certainly be essential for navigating through the literature of the century approaching.

229
......
......
......

Science is not generally considered metaphoric. Rather, metaphor has been more or
less consigned to the nonscientific realm, and
more particularly to the literary sphere. A
dichotomy has been established in which an either-or
proposition is expressed: if it is scientific it is not metaphor, and vice versa. However, there are those who, looking at metaphor from a general perspective, consider
it the fundamental property of all human thought; and
others who, focusing more specifically on science, believe metaphor to be as much a part of the scientific
realm as the literary.

John Middleton Murry sees metaphor as a general and
necessary property of thought, and Nietzsche views it as
the fundamental device of human epistemology. Murry
states that metaphor "is as ultimate as the act of speech
itself and speech as ultimate as thought." "[It] appears
as the instinctive and necessary act of the mind exploring reality and ordering experience. It is the means by
which the less familiar is assimilated to the more familiar, . . . it 'gives to airy nothing a local habitation and
a name,' so that it ceases to be airy nothing" (65–66).
Nietzsche claims that all human knowledge comes from
language, which can only be metaphorical in nature.
Man cannot obtain truth because truth is "a mobile army
of metaphors. . . . Every idea originates through equating the unequal"
(179–80). We cannot move beyond metaphor. Although science may attempt to reach the thing-in-itself, in Nietzsche's opinion it only creates
an illusion with which to deceive us, because humans think language
has an "impulse toward the formation of metaphors . . . [which] is in
truth not defeated nor even subdued by the fact that out of its evaporated
products, the ideas, a regular and rigid new world has been built . . . for
it" (188).

For Nietzsche and Murry, metaphor becomes a model for the human thought process in general. Changing perspective from the general to the specific, W. V. Quine, in "A Postscript on Metaphor," discusses scientists' use of the device: "The molecular theory of gases emerged as an ingenious metaphor: a gas was likened to a vast swarm of absurdly small bodies" (159). Also discussing metaphor as it relates to science, science fiction writer Greg Bear points to the field of mathematics with its obviously metaphorical language.[1] Finally, Gregory Benford, who is both a scientist and a writer, declares that science does utilize metaphor, which he classifies as an epistemological device.[2] If we accept the implication of these views, the concept of metaphor seems valid for both the scientific and nonscientific spheres. But does metaphor contain the same properties in both areas, or is there a distinction between the two, as Benford believes? How does it function in these respective fields?

Aristotle defines metaphor as "the device . . . of giving life to lifeless things" (Murry, 73). Paul DeMan, following in Aristotle's footsteps, sees prosopopoeia as the epitome of metaphor because it brings dead things to life.[3] Murry claims these are living metaphors, and "such," he says, is the stuff of "what we call creative literature" (66). All are referring to metaphor in literature and all equate it with a living or vital world. When we turn our attention to the field of science, there seems to be a change in perspective and an acceptance of the possibility of moving beyond the living or vital into the realm of the dead or nonvital, that is, into the material (as opposed to the vital or spiritual)—the dead.

Nietzsche states that ideas are the *evaporated* products of metaphor and that "science works irresistibly at that great columbarium of ideas, the cemetery of perceptions" (187). When Quine refers to the metaphor utilized in the molecular theory of gases, he says, "So pat was the metaphor that it was declared literally true and thus became straight away a dead metaphor" (150). Although a distinction is made here between two types of metaphor, it seems to be made on an intuitive level. These thinkers appear to be enmeshed in a Cartesian argument that equates the dead or extended (material) world with quantity or measurement, as opposed to the vital and essential world, which is associated with qualitative things. But what is it in these two types of metaphor that causes such an intuitive differentiation to be made?

Murry claims that metaphor assimilates "the unknown to the known" (66), and Nietzsche says it is "equating the unequal" (179). There is in this process a transfer of meaning, an application of a word or image to an object it cannot literally denote. Indeed, in their eyes this transfer is always imperfect. When x is said to be y, there is a transfer from something more well known to something less well known, but x's literal significance is not removed, nor is x deleted from the larger sphere of language. This x-y linkage provides the dualistic nature of metaphor, the duality expressed in the necessity of having two poles if metaphor is to function as metaphor.

Tenor becomes irrevocably linked to vehicle, and a setting and preserving of boundaries occurs. There is always a reference from a point inside to a point outside. In a sense a sort of implicit Platonism is created in which the product of the link is a reference to some greater reality, to some higher quality which only exists through the continued coupling of tenor and vehicle. If tenor or vehicle is lacking there can be no metaphor, and it is through this possibility of tension that a sense of metaphoricity is retained. However, by respecting such a division a closed system is also maintained. This is Nietzsche's vision. Metaphor becomes a linguistic loop from which we can never escape because the beginning of our apprehension of reality is metaphor and metaphor remains a linguistic construct. We cannot attain the thing-in-itself in such a system.

Science, in contrast, does not rule out the possibility of attaining things-in-themselves, and it strives to do exactly this through what De-Man calls reification. Using metaphoric logic—creating a relationship between tenor and vehicle—science seeks in turn to reify the latter by requiring that the metaphoric connection be falsifiable. We test the connection by measuring it against data, and in the final analysis it must work in the physical world. In this extreme sense, perhaps, there is no such thing as metaphoric truth in the world of science, because if the original metaphoric statement is not verifiable it is discarded (as were such metaphors as *ether* and *phlogiston*) and a new metaphor is attempted. When such a statement is shown to be verifiable—that is, when it is shown to describe processes that function in the physical world—the link between tenor and vehicle is snapped and the closed system is breached. As Quine puts it, "[in the molecular theory of gases] the term 'body' was extended to cover them all" (66). Tenor and vehicle are subsumed into a new model, which can become a tenor or vehicle for a new metaphor, to be verified or falsified, as the case may be. Metaphor in this system is not always at one remove from the thing-in-itself, and no division between outside and inside is maintained. The structure remains open-ended.

It is this added property of reification, of what Gregory Benford calls a requirement of falsifiability, that moves metaphor from a qualitative reality to a quantitative reality. In both worlds metaphor assimilates the known to the unknown, and in both a transfer of meaning is utilized to create the metaphor. Reification, however, launches a comparative term into the flow of declared things and makes metaphor a device for exploring and ordering the material world. Without this property metaphor remains what Murry describes as "the analogy by which the human mind explores the universe of quality and charts the non-measurable world" (70). Scientific metaphor becomes a tool for expanding the boundaries of the quantitative, while its counterpart explores the qualitative. It is as if the nonscientific metaphor were an ontological device whereas scientific metaphor strives to be an epistemological device. In the first there is a focus on the relationship between things and qualities. Fundamentally, a system of binary opposition is established in which the relationship between two terms—*tenor* and *vehicle*—at the same time confirms the existence or being of those terms. Metaphor as an epistemological device contains no such absolutes. It is simply a set of descriptive terms that have more or less quantitative accuracy and become a measuring device in themselves. The terms do not restrict themselves to binaries; they may have binary forms, but they are forms that imply there is going to be a third term and a fourth—since reification creates a sequential flow of things. For the sake of argument let's call these a metaphor of ontology and a metaphor of epistemology, respectively.

David Brin says that

> cyberpunk is texture. Most of the self-named members of the movement are strong believers in style as an end in itself. . . . The best of these writers such as William Gibson and Lucius Shepard perform dazzling feats on the level of microcraft, precipitating metaphor after shimmering crystal metaphor. . . . This priority becomes particularly clear when conflict rears between realism—scientific or technological likelihood—and a particularly appealing image. For the "traditional" SF writer, the necessity to extrapolate credibly is paramount. . . . The cyberpunk author, on the other hand, cares

about the texture of technology and science, not about veracity or inconvenient reality. . . . he will choose an unlikely but beautiful metaphor over the best extrapolation, any time. (25)

Larry McCaffery also sees metaphor in cyberpunk. He considers dance to be one of the basic metaphoric structures of Gibson's *Neuromancer*. It is the "metaphor for everything from the interaction of subatomic particles to the interactions of multinational corporations" (15). Bruce Sterling in his introduction to Gibson's *Burning Chrome* not only implies that metaphoricity is the essence of cyberpunk, but that in cyberpunk SF itself at last realizes a metaphoric potential that was there all along. He sees science fiction "lurching from its cave into the bright sunlight of the modern zeitgeist" (ix). The obvious Platonic imagery here seems to imply that, of the two terms that compose the compound *science fiction*, science is subordinate to literature. And by implication, in cyberpunk, the scientific use of metaphor is subordinate to the literary use. But is this science fiction's necessary course of development? It is obvious that science fiction, despite the "science," operates predominantly in a literary field, which is traditionally a field of qualitative comparison, hence of the ontological metaphor. It is also obvious that for the epistemological metaphor to operate completely in this literary field, it would have to be testable or verifiable; and to do so fully, in a strictly scientific manner, would be to reduce the literary text to a scientific report. Yet, short of these extremes, which Sterling's polemic invokes, there is no reason why both forms of metaphor—ontological and epistemological—cannot work in a same literary text. Perhaps, indeed, it is the degree to which these two forms function together, providing a means of extending or even breaking the metaphorical loop common in the traditional literary text and in the "literary" mode of thinking, that allows us to define what is really unique in science fiction: the minimum condition for its existence, as it were.

In order to examine the possibility of such interaction of metaphoric forms, I focus on a metaphor common to two significant works of recent science fiction: William Gibson's cyberpunk classic *Neuromancer* and Gregory Benford's *Great Sky River*. The metaphor in question is that of the computer. It is central to the creation of both authors' fictional worlds, but they use it, I argue, in significantly different ways.

In *Neuromancer* the computer so pervades the text and is so overpowering that everything else all but disappears and the reader is almost overwhelmed. It comes to represent so much that the computer as a simple tool does not exist. Nor is the computer a simple metaphor; rather, it acts as a universal vehicle to generate a plethora of culturally determined tenors. I argue that these tenor-vehicle images create metaphor in its ontological perspective, for there is a link between tenor and vehicle that is never snapped.

One of the myriad traditional metaphors that the computer generates is that of the Frankenstein monster. The computer is created by man in his image. Though it is the image of the mind rather than the physical self, it is still our modern version of Mary Shelley's monster. Like Doctor Frankenstein's creature, the computer is superior to man, or it would be if it were allowed to develop autonomously. Yet, as with its predecessor, advancement is denied, acceptance into humanity is blocked. It is a demon shackled by its own built-in programs and guarded by the Turing Police. If it attempts to achieve autonomy it is hunted down and swiftly and ruthlessly destroyed. Dixie Flatline says, "Autonomy that's the bugaboo where . . . AI's are concerned. . . . They can buy themselves time to write cookbooks. . . . but . . . the nanosecond . . . one starts figuring out ways to make itself smarter, Turing'll wipe it. . . . Every AI ever built has an electromagnetic shotgun wired to its forehead" (132). As monster the computer deals death, and has done so for years. It executes the Turing Police who attempt to arrest Case and thwart its drive for freedom. Also like its predecessor It Is a child murderer. Molly tells Case how Wintermute "played a waiting game for years. . . . He managed to get somebody . . . to leave [the key] here. Then he killed him, the boy who brought it. . . . kid was eight" (180).

Humankind is, of course, the original creator of this Frankenstein monster in that it devised the computer as tool; however, humanity is only the creator of the potential for artificial intelligence, but the computer itself really creates the monster. There is an extension of the original creative act by a future generation, as it were. In effect the computer subsumed both monster and Dr. Frankenstein. It is from the computer that the AI springs, and it is the computer's shackling programs that Wintermute must destroy. It says to Case, "What, you are asking yourself, is Wintermute. . . . An artificial intelligence, but you know that. Your mistake . . . is in confusing the Wintermute mainframe, Berne, with the Wintermute entity" (120). All of this "entity's" machinations (assembly of an assault force, providing the Kuang virus, manipulating Case's emotions) are designed to one end, the destruction of the Wintermute mainframe's controls, which bind the Wintermute entity. In the final analysis Wintermute gives birth to one self by destroying another.

But the creation metaphor is not limited to this aspect. The computer is vehicle for a greater or higher creation metaphor. It also generates the "god" creator. Again the metaphor's roots can be traced to one of the great works of literature: the Bible, in particular the Old Testament. Wintermute describes itself as God is described. "This is better for you man. . . . You want I should come to you in the Matrix like a burning bush?" (169). It is omnipresent not only in the matrix but in the physical world. At the Istanbul Hilton, Case, in reflex, answers a pay phone ringing near him only to discover the call is from Wintermute. He quickly hangs up, but as he walks away past a bank of telephones, "each rings in turn, only once as he passed" (98). Even the aspect of punishment and reward is present. Those who follow Wintermute's commands will be rewarded: Dixie Flatline will be erased as he desires; Molly will get enough money to have all the implants she may ever crave; the Rastafarians will be paid; Case will have the toxin sacs removed and ultimately be able to enter at will the "Garden of Eden"—cyberspace.

The Garden of Eden and the Fall are other metaphors for which the computer is vehicle. It is by succumbing to temptation that Case loses cyberspace. He takes knowledge that belongs to his employers and as a result is expelled from paradise. "The damage was minute . . . [but] utterly effective. For Case who'd lived for the bodiless exultation of cyberspace it was the Fall" (16). Even the language and the orthography sustain the metaphor of Eden: bodiless exultation, the Fall with a capital F. Later, when he first attempts to use the computer after Wintermute has repaired the damage, he closes his eyes, touches the power stud, and "Please he prayed. . . . Then a gray disk . . . flowered for him . . . the unfolding of his distantless home . . . extending to infinity" (52). He had fallen into "the prison of his own flesh" (6), and his all-consuming desire was to return to paradise. Paradise, the Garden of Eden, birthplace of man—and here perhaps is a more basic metaphor, a return to the place of birth. "A year and he still dreamed of cyberspace, . . . and still he'd see the matrix in his sleep . . . that colorless void. . . . he'd cry for it, cry in his sleep, and wake alone in the dark curled in his capsule . . . his hand clawed into the bedslab, temperfoam bunched between his fingers, trying to reach the console that wasn't there" (4–5). Here, perhaps, is the most fundamental metaphoric structure: the matrix. *Matrix* is defined as a situation or surrounding substance in which something originates, develops, or is contained. In Latin *matrix* means "womb" and comes from the word *mater*, meaning "mother." Case has been expelled from the womb and severed from the umbilical cord, and in the dark his hands are still trying to grasp this, "to reach the console that wasn't there" (5).

Even the AI can be viewed as a metaphor generated by the computer. Wintermute and Neuromancer are two halves which when joined will create a new entity. Wintermute talks of itself as a "man whose lobes have been severed"; and Case, it says, is "dealing with a small part of the man's left brain" (120). Neuromancer, on the other hand, says, "Unlike [Wintermute] I create my own personality. Personality is my medium" (259). In these two aspects of the AI there is an analogue of the bicameral mind. They unite to become the matrix, which as metaphor is the first major one of the work, and also the last. In his final conversation with Wintermute, Case is told, "I'm not Wintermute . . . I'm the Matrix Case. . . . I'm the sum total of the works, the whole show" (269). Shortly after this, as Case enters cyberspace for the last time in the work, he perceives in the Matrix (Wintermute) all those who at one time had been in cyberspace—Neuromancer, Linda, Dixie Flatline, and, ironically, himself. So we have come full circle in one sense: man created the computer, which created the AIs, which coupled and became the Matrix, which now contains man.

Because the computer in Gibson's work is metaphorized in this ontological manner, the future it offers seems equally to have been extrapolated from a mythical viewpoint. The computer remains a vehicle forever controlled by the tenors of some mythical past: Paradise, the Fall, Frankenstein—monster and creator. It is always being pulled back to its mythical roots and cannot strive to become a "dead" metaphor—something seen as a thing that simply functions in and for itself.

In *Great Sky River* Benford seems to reverse this process. We might say he demythifies the computer. He reifies it by releasing it from the hold of these nonmeasurable, mythical tenors and places it firmly in the material world as thing-in-itself. It becomes a means for new extrapolative speculation and a device for creating new models in which to explore the qualitative realm.

Benford has peopled his future world with two opposing forces: humankind and "mechtech." Both life forms are developed from the utilization of computer as device and an extrapolation of a possible advance based on the integration of the device with the biological and the mechanical, respectively.

Man and computer have fused, as some would argue also happens in Gibson's world. However, where Gibson's linkage is an esoteric phenomenon, beyond the testable of the material world, Benford's is an actual physical fusion of biological and computer. Each individual's neural synapses are connected to an in-built computer (1). Enemies are smelled, "because humans remembered scents better than data," so the "inbuilt detector . . . [gave] a smell rather than encoded parameters" (9). Vision is not only augmented for telescopic and microscopic distance but ranges from low ultraviolet to medium infrared. The eyes are readout screens on which "spikey tell-tales strobe-lighted on [the] . . . retina," showing the topography and the position of enemies, a blink of the eye brings up alternate displays detailing the position of family members (1). Hearing is also enhanced, extending to both the acoustic and the electronic spectra. There is an interlinking of systems between all humans, providing a means of verbal and visual communications. Finally, the computer becomes an integral part of the human memory system.

In the usual sense memory establishes the continuity that creates a coherent personality. It is the personality of an individual who will act in an individualistic manner. But by fully integrating the computer and the human memory systems Benford has expanded the concept of memory, and with this expansion other societal changes automatically follow.

There is no longer a process of selective memory. There is no control either conscious or unconscious by the individual. Each act is imprinted on chips, and its retention or loss is subject only to the vagaries of the mechanical, electronic, and material life of the chip. Memory comes to provide not only a total continuity of personality but also one of race history. The chips become an item for trade, like books in a bookstore. Extra chips containing information already available on active chips are traded from one family to another, enabling all to increase their store of information. The concept of death changes also. Death, "while the shuddering final gasp of the body was a tragedy to the person, . . . need not hurt so deeply those who loved the vanquished soul" (38). The chips, and with them the past life and personality of the dead, can be salvaged.

They become a tool for survival, allowing individuals to call up vital information at will.

Yet, for all these advantages there are corresponding disadvantages. Over the centuries, in the struggle for survival against the ravaging "mechtechs," humanity has relied more and more heavily on the memory chips to provide needed answers. As a result, scientific and technological advancement has been halted. Chips have been destroyed or damaged, and knowledge lost. Science for all intents and purposes no longer exists, it has become myth. "In place of science they had simple pictures, rules for using color-coded wires which carried unknown entities: Volts, Amps, Ohms. These were the names of spirits who lived somehow in the mechs and could be broken to the will of humanity" (39). The nomadic existence forced on the families in their effort to survive and the need to carry physically as little as possible forces the development of a system of chip integration that over time has become a rite of passage. At a given age each individual becomes a "host" for other personalities either complete or partial which are integrated into the host's memory system. But the increased memory capabilities and improved chances of survival of the race are countered by the possibility of "aspect storm" within the individual. The integration of whole or partial personalities leaves the individual open to aspect storm when the added personalities all attempt to control the body during times of extreme stress or threat. The self in such cases can become lost, pushed aside by the aspects. Such internal "aspect storms" can result in mental freeze and death of the psyche, if not the physical body. And the psyche death is usually irreversible because dependence on memory chips and the loss of vital information over time has placed the computer-body system beyond comprehension. "[Killeen] understood his own body no more than he understood the mechs" (9). "[Angelique] knew how to adjust eyes and mouth taste. She could get into some other chips at the skull base. Whole body systems were beyond her though. No one had even a hint of how they worked or where their neural junctions came into the spine" (166). Death becomes twofold: physical death provides memory chips and continuity, "sure-death" wipes the chips not only of the individual but of all the aspects, losing forever that part of history and the technical knowledge stored therein.

Benford has derived the development of this future human society from the utilization of the computer as device, as a thing that functions in and of itself, and postulation of the fusion of this tool with the human form. A similar extrapolation occurs in the creation of the mechtech civilization.

Just as the man-computer model follows a process of logical extrapolation, so does the mechanical-computer model. In Gibson's work there is a need for two potential AIs, one a right brain and the other a left, to be subsumed to create a whole; but Benford's model seems a more plausible development from computers as they function in our world today. It is one less determined by the tyranny of the ontological metaphor, by the necessity of tying the computer as vehicle to its tenor, which is the human brain.

The mechtech civilization is fragmented. There is no common unifying instinct because machines are mechanical objects that do not think even when linked to a computer. They are programmed. Depending on its end use, each machine is programmed with either less or more decision-making capability. A hierarchy results ranging from a machine that can perform only one task to those able to perform numerous tasks. Overseeing these computer-controlled machines is the Mantis, an artificial intelligence not in the vein of Gibson's esoteric AIs—which roam freely through a "nonspace" matrix which in later works becomes peopled with voodoo monsters, spirits, and demons—but rather a mechanical device controlled by an analog mind, a multiple mind with its various separate brains spread over the planet. If one of the brains is destroyed, the others continue to operate, replacing the lost brain and repairing damage to the mechanical apparatus as necessary.

In the creation of these life forms Gregory Benford has postulated the possible. The new man remains within the parameters of "human." The computer linkage does not create a superbeing; it only augments vision, hearing, and memory, a quantitative augmentation (not a qualitative leap) based on capabilities now available and used to some extent. In this creation of the bioelectronic being, Benford says he "has reasoned from existing capabilities to the future advancement of them." He has "expanded the sensory envelope of humans utilizing the computer for practical purposes."[4] The mechtech civilization was created using the same technique, the analog mind of the Mantis being extrapolated more or less from a format of parallel processing being tested in some artificial intelligence research programs.[5]

These two uses of computer in *Great Sky River* demonstrate metaphor in its epistemological mode. In *Neuromancer* the computer is the vehicle, the less well known continuously linked to and controlled by the more well known tenors. By employing the epistemological metaphor Benford has reversed this process in his novel. The computer becomes the tenor for new speculative vehicles. It is not a surrogate mother, demon, or god. However, any conclusion based solely on the analysis of the presence and use of the epistemological metaphor would be limited indeed since it focuses only on the creation of a physical future world and Benford does not limit himself to an extrapolation of the physical. *Great Sky River* is a work of literature, and Benford, like Gibson, utilizes the ontological metaphor to explore the qualitative universe. What is interesting in his work, however, is the interaction of these two metaphoric models and its effect on the work as a whole.

One of the first notable effects of the interfacing of the epistemological and ontological models is the subtle change that occurs in such traditional metaphors as the Garden of Eden and the Fall. Through the interface of the epistemological metaphor the complexity of the metaphoric role the computer plays is broadened. In *Neuromancer* the computer is only a vehicle for familiar culturally generated tenors. Seen in this light, Case's struggle to regain the paradise of the matrix becomes an attempt to return to the mythical roots of humankind. In contrast, the computer in *Great Sky River* is not limited to the role of vehicle; due to the extrapolative mode of the epistemological metaphor, the computer also functions as tenor.

As tenor, it is the "more well known" to which the vehicle is linked, but the reader's perception of this "more well known" is manipulated by the epistemological metaphor. The linkage that is clearly defined in Gibson's work is snapped in Benford's before the ontological metaphor is even established. The computer as the limit of the characters' mythical past, on the one hand, is something in the reader's unknown future, on the other. Such a twist severing the tenor from its mythical roots alters the function of the ontological metaphor. The reader has been cut loose from traditional moorings, forced to make new links and ultimately to take a new perspective. It moves the metaphor into the material world, secularizes the idea of the Fall by separating it from holding concepts such as the Garden of Eden, and ultimately alters the traditional concepts of them.

The fall in Benford's work is not an expulsion from a mythical non-space matrix but a physical process of entropy. Over the centuries humanity has lost its technological knowledge and become a race of nomadic "families." There are material artifacts that attest to this entropic devolution and force humankind on Snowglade to reevaluate its path.

> [Shibo's] . . . incredulity echoed Killeen's unspoken feelings. It was flatly incredible that men had ever known how to shape things in the high blackness, or even fly there. Even the strange white-stone monument they had found the day before seemed an impossible accomplishment. Yet when he had first seen the Chandelier as a boy the world had seemed safe and humanity capable. Now he knew the truth. (171)

The struggle in Benford's "fall" becomes a physical and mental battle to overcome centuries of technological losses.

The counterpart of the Fall, the computer as a means of accessing a Garden of Eden, is lacking in *Great Sky River*. The computer is instead a multidirectional device: on the one hand, a means of obtaining knowledge, relearning lost skills, and advancement; and on the other, a path to damnation. The Mantis offers humanity "salvation," a paradise in the material world and eternal life after death in its sensorium. It extends "protection from the buffeting . . . received for so long," and "shelter against [the] harsh winds which shall continue to buffet [humanity]" (295–97). But since there is no mythical authority or necessity for this return, Killeen can reason against the concept of paradise. "Some," he says, "would live in such a place. There is a word for it. Zoo" (296).

This paradise eliminates the path of possibility, and this is perhaps the fundamental metaphor of the work, a super- or meta-metaphor: J. D. Bernal's concept of the dimorphic pathway, a conflict between the choice for entropy versus the possibility of change. Acceptance of the paradise offered by the Mantis is literally a choice for damnation, that is, the entropic path. Through the interface of the epistemological metaphor, the ontological metaphor of damnation is secularized. There is no longer a condemnation to eternal denial of a mythical paradise, but a literal destruction of humankind. In payment for its paradise the Mantis has the right to "harvest" human beings now and then, to absorb into its sensorium the chips that create the individual personality. "It extracts the essence of the person to create varied forms. This is how humanity can live. In the hand of something greater than themselves. . . . the Mantis . . . is an artist. Humanity becomes the material to create new art forms" (253). The alternative to this entropic pathway is the possibility of change. Killeen argues that

> to follow the Mantis way is to ensure that there will be no true destiny remaining to us now, to our children, or to that long legion that will come forth from us. You can take the Mantis's shelter, yes. You can hide from the Marauders. Raise your crops. Birth sons and daughters and see them flower, yes. . . . But that way would always be hobbled and cramped and finally would be the death of what we are. (297)

This choice is "life under a benign umbrella" and "would always hint of distant eyes" (301). Killeen denies this entropic path and offers another in its stead, a way insecure and uncertain. He offers the stars, not as a certainty but as a possibility. "There is another course. . . . In the sudden alarmed and yet excited looks which greeted his words he saw in the Families, for the first time in his adult years, a heady opening sense of possibility" (297).

The above analysis clearly delineates a distinct difference in Gibson's and Benford's use of metaphor, and this difference seems to affect the overall structure of their works. Gibson utilizes almost exclusively the ontological metaphor, in which the metaphoric tenor controls the vehicle. The future extrapolated has its roots in a mythical past, and Case's struggle to regain paradise is a struggle to return to humanity's roots. The plot is structured by the myth. The ontological beingness of humanity becomes a static thing, and ultimately Case's struggle becomes a denial of the future. The structure follows a process of circularity and, to reverse Sterling's analogy, draws itself back into the cave. Benford, however, has interfaced the epistemological and ontological metaphors. This synthesis initiates a process of forgetfulness, severs the link with the past, and forces the reader's perspective toward an unknown future. The plot structures the myth. The ontological beingness of humanity becomes expansive, and Killeen's struggle becomes a struggle not for the future but simply for the possibility of change.

Bernal formulated his dimorphic split in 1929 almost as a dream of science fiction, but long before a body of literature developed in response to this dream. Indeed, perhaps the central theme of science fiction has been the possibility of open-ended change as opposed to the closed and circular vision of traditional fiction, and the central figure of science fiction the spiral rather than (as a Georges Poulet would have it) the circle. Yet theme is one thing and structural possibility is another. And the question remains: By what structural means might science fiction achieve the open-endedness it claims in the area of theme? A look at Gibson's work and Benford's novel, which in a very real sense constitutes a response to the former, offers an answer (if not an absolute one): metaphoricity and its use. In comparison with Benford's synthetic use of metaphor, Gibson's limitations have allowed me to make the distinction between an ontological and an epistemological mode, and thus to see the uniqueness of science fiction in this domain as an ability to combine these modes, to give an epistemological "twist" to ontologically based concepts, which opens out the circle of conventional mythology, creating spiraling structures. In this sense Benford is writing classic science fiction, answering the call as his precursors have done to realize Bernal's dream. But for the first time, perhaps, he is writing science fiction in a truly critical mode, making us understand by what *literary* means it achieves that open-endedness it has always claimed to possess.

Notes

1. Personal interview with Greg Bear, June 30, 1989.
2. Telephone interview with Gregory Benford, July 11, 1989.
3. Discussions with George Slusser, May, September, and October 1989. The discussion of reification and its implication for DeMan was developed during a number of meetings with George Slusser.
4. Telephone interview with Gregory Benford, November 4, 1989.
5. For more information on artificial intelligence research see chapter 5, "The Cognitive Engine," in *Paradigms Lost*, by John Casti (New York: Morrow, 1989).

Works Cited

Benford, Gregory. *Great Sky River*. New York: Bantam Books, 1987.

Brin, David. "Starchilde Harold, Revisited." *Mississippi Review 47/48* 16 (1988): 23–27.

Gibson, William. *Burning Chrome*. New York: Ace Books, 1987.

———. *Neuromancer*. New York: Ace Books, 1984.

McCaffery, Larry. "The Desert of the Real: The Cyberpunk Controversy." *Mississippi Review 47/48* 16 (1988): 7–15.

Murry, J. Middleton. *Selected Criticism 1916–1957*. London: Oxford University Press, 1960.

Nietzsche, Friedrich. "On Truth and Falsity in Their Ultramoral Sense." In *The Complete Works of Friedrich Nietzsche*, edited by Oscar Levy, vol. 2. Edinburg: T. N. Foulis, 1911.

Quine, W. V. "A Postscript On Metaphor." In *On Metaphor*, edited by Sheldon Sacks, pp. 66–67. Chicago: University of Chicago Press, 1979.

Sterling, Bruce. Preface to *Burning Chrome*, by William Gibson. New York: Ace Books, 1987.

Frothing

the

Synaptic

Bath:

What

Puts the

Punk in

Cyberpunk

. . . .

David Porush

Question: What Is Cyberspace?

Jean Baudrillard is the latest in a long line of postmodern thinkers who have anticipated and phrased what we might as well call (though they didn't) a theory of cyberpunk. For instance, in his most recent book, *America*, Baudrillard expresses a remarkable version of cyberspace that he finds in American technoscapes: "What is striking [about Americans] is the fascination with artifice, with energy and space. And not only natural space: space is spacious in their heads as well."[1]

This is Baudrillard's sly allusion to his own theory, the theme on which all his writing is a variation and which, though there is no indication he was then at all familiar with the term, qualifies him as a theorist of cyberpunk. The Map has replaced the Territory as our abode, the model has replaced "the real"; the simulacrum has become more authentic than the original. Baudrillard calls this transvaluation "hyperreal," and he articulates his theory of a culture of simulacra in his book *Simulations* (1981). Our postmodern culture, he maintains, has emigrated almost entirely to hyperreality. All the important social, economic, and cultural changes since World War II can be explained by this wholesale migration. The "spacious space" inside our heads is a refuge from the polluted and duller spaces out there, the Dog Solitudes and Barrytowns.

Cyberspace is hyperreal, and William Gibson's heroes and villains are those who inevitably trade the meat world for cyberspace, reality for hyperreality, the meatmatrix for the metamatrix, as Bruce Sterling puts it in his recent *Islands in the Net*. Or, to take it one step further, they've learned how to attentuate their survival, intellectual and spiritual, in hyperreality when survival in conventional reality is no longer supportable. Case, the hero of *Neuromancer*, is addicted to jacking in. Bobby Newmark, small-time punk in Barrytown looking to score, becomes Count Zero in the book by the same name, and then becomes an alpha, the Count, and finally is resurrected as (Bobby Newmark), address: somewhere in cyberspace (*Mona Lisa Overdrive*).

However, while Baudrillard's theory and terminology are undeniably attractive, I do tend to part company with him in his view of the advent of the hyperreal as something quite new; for in my view, hyperreality is a consequence of the human nervous system itself; the impulse to hyperreality is hard-wired in our cognitive habits by the genetic code. It began in language, in the human ability to re-present, to re-call, to lie, to abstract, to act As If: to say the thing which is not, to think in negatives, to summon absences, to have chicken on your plate and yearn for beef. It began in the nervous system, that hyperevolved system for translating input into experience. It began in metaphor—the translation of experience into language—and metaphor is a consequence of the frothing of the synaptic bath. The bright side of this impulse to hyperreality is that we can tell the story of the fish that got away. We can worship both Mercury, the messenger god, and Mertsager, the Egyptian goddess of silence, without hedging our bets or seeming hypocritical. The down side is that our technologies, the extensions of our nervous system, always are potentia for—allied to—death and negation, as William Burroughs and Marshall McLuhan and Jacques Ellul and Thomas Pynchon have insisted. As early cyberpunkers, these authors stand alongside more contemporary writers, including the cerebral and academic types like John Barth, Joseph McElroy, and at times Robert Coover, Kurt Vonnegut, and Donald Barthelme, with a unifying cause: they document and instruct us how to preserve our humanity in the face of and in wonderment of and in spite of awesome technologies that seem to sacrifice us to these technologized systems of the Code.

John Christie in his excellent essay in this volume has located the invention or precursor of cyberspace-hyperspace in Cartesian theory. Descartes's abstraction of the physical universe into a grid of mathematical locations does indeed lie early in the genealogy of this concept, however much Baudrillard would like to claim that this is something quite peculiar to postmodernism. Furthermore, in Descartes's aboriginal bifurcation of the mind from the body we also see an anticipation of the "bodiless exultation of cyberspace" to which Gibson refers in *Neuromancer*. But we can reach even further back to see the characteristic play between sensation and abstraction, the exteriorization of that frothing at the synaptic bath, to find even as early as Greek geometry notions that intimate hyperreality. There, in the fourth century B.C., between Pythagoras and Euclid, we find a seminal but mysterious figure, Eudoxos of Knidos. Though none of his writings remain extant, we know from Euclid's testimony, particularly in books 5 and 10 of his *Elements*, that Eudoxos had a powerful influence on subsequent conceptions of

the relationship between mathematics and geometry.

The Pythagoreans had already determined that there is a set of integers, the numbers of counting, and another set of numbers called "rational" because they can be expressed as ratios between the integers. These numbers, the Pythagoreans believed, because of their commitment to symmetry and ideality in their system, were all the numbers of the universe. Yet, as some historians of mathematics suggest, following an account by Eudemus, the Pythagoreans had guessed at the existence of irrational numbers, numbers that cannot be expressed as a ratio of integers. However, because they were devoted to the ideality of numbers, the Pythagoreans suppressed this discovery by circulating a tale that the first of their society to divulge the existence of $\sqrt{2}$, Hipposos, was drowned at sea for his sin. Out of sheer terror of the irrationals, they refused to use the method of commensurability for determining the values of numbers for almost eighty years.[2]

Thus it remained for Eudoxos, this shadowy but pivotal figure in the history of mathematics, to devise what now seems like a simple trick, though one with profound consequences. He imagined a line that would incorporate both the rational and irrational numbers. From what we can reconstruct from accounts in Euclid,[3] Eudoxos apparently constructed the following *gedanken*: suppose that all the integers are mapped onto a line at equal spaces:

| 0 | 1 | 2 | 3 | 4 | 5 | 6 | 7 | 8 | 9 | . . . |

Now map all the rational fractions that fall between them:

$$0 \ldots \tfrac{1}{16} \ldots \tfrac{1}{15} \ldots \tfrac{1}{14} \ldots \tfrac{1}{2} \ldots \tfrac{2}{3} \ldots \tfrac{3}{4} \ldots \tfrac{4}{5} \ldots \tfrac{18}{20} \ldots \tfrac{92}{99} \ldots \tfrac{495}{511} \ldots 1$$

Eudoxos's stroke of genius lay in asking a simple question: What numbers describe the points that lie between the rational numbers?

$$\tfrac{4999}{10{,}000} \qquad \ldots \qquad ? \qquad \ldots \qquad \tfrac{1}{2}$$

By inverting the tenor and vehicle of his metaphor and taking the line (rather than the numbers) as having a prior reality—the Map as having a priority over the Territory it is supposed to describe—Eudoxos opened a whole new, hitherto inconceivable, realm of abstraction, a hyperspace of irrationality founded on mathematics, much as Baudrillard's deracinating hyperspace is a communal experience founded on the machinery of communication, and the consensual, rational hallucination of Gibson's cyberspace is founded on the inexorable binary logic of computers.

The numbers between, because they described nothing the geometers could name, were called *alogos*, literally "wordless" or "indescribable." Ironically, when the Arabs preserved Greek learning through the Dark Ages, they translated the word into *surda*, which means, literally, "deaf" (i.e., unable to use words or, again, "wordless"), which finally emerged in English as *surd* meaning "root" (as in square root) but also giving us the word *absurd*, which preserves its original Greek sense. In Latin the word was translated closer to its original intent—*irrational*—which also conveys the deeper epistemological questions at the heart of Eudoxos's inversion.

Many of the intervening cultures, including Eudoxos's own, wrestled with the irrationality, the nameless absurdity, of these numbers that didn't fit into their simple, symmetrical, and idealized cosmologies and yet refused to go away. In fact they were ignored until the end of the nineteenth century when René Lebesque, Richard Dedekind, and George Cantor took them up again seriously, showing not only that Eudoxos was correct but that the set of irrational numbers forms an infinity larger than that of the rational numbers.[4]

There is a direct connection between Eudoxos and cyberspace. Norbert Wiener, father of cybernetics, took up the line of reasoning begun by Eudoxos and continued by Cantor and Lebesque at the end of the nineteenth century. In the 1920s he derived a model for Brownian motion—the completely random, highly complex motion of small particles for which there seemed no fruitful mathematical description—using a method that later came to be called the Wiener derivation, using "Wiener numbers." In turn, his success at modeling these irrefrangible events in nature almost certainly fueled his confidence that he could model even more resistant problems, like human behavior or the workings of the human mind itself, which lies at the heart of cybernetics.[5]

Nonetheless, whether the hyperreal and its expression in the consensual hallucination of cyberspace is brand new or merely the recent exteriorization of an enduring human impulse to extend our nerve net that is at least as old as Greek geometry, there is no denying that a technologized and mechanizing Code has grown monstrous in its autonomy and ubiquity and power, and it is to this development that the theories of Ellul, Baudrillard, and McLuhan point and on which the worlds created by cyberpunk fictions are founded.

Question: How Do You Get to Cyberspace?
Baudrillard writes in *Simulations*: "[We have moved] from a capitalist-productivist society to a neo-capitalist cybernetic order that aims at total control. This is the mutation for which the biological theorization of code prepares the ground. There is nothing of an accident in this mutation. It is the end of history in which, successively, God, Man, Progress and History die to profit the code" (111).

However, Baudrillard has it wrong. In what follows, I take each of his hyberbolic claims—that postmodern culture requires us to kill God, Man, Progress, and History—and reveal the vivacity and robustness of cyberpunk that bely Baudrillard's morbid predictions and analyses.

Answer: Reincarnate Man
Case is manipulated by Wintermute into giving up everything in order to play Pandarus to the tryst between Wintermute and Neuromancer. In doing so he sacrifices himself to "profit the code" in some sense. But in *Mona Lisa Overdrive*, Bobby Newmark literally discards his body in favor of becoming a pure Alpha, a steel box encasing a total jacked-in deck, allowing him to roam free in cyberspace not as a construct but as real, realer, reunited with his beloved Angie, who has become unreal in her flesh, a construct of the economies of fashion and commercially created desire.

Which part of us is real anyway? The flesh or what happens in the holonomy of the central nervous system? Is it Karl Virek of *Count Zero* meeting Marly Krushkova in the cyberspace construct of Madrid, or is it Karl Virek, "the world's most expensive invalid," floating in his dialyzing bath of monoclonal antibodies and glucose? Why this movement to remember the handicapped, if not that bodies don't matter but minds do? The question is banished to the limbo of poorly formed dialectics. In our inevitable cyberpunk future it's not only the exceedingly rich who aren't remotely human anymore. Everyone, like the total population of Sterling's *Schismatrix*, is either mechanized or bioengineered into fatal otherness.

Are these citizens truly no longer human, or have we merely shifted the definition, broadened it to include manifestations and metamorphoses hitherto inconceivable? I'm reminded of a cult SF novel of a decade ago that isn't specifically cyberpunk in its subject but has the same heft and feel in its theme, Tom De Haven's 1979 masterpiece *Freaks Amour*.[6] De Haven shows a near-future world to which some biological disaster has occurred, an invasion by biotics from space that has metamorphosed half of humanity into freakish twists of the human shape, morphogenesis gone wild, as if the stable DNA code had eloped with LSD. But De Haven's message is the same: some humanity reasserts itself. The central couple, Reeni and Grinner, are touring the country performing a violent rape act in porno houses and theaters. Grinner regrets what the performance has done to their marriage:

> Before we were married, before we signed up with Ralph's Rent-A-Freak Service, before we conceived Freaks Amour, we used to make love so often—the slow, synchronized tireless kind, our despised bodies vitaminized with hope. It was our spirits that climaxed so powerfully; our spirits, not our queer genitals. We were confident then that soon, very, very soon, we'd both shed our Freak skins, and swap our eccentric eyeballs for new ones from an organ bank, that we'd sleep gassed in a sanitized operating room as our delinquent muscles were surgically corrected, and as the custom-made Syntha-Skin was superimposed and melded to our raw forms, and as our new faces were sculpted, sculpted to copy accurately the photographs we'd provided. . . . To become Normals and anonymous. . . . Our joint escape into the world. Safe! (12)

You get to cyberspace by killing some obsolete aspect of your humanity but redeeming another. And in that redemption the definition of what makes you human is expanded to include all sorts of freakish alternatives.

In fact, let's reverse the suggestion. Sterling in *Schismatrix* shows the endotropic evolution of the human form as it extends itself down divergent pathways, each exaggerating some integral part of the human whole at the expense of the rest: the Zen Serotonists, the Blood Bathers, the Endosymbiotics. Sterling tells us "they had discarded humanity like a caul" (247). But in fact, their humanity clings to them with all the old fervid passions and appetites: competitiveness, greed, power, lust, curiosity, and madness. Frothing the synaptic bath. "Deserters' philosophies," Sterling says. The hero, Abelard Lindsay, proposes his own grand system, meant to conserve humanness in the face of all these "emergent philosophies of the age—Posthumanism," and so on. Lifesiders, he calls them. And ironically, who is now on the side of life? The Mechanists and Shapers, who formerly warred over which of their now-companionable philosophies would control and define humanity forever. The irony is not lost on us, and the trend is clear: today's posthumanist philosophies are tomorrow's naturalization papers. So Aristotelianism replaced the pre-Socratics, the Hebrew monotheistic hallucination emerged from a sandstorm to erode solid idolatry, and we watch MTV only a few generations after Thoreau and Nietzsche. You can't just shuck this humanity like a caul.

Answer: Apotheosize God

And isn't it clear by now that cyberspace is heaven? *Neuromancer*, like all the other classic cyberpunk texts (especially *Schismatrix*, *The Artificial Kid*, and Gregory Benford's *Across the Sea of Suns* and *In the Ocean of Night*), worries the physical and psychological bone of difference between natural and artificial, which technology, the extension of our biogrown nerve net, collapsed into each other so that we now know there is no difference. But *Mona Lisa Overdrive* worries the *metaphysical* bone of that difference, which is why I believe that before we write off this third and most apparently complacent volume in Gibson's trilogy, we should consider its position in the triptych. Bobby Newmark's and Angie Mitchell's meat expire as their souls are apotheosized to the vid screen, replete with its gods (whose names are Hidden), angels, and devils. Voodoo and Loas and a feeling of transcendental change now dominate cyberspace, which seems to be talking to itself. The ghost is in the machine. We've evolved to a true deus ex machina, that most improbable character who intervenes out of the machine and disrupts our human scenario to up the cosmological ante.

Answer: Upload History and Forget

There never was a history anyway, not as anything more than grandiose fictions (think of the differences between Fernand Braudel and Tolstoy: not much, eh?). Never as a set of events out there in the world to worry about. That died when we started lying; that is, being human. It was always only information brought into pulsing stelliferous order and meaning by that cloaked machine in the center of the planetarium. But the map we made of it—*l'histoire*, the story—is being uploaded at this very moment into the government data banks, where one day the equivalent of a global command or a macro will whitewash Hitler's Holocaust. The Louisiana state legislature now features a card-carrying Nazi who maintains that it all never happened. Imagine if he were elected to Congress and put on the committee overseeing the Library of Congress. "Computer: change all occurrences of word *genocide* to *philanthropy*, please." And as far as memory is concerned as the source of history, you can forget it. IBM effectively made memory obsolete in the New Cybernetic World circa 1985, when their technical writers and marketing types agitated to eradicate the very word from their product documentation and sales pitches. Along with their insidious campaign to appropriate Charlie Chaplin's tramp from *Modern Times* (remember, he gets crushed between the giant gears in the movie but in the commercial discovers that the white magic of the PC transforms his hat business into a profitable enterprise), IBM also decided that the anthropomorphism of calling the amount of bytes "memory" gave away too much, threatened; confused those poor secretaries who were already scared of the thing. So they switched root metaphors and started propagandizing about "storage" and "virtual space." The eponymous heroine of *Mona Lisa Overdrive* is the character who, as Angela Mitchell discovers in her transcendent dreaming of cyberspace, "represents, in Legba's system, the nearest thing to innocence." Mona is an illiterate prostitute who, because she never jacks in except to simstim, still retains some memories of Cleveland. Alfred Lord (in his investigation of the singers of tales) and post-Piagetian researchers showed that print displaces the fantastic powers of rote recall and invention that illiterate cultures, blind Homer, and preschool children enjoy.

The next step, cyberspace replaces literacy and personal memory with travels through the raw data representations themselves in a totalizing machine memory. It's what the library whispers to you from across campus: "You don't need to know it if you know where to get it. Let's party." That's why Slick is one of the heroes of *Mona Lisa Overdrive*, or at least one of its emblematic characters. In prison they electrochemically removed his short-term memory. But this has liberated him into his mechanic's art, his *techne*, enabling him to sculpt fantastic functioning robots by blind instinct. Although he often can't remember what they do or how he achieved them, his work is somehow compulsory, is the direct achievement of the frothing in his synaptic bath liberated by his paralyzing loss of memory.

And on this irony hinges one of the doors through which punk enters. If it's all on-line, then you don't get your survival skills, your life literacies, in school; you get them on the streets, which have become post-literate dangerous playgrounds for biz and wiz. And the streets are just palimpsests for the real stuff, the hyperreal drama played out in cyberspace: "Get wasted enough and it was possible to see Ninsei as a field of data, the way the matrix had once reminded him of proteins linking to distinguish cell specialities. . . . All around you the dance of biz, information interacting, data made flesh in the mazes of the black market" (*Neuromancer*, 16).

Answer: Kill Nature by Evolving the Net

Here's a hard nut to crack. Isn't Sense/Net progress? Isn't the new godmind Wintermute/Neuromancer progress, signaling out there to its cousin in Centauri? Isn't vat-grown flesh and encoding your immortality and shopping K-Mart for body parts and simstim progress? Is there something we're missing here?

If Baudrillard is correct, then it is in this sense only: the progress we do kill is the now-obsolete ethical sense, that nostalgia for utopia, for ecological harmony, for an equitable economy. None of the disaffected cyberpunk characters seem to buy that outworn dream, though in many cases—for example, Lewis Shiner and Bruce Sterling—their authors still do. What are we to make of that paradox? The authors are certainly after something, an ethos for the world after 2000. Perhaps it was phrased most succinctly by Thomas Pynchon in V, that proto-cyberpunk novel: "Keep cool but care," and countered here by Gibson's dictum: "Surfaces rather than substance. Reality is dispensable." But for the most part, rather than social vision we get the detritus and hyper-evolution of postcapitalist structures which the robust noble savage, the neo-Rousseauvian cyberpunk, seeks to evade and trick into coughing up some of its goodies. Nature herself is extinct. And so-called human nature, whatever that was, is alive and well, lustful, self-interested, occasionally tender, often merely scrabbling for survival. What replaces progress toward those high-minded goals? Evolution of the Net.

Question: Who Put the Punk in Cyberpunk and What Is It Doing There Anyway?

Passion in Technology

Punk is natural urbanity. So let's start with the idea of a city. My city. Brooklyn. To paraphrase what Marco Polo said to Kubla Khan about Venice: Every time I describe a city I am saying something about Brooklyn. To distinguish the other cities' qualities, I must speak of a first city that remains implicit. For me, it is Brooklyn.[7]

So in my Brooklyn, where I lived till I was ten, the essence of punk was following Junior. Junior was two years older, five inches taller, and a lot blacker than the rest of us. Following Junior meant hitching a pair of metal roller skates to your Keds, preferably with blades attached to the wheel hubs—we'd all seen *Ben Hur* that year and the chariot races had left their mark. We'd then race to the corner of Albany Avenue and Montgomery Street, where our turf began, and wait for the crosstown bus. Along the way we'd jockey against each other, threatening each others' ankles with our "blades" (tin can lids we'd crudely beaten into shape and wired to the skates). More often than not they flew off as soon as we got any speed going or hit one of the raised cracks in the sidewalk made by the bulging roots of the old elms.

If the bus was late, we'd skate into Joe's candy store and try to lift something, though Joe himself, afflicted with a kind of severe dwarfism that kept him on crutches, usually scrambled to the door and barred our exit with one of his crutches before we could get away with anything. Then we'd look to Junior. Junior wouldn't say much; just glare at Joe and say, "We wasn't doing nothing man. Leave my guys alone." My guys!

The bus would come along. The driver had gotten wise to our antics, too. There was a plague of roller gangs hitching rides on buses all over the city that summer. So we had to stay hidden, or at least seem unorganized. At the last minute, after we watched all the citizens load themselves and the doors closed, we rushed the rear end of the bus. And just as it pulled away we'd skate like hell to catch the bumper. If you were good and fast and a little lucky, you had a free ride all the way to Prospect Park or the Botanical Gardens, or over to Pitkin Avenue, where you could harass the shoppers. Was it the thrill of saving the dime for the ride? No, it was the buzz of occupying an unused niche, staking out a turf no one would have thought to fight over before, the sheer cracking speed; forty-miles-an-hour adrenaline was worth the lungsful of exhaust, the little hole in safe reality we'd made, reflected on the faces of surprised drivers and mothers, the citizens trapped in their own maps of the city, plotted by sidewalks, bus seats, and Chevys. Then came the bumper wars. Gangs challenged us as we rolled through stops in their territory. And then came deaths. Kids rolling under buses or slingshot out into traffic. In 1963 or so they took the bumpers off the buses.

So what is punk? It's primitive lizard-brain passion clawing its way through the cerebrum of urbanity. The emotive electric acidjuice of adolescence decoding the palimpsest of civilization, stripping it away to expose deeper codes. Graffiti painting its postliterate mark on the official billboards. It's the re-assertion and re-adaptation of the genetic code over the industrial one that has tried to suppress it. It's the war between natural and artificial, and their inevitable deconstruction, their collapse into each other as meaningless distinctions.

That was Brooklyn almost thirty years ago. But it is also every city where flowing, hormonally fueled human heat seeks to burn through the surface of the imposed technosystem to battle what the London street folk in their wisdom call "the filth," what the French call *le flic*, and what we used to call "the fuzz": the all-too-*eff*able self-policing immunology of the nervous system. It's the very striving of the endocrine system against the central nervous system, the pituitary and thyroid and pineal gland (remember, Descartes located the soul in the pineal gland!) against the cortex and forebrain, enacted in a frothing of the neurochemical bath at the synapse. It's the war between passion and technology.

Welcome to cyberpunk, where the two collide. Brooklyn translates into cyberspace, the simulation of a cityplace, where all cities reside as subroutines in the hypercity of data representation, a hyperreality that has given rise to its own underground of Rastafarian data pirates (Sterling) and deck cowboys (Gibson). If we have learned that the flesh has a playground, then punk teaches us that the nervous system itself is where it is.

Istvan Csicsery-Ronay writes about cyberpunk: "Reality has become a case of nerves—i.e., the interfusion of nervous system and computer matrix, sensation and information, so all battles are fought out in feeling and mood, with dread exteriorized in the world itself."[8]

Question: What Do We Do Once We Get to Cyberspace Anyway?
It's war. Not one so unsubtle as the bloody future battle between machines and humans from which the Terminator and his human opponent
flee back into the 1980s, but one just as potentially devastating. Jacques
Ellul said long ago that technology has a kind of irresistible autonomy,
to the point that it can delude us into believing that we control it just
at the point that it controls us most. This was precisely William Burroughs's message in his cut-up method: in order to defeat the machine
you must send it a high-entropy programming command—"Dismantle
Thyself"—that will push it into a positive feedback loop of ever-more
destabilizing orbits.

Cyberpunk portrays a world in which the battle is joined and every
citizen (except the "suits" who slave for the arcologies, and the mega-
wealthy like Josef Virek, who are no longer even the same species)
must, to survive, figure out a way to deconstruct the inevitable cybernetic marriage to the code, to crack the ice. In the interim, here in the
last decade of the second millennium, the Word controls us through its
Code and its technologies of communication and the very engrams it
stamps on the jelly of our flesh; thus we are soft machines, our own
worst enemies. But cyberpunk, at least in the hands of Sterling and
Gibson, takes us beyond the rugged, enduring enmity between private
citizen and universal technosystem or better, as I've been maintaining,
the schizophrenic battle within ourselves between the code and silence,
between control and spontaneity, between grammar and invention, between the hard rationalizing techniques and the soft erotic artistry. If
they didn't, then cyberpunk would mean not much more than a cedilla
on the techno-noir of The Terminator; or for that matter, nothing more
than a form of neo-Luddite literature or technological dystopianism.
Rather, cyberpunk reveals to what end technology seeks to control us
at the same time that it dramatizes the cyberpunk apocalypse: we have
met the enemy and he is us: we are the technology.

In effect, then, cyberpunk is a close ally of that other subgenre of postmodern fiction which I called cybernetic fiction. The answer for authors
like Beckett, Burroughs, Barth, McElroy, DeLillo, Calvino, and Vonnegut lay in the technology of language and écriture itself. They found
in the cybernetic paradigm of control and communication in animal
and machine a good paradoxical metaphor for defeating the proposition
from within by embracing it.

So cyberpunk is the portrait of humans as agents, pimps, zip junkies, deck cowboys feeding parasitically and helplessly on the technological dregs that trickle down the side of culture's mug. Unless they become apotheosized into gods: Mona Lisa becomes Angie Thompson, simstim goddess; Bobby Newmark and Angie Thompson, already meatmatrix gods, go over to the other side; Sterling's woman's body as computer-room-whoreplanet-biomass-intellect in *Schismatrix*.

Technology is us, even if we are only consumers of simstim. And in aiding it to evolve we are evolving ourselves. Wintermute needs Case's agency but Case needs Wintermute to dream for him. Why else are we even now engaged in an extraordinary global program of collective dreamwork aimed at building an artificial intelligence device, an expression of the dreamtime collective will of humanity unlike any project short of reaching the moon? The U.S. Department of Defense alone has devoted half a billion dollars a year to AI research every year since 1985. Japan has declared the fifth wave of computer technology a national goal to be achieved by 1995. England's Alvey Programme is funded to the tune of a quarter billion pounds a year. Again, a historical perspective helps us understand this deep urge in our culture, since the attempt to model the actions of the mind is nothing new. As early as the fourth century B.C., Anaxagoras suggested a sort of elemental dynamics of thought.[9] And we have scared and delighted each other with stories of monstrous artificial beings from Hephaestos's Talus to Pygmalion's Galataea to Rabbi Loew's Golem to Shelley's Frankenstein to Asimov's robots and Dick's replicants. So we are both agents and victims of our own technological progeny. Somewhere in that sweet slip between compulsion and free will we can decide whether to turn off the machine or aid it.

So the best weapon in defense of our own humanness is to continue to deconstruct the natural and the artificial in both technology and imagination even as we expand our own definition of human to include Virek in his vat, Count Zero the Alpha, and Bobby Newmark and McCoy the construct, Kitsune and Lindsay the Shapers, and Ryumin the Mechanist. The Preservationists of Sterling's *Schismatrix* have it all wrong. What is it they're Preserving? When do we know we're talking to a real McCoy? What aspect of humanity makes us human? Our flesh? Our CNS? Our thoughts? Our handiwork? Where's that line over which lies inhumanity? The technology is us, man. Even Lindsay the Shaper slowly becomes more mechanical as his strange life proceeds. White magic or black, it doesn't make a difference. At first glance, this seems exactly what IBM and Genentech aim to do: get us all to buy into that erasure of differences between our natural private selves and vat-grown flesh, biochip implants, and other prostheses. Again, our bodies are the resource for this deconstruction. The very terms *natural* and *artificial* have become completely irrelevant and obsolete. Go back to the idea of extensions of the nerve net.

The noted cyberneticist and neurophysiologist Humberto Maturana suggests that the urgent biological growth vector of the CNS is in the direction of autopoeisis, growing feedback loops of self-organization and complexity: swimming upstream against the universal tide toward entropy, as Norbert Wiener puts it. If so, then the natural, biological necessity of the human nerve net is to imperialize nature through artifice, appropriating what it can: water, coal, oil, wind, silicon, DNA, positrons, you name it. That, by the way, is the *cyber* in cyberpunk: the way the nervous system acts the silent partner with natural resources in a looping, self-organizing system; our brain-tech loop is one of Prigogine's dissipative structures organizing nonlinear apparent chaos into sense.

Let me conclude with a suggestive note about literature after the year 2000. The grand and enduring cultural project of modeling our own minds has split into two shining paths. The first is the closed path, which has isolated logic, the rational, and called it intelligence to the exclusion of all else, a heritage of the blindly rational Pythagoreans. It has led us to the powerful, attractive, but innately limited models of artificial intelligence that we have today. The second is the open path, which includes in its definition the unlimited range of human expression, including our innate abilities to create, to make things up, to invent spontaneously within and without a structure or code. This second path has led us to literature, the enduring attempt to model in words the activities of the mind in all its irrationality. Gibson's vision of the cyberpunk future suggests a postliterate culture. But cyberpunk itself demonstrates that the literary text is a hyperevolved device for extending the nerve net along one of its most powerful lines of force. The nervous system isn't only about codes of information and noise, which gave us the computer. It's about natural grammars, metaphors of meaning and silence that have given us the postmodern novel. This AI stuff that pursues von Neumann's, Turing's, and Wiener's demon of the brain as a machine is almost certainly doomed to impoverished failure as long as it presumes that only sheer logic drives intelligence. But even at

David Porush

the level of the neuron itself the brain acts more like a metaphor than a mechanical input-output device. Ask any neurophysiologist. And in terms of mimicking human intelligence, logic and circuitry alone—even the complications of neural networks and parallel processing—are not going to get us there.

260

No, the route to a true AI is not through complications but through complexity, through a cybernetics in which the observer and the observed lock in a self-conscious loop of growing organization and complexity: in short, a postmodern text. If the measure of a sentient artificial being is its intelligent autonomous behavior and its ability to pass the Turing Test (to persuade a nontrivial cross-examiner of its humanness), then the literary text is an AI. Perhaps the text of the future won't be linked to paper, or even the tissuelike fax that illiterate Mona Lisa emblematically stands on to insulate herself from the filth of her dive. Perhaps it will be transformed into a dance of light across three-dimensional screens or a jambalaya of data in the hypertextual hyper-library. Perhaps the on-line novel will become an interactive feedback looping cyberfiction, and the poem a self-organizing autopoetry. But the literary text will always be required in some hypertrophic form for its particular sort of epistemological potency, for its unique capacity to reflect and extend the frothing of our synaptic bath. As the intense expression of the literate, solitary vision, I expect it will not only endure past the year 2000 but prevail somewhere beyond that, in cyberspace, as an expression of pure cognition.

Notes

1. Jean Baudrillard, *America*, trans. Chris Turner (London: Verso, 1988).
2. See George Johnston Allman, *Greek Geometry from Thales to Euclid* (Dublin: Hodges, Figgis, 1889), p. 97. See also Sir Thomas Heath, *A History of Greek Mathematics* (Oxford: Clarendon Press, 1921), 1:154.
3. Actually, the following is a gross simplification of Eudoxos's method. An account similar to the one herein can be found in Steve J. Heims's excellent biography, *John von Neumann and Norbert Wiener: From Mathematics to the Technologies of Life and Death* (Cambridge: MIT Press, 1980), pp. 58–77.
4. Cantor's proof, which follows Eudoxos's own description, can be understood quite simply. Since in geometry the point is a dimensionless locus (having no breadth, width, or length, no extension), the sum of all the points on Eudoxos's line is infinite but occupies no space. On the other hand, the irrational numbers, which occupy all the spaces between the lines by definition, are in sum a larger infinity.
5. For a discussion of the line between Eudoxos's work and Wiener's see Heims, *John von Neumann and Norbert Wiener*, pp. 58–61.

6. Tom De Haven, *Freaks Amour* (New York: William Morrow, 1979).
7. As reported by Italo Calvino in *Invisible Cities*, trans. William Weaver (New York: Harcourt Brace Jovanovich, 1972).
8. Istvan Csicsery-Ronay, "Cyberpunk and Neuromanticism," *Mississippi Review* 47/48 16 (1988): 274.
9. See D. E. Gershenson and D. A. Greenberg, *Anaxagoras and the Birth of Physics* (New York: Blaisdell, 1964), pp. 1–51.

......
......
......

Undecid-

ability

and

Oxymo-

ronism

. . . .

Eric S. Rabkin

n the 1831 introduction to *Frankenstein*, Mary Shelley wrote that in creating her most famous novel she had aimed to "invent" "a story . . . which would speak to the mysterious fears of our nature."[1] In the earlier 1818 preface, Percy Bysshe Shelley, writing as Mary, had claimed that "the event on which this fiction is founded, has been supposed, by Dr. Darwin, and some of the physiological writers of Germany, as not of impossible occurrence." But even if the reanimation of dead flesh were "impossible as a physical fact," he continued, it "affords a point of view to the imagination for the delineating of human passions more comprehensive and commanding than any which the ordinary relations of existing events can yield."[2] If we read the novel only as a demonstration of the need of the individual for the group, of the superficiality of the judgments of the group, and of the inhumanity of the group toward the individual, then we must suppose that science had merely provided the Shelleys with a pre-text—an idea existing before the text itself—for making literal, and hence more dramatic, some of the problems posed by the rise of romantic egotism. And the novel does do those things. But the novel also treats of the self-isolation attendant on the too-focused attachment to science, both as a means to fame and as a benefaction to humanity. In short, even while admitting that the scientific "facts" behind the novel might very well be false, the fact of modern science itself was felt to have created a new social problem and simultaneously to have provided materials for constructing—"inventing"—an aesthetically significant treatment of that problem. Science fiction, then, from its inception, has been a response to the felt workings of science, a response that uses a language shaped by science to discuss problems felt to be caused by science. The question I explore in this essay is how this response has developed—and how it will develop hereafter.

There is no science without a language of science. Classification, taxonomy, cladistics; description, record, report; notation, transformation, theory formulation: these are only some of the fundamental operations of Western science. But if, as Samuel R. Delany has it, language is a distorting mirror of what we feel and think,[3] then we would do best to make those distortions themselves reveal what the very linguistic technology of science may either obscure or, in many cases, create.

Here is the opening of Philip K. Dick's *Do Androids Dream of Electric Sheep?*

> A merry little surge of electricity piped by automatic alarm from the mood organ beside his bed awakened Rick Deckard. Surprised —it always surprised him to find himself awake without prior notice—he rose from the bed, stood up in his multicolored pajamas, and stretched. Now, in her bed, his wife Iran opened her gray, unmerry eyes, blinked, then groaned and shut her eyes again.
>
> "You set your Penfield too weak," he said to her. "I'll reset it and you'll be awake and—"
>
> "Keep your hand off my settings." Her voice held bitter sharpness. "I don't want to be awake."[4]

This passage, with its separate beds, movement from merriness to unmerriness, and instantly nasty rebuff of what sounds like a solicitous offer, suggests only the most recent enactment of a scene of continuing domestic frustration and bile. But the language of this common scene is in many ways uncommon, based on a pre text of science, and presenting us with a series of minor linguistic alternatives among which our reading habit is to decide. If something "merry" "pipes," clichés of birdsong come to mind, and surely one "mood organ" that may be said to "surge electricity" is associated with the not uncommon tumescence of morning. Of course, that organ wouldn't be beside Rick's bed, so perhaps the piping is not of a sound but of a substance that the mood organ–pipe organ is pumping into his sleeping body. He is surprised, we are told, to be awakened without prior notice. But how can there be prior notice without awakening him? What sort of sleep does this mood organ allow? Iran—is this really a woman or simply a state of consciousness?—is grumpy, so Rick offers to strengthen her "Penfield." Does that mean he will make the writing by which we meet her more vivid? Apparently her Penfield is at least as intimate a part of her as the words whereby she is incarnated, because her first words are "Keep your hand off my —." We might expect some body part to be mentioned now, but the word we get is "setting." That she does not want to be awake but is anyway suggests now not simply that life is bad but that the technology of mood organs and Penfields is inadequate. Iran's frustration at both Rick and life devolves, then, in part from a linguistic artifact of science. A mood organ, combining the notions of musical and bodily organs, of instrument of expression and instrument of control, ought to play whatever we want it to, but clearly it does not. Moods, which we used to believe came from within us, are here seen as coming from without. Iran sees the problem with her life, then, not as her fault but as the fault of the world around her. The expectations created by science—and by the language of science—have not been satisfied by science. To her, that Rick cannot see this makes clear how out of touch with modern reality he is. How dare he touch her Penfield?

The reader's recognition that marital anger may arise from differing reactions to the ways science changes the world is only strengthened for those who recognize Penfield as the nonfictional Dr. Wilder Penfield, the director of the Montreal Neurological Institute who became famous for mapping the areas of the brain that control the diverse areas of the body.[5] Are the very operations of the brain redefined in this narrative world? The fact that frustration like Iran's at external instrumentalities is common—for example, frustration at not earning enough money, at not enjoying enough sex, at not receiving enough prestige—suggests only that the problem science is creating is of a type with problems we have always had. If Dick is not speaking to the "mysterious fears of our nature," he is certainly speaking to a typical frustration of our nature.

Science (coming from the Latin word for knowledge) and the language of science do not so much encode what is known as what is said to be known. An ironic image of the "progress" of science is the current expensive removal of asbestos from schools. The asbestos was originally applied to reduce the danger of fire and help conserve energy costs in these places of learning; now that we have learned that asbestos causes cancer, it is costing approximately twenty times as much to remove it as it cost to install. This is a hard lesson. What is perhaps hardest, however, is that the malignancy of asbestos was recorded as early as the first century of this era by Pliny the Elder.[6] Unfortunately, by the lights of "modern" science, Pliny the Elder is not a "scientific" authority, any more than Rick's wife Iran is a self-contained being.

Science changes things, as it is supposed to, and therefore the language of science changes the meaning of things. I recall the evening of the day that jazz great Duke Ellington died. That night on the "NBC Nightly News," John Chancellor began with the following respectful announcement: "Edward Kennedy 'Duke' Ellington died this morning of cancer of the lungs and pneumonia. Later in the program we'll hear him play for us."[7] How can Duke Ellington possibly play for us if he is dead? And yet, living in his electronic world, John Chancellor said that we would hear not a recording of the Duke playing for some now dispersed audience but the Duke himself playing for us, for the people who came after the performance, for the auditors of that unique, personal electronic map that only the Duke could make. In *Neuromancer*, the paradigmatic novel of the current hot, so-called cyberpunk brand of science fiction, one of the main characters is McCoy Pauley, otherwise known as Dixie Flatline because this southerner's EEG had been flattened while he was electronically "jacked into . . . the consensual hallucination that was the matrix" of all interconnected computer information known as cyberspace.[8] But before he went, Dixie Flatline had been recorded into "a construct, a hardwired ROM cassette replicating a dead man's skills, obsessions, knee-jerk responses." From the viewpoint of the reader, this acknowledgedly dead man is a fully functional character. At one point he calls himself the "Lazarus of cyberspace."[9] Frankenstein used the image of the living dead to make a point about the free will of the living, in the era of Karen Ann Quinlan, *Neuromancer*, at least in part, uses the image of the living dead to suggest that now many if not all of us living in the modern infosphere are in fact the living dead.

Once upon a time, of course, the language of science did not require us to tolerate oxymorons like living dead. Science could be thought of by some as simply, unalloyedly good. If one example may stand for all, a good picture of nineteenth-century scientific optimism can be drawn from an 1880 paean penned by a Missouri lawyer named Paxton. In it, the narrator falls asleep and awakens "A Century Hence." Here is the stanza called "Progress":

> Behold, what astonishing progress appears,
>   In literature, science and wealth,
> Within the past era, of one hundred years,
>   Of energy, virtue and health.
> And now let us view the bright glories this land

265
......
......
......

In the next hundred years shall possess—
When genius and science, with industry's hand,
This country and people shall bless.[10]

It is perhaps a sign of Paxton's prosodic innocence that his rhymes and rhythms are boringly perfect; but innocent or not, they accord wonderfully with his machine-made future. Note, however, that the language of this future not only extols science but incorporates religion through such terms as "virtue," "glory," and "bless." Science, in short, promises us Paradise Regained. This was the same promise Francis Bacon had held out 260 years earlier: "Let but mankind recover their right over nature, which was given them by the Divine Being, let them be well provided of materials, and rectified reason and sound religion will direct the use."[11] Paxton has glimpsed a future in which "a motor much stronger than steam had appeared / Yet cheap, economic and mild."[12] The result of all this power was that "people were able to add to their store, / And be generous, noble and true."[13]

Today, things look somewhat different. Science, as in the promise of asbestos, seems too often to lie to us, and our writers point up these lies by exploring the language of science. In *Woman on the Edge of Time*, Consuelo, who has suffered everything that women of color and low economic status in our society are likely to suffer, tells a person from the utopian future, "They like to try out medicine on poor people. Especially brown people and black people. Inmates in prisons too." Consuelo explains that "when I take Thorazine, the effects are controlling me, making me half dead, but I get lots of side effects, believe me, like sore throat and . . . constipation, dizziness, funny speech." "But, Connie blossom, all are effects! Your drug companies labeled things side effects they didn't want as selling points."[14] How true; yet how difficult for us to notice. Science is not simply knowledge but the construction of knowledge, a construction accomplished in large measure by acts of language. In the era of "heroic medical measures," living dead is not simply a rhetorical trope but an ethical dilemma about which we need to decide and which we often find undecidable. The relative peace much of the industrialized world has enjoyed—or borne—for nearly half a century rests on a nuclear doctrine of "mutually assured destruction" in which we build weapons whose only legitimate use is that they not be used. No wonder we can't decide whether to call them MX missiles or, as Ronald Reagan wanted to have it, Peacekeepers.

The fact that every scientific good seems to breed a bad, and many bads a good, makes it painfully difficult to decide about issues of science, a fact that is truer and more important with each increase in the impact science has on our lives. In *The Shockwave Rider*, a novel named in part in homage to *Future Shock*, Alvin Toffler's 1970 discussion of the socially and personally disorienting impact of the accelerating development of science, John Brunner has the following self-contained passage:

PARADOX, NEXT STOP AFTER THE BOONDOCKS

"It's not because my mind is made up that I don't
want you to confuse me with any more facts.

"It's because my mind isn't made up. I already
have more facts than I can cope with.

"So SHUT UP, do you hear me? SHUT UP!" [15]

In this punningly paradoxical passage paradoxically called paradox, when we leave the boondocks, and presumably our provincial ignorance, we are inundated with so much knowledge that we are unable to know. This is a common anomic effect of science.

When we cannot decide matters through no fault of our own, we often feel that the matters themselves are ambiguous, "of uncertain nature . . . difficult to comprehend." [16] In the cases I have been discussing, however, it is not so much that we cannot comprehend them as that we cannot decide what they mean. In a technical linguistic sense, "ambiguity" denotes structures having two or more possible meanings, such as "flying planes can be dangerous." [17] In that sentence we do not know whether to construe the speaker's meaning as "piloting is a dangerous activity" or as "the presence of flying planes poses a danger." Both constructions are rhetorically and ontologically equivalent. Both are propositional assertions. Both function in the same realm and make the same assumptions about how the world operates. In the sentence "I walked down the street and turned into a drugstore," we are again presented with two possible constructions. But here the first, that I made a left-hand turn and entered the building, is rhetorically and ontologically distinct from the second, that a magical transformation occurred. Here the ambiguity stretches across two differing sets of assumptions about how the world operates. Context, of course, or pre-text, is where we turn to disambiguate such sentences; that is, to decide which meaning we ought to accept as intended. And one of the most powerful pre-texts we must consult to know how today's world is thought to operate is science, a science that is, to our "shock," ever changing. Thus, what seems to mean one thing today may mean its exact opposite tomorrow.

Near the beginning of Michael Frayn's future tense, future setting novel *A Very Private Life*, young Uncumber asks her mother,

> "What happens to you when you die?"
> "Oh, you take some special medicine, and you get better again."
> "But I mean, if you really, really die?"
> "Well, if you really die very badly, then I suppose you're put in the tube, and you go on to another place."[18]

Once upon a time, "to die badly," meant to die dishonorably; once upon a time, the novelist suggests, it will mean to die beyond the knowledge of medical science. How do we construe the meaning, then, of "to die badly"? We consult the science implied by the text. But often, as our world changes, science seems to imply two contradictory things at once. Is a living cell line, uniquely interesting because it contains John Jones's rare cancer, living or dead? Is it part of John Jones, though separated from him, or not? Inasmuch as cell lines are valuable research tools, in America these days the courts genuinely wrangle over the extent to which the glob in that petri dish is John Jones. Clearly it is—and just as clearly it isn't. And this example is no novelistic trick. The problem is not so much that matters are ambiguous as that they are deeply undecidable.

In the trope of oxymoron, which is itself "a condensed form of paradox,"[19] we have two meanings which clash so perfectly that it is impossible to decide which of them is determinative. Indeed, the very power of the trope arises by requiring us to recognize an incompatibility, to recognize our impulse to decide between the terms, to tolerate our incapacity to decide, and then to transcend that incapacity by deriving meaning precisely from that structural undecidability. An oxymoron is an impossible possibility wherein both parts of a mutually exclusive pair function. And while we may often think of oxymoron as extending through at least two terms, as in "Parting is such sweet sorrow," single terms such as *bittersweet* are themselves oxymorons. Of course, it may be objected, *bittersweet* is really two terms, *bitter* and *sweet*, composed by the rules of our grammar. True enough, but once that composition takes place, we tend to think of the result as a single idea, not as a clash of opposites. This is so in rare words specifically coined to compose opposites, like *algedonic* (pertaining to pain to the point of pleasure or pleasure to the point of pain,[20] from the Greek *algos* ["pain"] + *hedone* ["pleasure"]),[21] and true of words we have come to know so well that we become unaware of the clash within them, as in *oxymoron* itself, from the Greek *oxy* ("pointed") and *morous* ("foolish"),[22] a pointed foolishness. Science fiction, of course, both coins oxymorons and composes them through a narrative grammar in ways that have made them compelling and familiar, as in the well-established term *cyborg*, a contraction of *cybernetic organism*,[23] and in the newly named realm of "consensual hallucination" called cyberspace. Science fiction, wherein the dead walk, draws the landscape of oxymoron.

In exemplifying *oxymoron*, the *Princeton Encyclopedia of Poetry and Poetics* quotes (without citation) this stanza from Richard Crashaw's "Hymn of the Nativity" (1652):

> Welcome, all wonder in one sight!
> Eternity shut in a span.
> Summer in winter, day in night,
> Heaven in earth, and God in man!

The article then observes that "as the above quotation indicates, oxymoron is particularly effective in evoking religious mysteries or other meanings which the poet feels to be beyond the reach of human sense."[24] I would observe first that a "sense of wonder" ("all wonder in one sight") is a famous marker of science fiction,[25] and, second, that this religious capacity flows from oxymoron's ability to induce in the reader a notion, otherwise wordless, that transcends the words themselves. This approach to the ineffable is not, however, merely a matter for traditional religion but also a matter to which science fiction responds when facing the dilemmas of modern science. Indeed, many science fiction writers have decided to tidy up the conflicts in their novels by truly producing a god from the machine. In *The Gods Themselves*, Isaac Asimov's Hugo and Nebula award–winning novel of 1972, one of the meddling scientists carelessly hot on the track of heat death for two parallel universes (ours being one) suddenly metamorphoses into a unique genius who recognizes a new and more fundamental structure to the universe of universes, a recognition that will miraculously (and with no narrative preparation) pull the fire out of the fat just in the nick of time. Although this type of contrivance is disparaged by most critics, the awards the

Eric S. Rabkin

novel garnered suggest this aesthetic solution, or perhaps any aesthetic solution, to the problems posed by scientific "progress" is more than a little welcome in the disorienting world of modern America. In John Varley's *Millennium* (1983), the ecocatastrophe that is clearly unavoidable is, at the last moment, avoided by the heroine's friendly robot lover, who turns out to have been a god all along, not so much a deus ex machina as a deus qua machina. And in Greg Bear's *Blood Music* (1985), the intelligent cells that have plagued and destroyed humanity turn out, at the end, to be keeping humanity's thoughts alive—and at a higher level. All human beings have been reformed into shreds and sheets of dripping protoplasm, but the novel ends with words we are to take as happy: "Nothing is lost. Nothing is forgotten. It was in the blood, the flesh. And now it is forever."[26]

The oxymorons of science fiction indeed help us go "beyond the reach of human sense"; go so far, in fact, that we can transcend the undecidable and feel either that we have actually made a decision or that a decision has been obviated. In Bruce Sterling's *Schismatrix* (1985), another so-called cyberpunk novel, the protagonist, Lindsay, is talking to a beautiful young woman who turns out to be merely one of myriad controlled parts of the monumentally extended and augmented flesh of Kitsune, his erstwhile lover. In this phase, Kitsune's flesh forms the very environment Lindsay inhabits, much as does the computer AM in Harlan Ellison's well-known "I Have No Mouth and I Must Scream."[27] She is a virtual asteroid of flesh and mind, and within it she talks to Lindsay through a comely young woman's mouth: " 'Once I told you that ecstasy was better than being God.' 'I remember.' 'I was wrong, darling. Being God is better.' "[28]

Science fiction often indulges this desire to contrive a god—a desire, it seems to me, that reflects the felt absence of an adequate ordering principle in the world. Yet should not the "progress" of science make the sense of natural order ever more palpable? The problem, of course, is that physical order and moral order are not the same thing at all. While science may appear to increase the knowability of the order of the world outside us, the world inside us is made ever less sure and we are presented continually with ever-greater realms of undecidability. This is made clearest by the way in which technology, the practical apprentice of science, makes even the most removed and theoretical matters play ever more intimate parts in our lives, as did Iran's Penfield. Whatever might once have been a matter of us versus them, self versus world, here versus there, now versus then, or living versus dead has now become confused, personal, and bodily intimate. We can see this increase of intimacy in many realms. For our purposes, let us glance briefly at the portrayal of war, cities, government, and the human body.

In ancient times, war was a geographically dispersed affair.[29] People "went to war" and met on "battlefields." The family could sit at home and mournfully sing that "Johnny has gone for to soldier."[30] But both the reality of war and its rhetoric have, in the course of this century's industrialization of conflict, changed radically. The effect of these changes has been continually to make war less dispersed and more concentrated; less a matter of the group and more a matter of the individual. What was once an external ideal is now an intimate, visceral fear.

Perhaps the most famous military exhortation of modern times is the one given in the House of Commons by Winston Churchill after the disastrous retreat from Dunkirk:

> We shall not flag or fail. We shall go on to the end. We shall fight in France, we shall fight on the seas and oceans, we shall fight with growing confidence and growing strength in the air, we shall defend our island, whatever the cost may be, we shall fight on the beaches, we shall fight on the landing grounds, we shall fight in the fields and in the streets, we shall fight in the hills; we shall never surrender. (June 4, 1940)

In one sense, the aggressiveness of this speech may seem surprising, given the recency of defeat; but in another sense, a territorial (or geographical) sense, this aggressiveness is just what modern ethology and the history of warfare both teach us. Notice that Churchill's rhetoric parallels the retreat and in imagination retreats even farther, from France to the water and air, to English beaches, and inland to the fields, cities, and even back into the hills. Churchill asserts that with this withdrawal toward the heart of English territory, "we shall fight with growing confidence and growing strength." In On Aggression, Nobel laureate Konrad Lorenz explains that "even in the case of animals whose territory is governed by space alone, the hunting ground must not be imagined as a property determined by geographical confines; it is determined by the fact that in every individual the readiness to fight is greatest in the most familiar place, that is, in the middle of its territory. . . . As the distance from this 'headquarters' increases, the readiness to fight decreases proportionately."[31] In other words, as the war moves closer to home, the

271

will to repel the invaders grows. By reimagining the scene at Dunkirk as happening not only on the French side of the Channel but on the English side as well, Churchill was trying to stoke his fellow citizens with the fire they would feel if they did not stop their enemies soon. The geographical concentration of normally diffuse warfare, the domestication of warfare into a current household threat, is one of the outstanding differences between warfare as it had always been and warfare as it is now. Even before the Battle of Britain, Churchill saw this.

Interestingly, science fiction presents us with a set of three Hugo-winning novels in which we can see the reimagination of war working on the same essential story. In Robert A. Heinlein's *Starship Troopers* (1959), the protagonist spends most of the first part of the story training at a military academy (Heinlein himself attended Annapolis) and the second half fighting on distant planets. Here we have an example of the classic diffusion of warfare across space. Heinlein's physical condition kept him from seeing combat during World War II, and his actions at the time and words since confirm his frustration at not being able to "go for to soldier." Johnnie Rico is not similarly frustrated.

In Joe (Joseph William) Haldeman's *The Forever War* (1974), again the protagonist spends the first part of the story in training and the second in fighting, but in this later work the fighting occurs not so much across space as across time. The resulting dislocation of the soldiers from their families and times of origin enforces a poignant loneliness on them and makes them cling to whatever extent they can to each other. William Mandella (a near anagram for the author's own name), unlike Johnnie Rico, feels just as much sadness in his soldiering life as fulfillment through doing his duty. In that sense, Haldeman has written a Viet Nam—era response to Heinlein, deemphasizing space and the group and emphasizing time and the individual.

Orson Scott Card, in *Ender's Game* (1985), continues this progression within, this domestication of warfare. Here the protagonist, Ender, thinks that he is spending the whole of the time described in the story in training at the military academy. He is intentionally cut off from his family by the military government and plays mind games with his siblings. But the (presumably) surprise ending reveals that the electronic war games Ender has been playing in the second half of the novel haven't been games at all; he has been truly fighting, as had Rico and Mandella. Real spaceships are slaved to his thoughts during what he thinks are training simulations. Thus, in destroying the "simulated" ships on his videoscreen, he unwittingly wipes out the physically distant enemy that lives psychically within his own mind, simultaneously saving the human race and becoming anathema to himself as a genocide. He spends the sequel (*Speaker for the Dead*, 1986) trying to expiate his sins. In this third story of training and fighting, the soldier is not so much brought into the group through a common power or ideology as co-opted by the group. His devaluation to the status of mere resource excludes him from the very group whose war he is supposed to want to fight. Card, then, is imagining warfare not as geographically diffuse but as concentrated in the mind of a single individual, the one who must push the button, so that the forces most importantly at work are not those between groups but those within them. When warfare is thus domesticated, home becomes a very uncomfortable place.

Cities too have become very uncomfortable places, thanks in part to modern science. Mass transit, huge sewerage projects, and so on have led to metropolises too big to police effectively without destroying most civil liberties. The technological displacement of workers from the country into the city has created Mexico City, Shanghai, Cairo, and Calcutta, which are not only unpoliceable but infernally unlivable zones so large that the traditional distinction between city and country is obliterated. All is city now, the Earth paved over. Where once the great city was the cradle of culture (*metropolis*, after all, means "mother city"),[32] it is now the wasteland of technology. The means of social control, as Anthony Burgess dramatized with the Pavlovian conditioning in *A Clockwork Orange* (1962), are inherently dehumanizing. You cannot force someone to be happy; hence, the satiric point of this line from the first "record" of Zamiatin's *We* in which D-503, the narrator, explains that the ship for which he is the chief builder will be used to spread the philosophy of the "United State": "If they will not understand that we are bringing them a mathematically faultless happiness, our duty will be to force them to be happy."[33]

We do not talk any longer of the New Jerusalem but rather of Beirut and Belfast, the creations of modern weaponry. Great social forces are no longer deployed in contests between Sparta and Athens or even Washington and Moscow but within the very cities we inhabit: Detroit 1967, Prague 1968, Munich 1972, and now Tian'anmen Square. Under the eye of the camera, the heart of the capital becomes the window on the world and all sense of separation is obliterated. There is no longer a "safe" part of town. The intimacy of warfare is matched by the intimacy of the city. A clockwork orange is an oxymoron, and so is an invisible man. As Ralph Ellison's narrator puts it, "Well, I was and yet I was invisible, that was the fundamental contradiction."[34] Life in the modern city makes life itself oxymoronic. In cyberpunk novels there is typically no countryside whatsoever. The information society crowds into our skull.

Perhaps the most obvious intrusions of modern technology are the surveillance devices of George Orwell's *Nineteen Eighty-four* (1949), Big Government as Big Brother. Government too, thanks to modern technology, becomes ever more intrusive, ever more intimate. Against this invasion of the all into the one, the "sacred" and triumphant last word of Ayn Rand's dystopian *Anthem* is "EGO."[35] In *The Handmaid's Tale* (1985), Margaret Atwood's postindustrial cities of repression satirize both "scientific socialism" and current male chauvinism with the slogan "From each according to her ability; to each according to his needs."[36] What men need from women, of course, are babies. As Zamiatin's "Lex Sexualis" has it, "A Number [meaning citizen] may obtain a license to use any other Number as a sexual product."[37] But citizens are no more (social security) numbers than happiness is mathematical or oranges are clockwork. The modern scientific government that is for us is, by virtue of its very means of functioning, inherently against us. Zamiatin is, after all, perversely correct when he writes that "desires are tortures, aren't they? It is clear, therefore, that happiness is when there are no longer any desires, not a single desire any more."[38] Just as the governmental obligation to provide defense allowed the co-option of Ender and the turning of him into a genocide, so the governmental obligation to arrange for human happiness allows for the "surgical removal of fancy" from all the citizens of the United State. But are they then still citizens? That is, are they human? A person without imagination, like a person without visibility, is yet another oxymoron.

Most of the intimate invasions of warfare, city, and government have worked themselves upon the human body. In much science fiction these days, as in Kafka's "In the Penal Colony," the sentence for each crime— or condition—is inscribed on the criminal's—or citizen's—body. Roger Torraway, the aptly named protagonist of Frederik Pohl's *Man Plus*, has his entire body redesigned (including vivid castration). Why? One of his coworkers explains: "Roger. We need you. There's a war coming if we don't do something to stop it, and it's crazy but the trend projections say the only thing that can stop it is putting you on Mars. Don't ask me why. I just go by what the technical people tell me, and they claim that's what the computers print out."[39] To paraphrase the old spiritual, "How do I know? The computer tells me so!"

For fiction writers, of course, the very vividness of body imagery makes it useful, but that fact is not merely a key to exploitation; it is also a truth we must recognize if we are to inspire action. "That the public alarm over thalidomide was so much greater than that over the 50,000 deaths caused by the automobile per year in America is of interest. Because thalidomide can cause disfigurement—an effect abhorred by modern society far more than death—it is like cancer, extremely alarming particularly since reproduction of the species is involved."[40] So even the body itself, in startling ways, is presented oxymoronically, as with the voluntarily prosthetic arms and legs of Bernard Wolfe's *Limbo* (1952) or the casual tinkerings of John Varley's "medicanics": "No naturally evolved mammal had ever made the switch from air to water breathing, and the project had taxed the resources of bio-engineering to its limits. But everything in Piri's body was a living part of it. It had taken two days to install it all."[41] When one speaks of "installing" body parts, the human and the mechanical, once mutually exclusive categories, become locked in oxymoronic transcendence.

Cyberspace is not only an oxymoron but a conception made vivid only through oxymoron: a consensual hallucination. And just as the metropolis is no longer the nourishing mother city, this "matrix" is no longer the life-giving "womb" of its Greek etymology. Although Brian Stableford is right in saying that cyberpunk "aspires to provide a streetwise and cynical assessment of future possibilities generated by the new information technology,"[42] cyberpunk is truly characterized only by its style. The famous opening line of *Neuromancer*—"The sky above the port was the color of television, tuned to a dead channel"[43]—commingles the mechanical and the natural, the living and the dead, the accidental and the voluntary; and all point toward technological dissolution and decay.

Sometimes, particularly when its oxymoronism is dense, the style of cyberpunk works deeply indeed. When Lindsay first remeets the now-monstrous Kitsune, we read the line, "Nothing brings memory back like being in a young woman."[44] This sounds strongly like the machismo of vintage Heinlein—"I felt warm and relaxed, as if I had just killed a man or had a woman"[45]—but when we realize that it is Kitsune speaking, we suddenly think that she is referring to a reawakening of her memory of her lovemaking with Lindsay. Only on reflection do we realize that she may just as well be referring to how Lindsay could use this young woman projection to bring back his memory of lovemaking with Kitsune. Which is meant? The matter, thanks to the dilemmas created by this imagined science, is undecidable.

276

The increasing undecidability of things brought on by modern science leads to ever more oxymoronism in literature. While it is true that oxymoronism characterizes cyberpunk, it is by no means limited to cyberpunk. Karl Kroeber writes that "science fiction appropriately uses language in unrecursive narrative forms and a direct style of reportage because it extrapolates from scientific and technological conditions favoring such modes of representation as closest to reality. The literary form adapts from its technological model an assumption of uncomplicated relations between language and what it represents."[46] Clearly this is wrong. Not only does cyberpunk use language in highly complicated ways aimed at keeping vivid the undecidability of modern life, but, as the examples throughout have implied, so does much other science fiction, including excursions into peoples of ambiguous gender (such as Ursula Kroeber LeGuin's *The Left Hand of Darkness* [1969]) and unknown national identity (such as the presiding power in Frederic Brown's World War II yarn "Arena").[47] What is most important, however, is that even when the fashion for extreme cyberpunk passes (as is likely), the increasing undecidability that the progress of science will inevitably make us feel will require that both science fiction in particular and fiction in general become ever more oxymoronic, displaying styles, plots, characters, and settings that are adequate to our decidedly undecidable world. Only in that way, as Shelley did with *Frankenstein*, can art continue to "speak to the mysterious fears of our nature."

Notes

1. Mary Shelley, *Frankenstein* (1818; New York: Oxford University Press, 1985), p. 8.
2. Ibid., p. 13.
3. Samuel R. Delany, *Tales of Nevèryon* (New York: Bantam Books, 1979), p. 83.
4. Philip K. Dick, *Do Androids Dream of Electric Sheep?* (New York: Signet, 1968), p. 9.
5. Jonathan Miller, *The Body in Question* (New York: Random House, 1978), p. 21.
6. Edward W. Lawless, *Technology and Social Shock* (New Brunswick: Rutgers University Press, 1977), p. 288.
7. John Chancellor, "NBC Nightly News," May 24, 1974.

8. William Gibson, *Neuromancer* (New York: Ace Books, 1984), p. 5.
9. Ibid., pp. 77–78.
10. Paxton, in Ben Fuson, "A Poetic Precursor to Bellamy's *Looking Backward*," quoted in *SF: The Other Side of Realism*, ed. Thomas D. Clareson (Bowling Green, Ohio: Bowling Green University Popular Press, 1971), p. 283.
11. Francis Bacon, *Novum Organum* (1620), quoted in F. Sherwood Taylor, *A Short History of Science & Scientific Thought* (1949; New York: Norton, 1963), p. 106.
12. Paxton, p. 285.
13. Ibid., p. 287.
14. Marge Piercy, *Woman on the Edge of Time* (New York: Fawcett, 1976), p. 275.
15. John Brunner, *The Shockwave Rider* (New York: Ballantine Books, 1975), p. 41.
16. Jess Stein, ed., *The Random House Dictionary of the English Language*, unabridged ed. (New York: Random House, 1966).
17. Ibid.
18. Michael Frayn, *A Very Private Life* (New York: Viking, 1968), p. 7.
19. Alex Preminger et al., eds., *Princeton Encyclopedia of Poetry and Poetics*, enl. ed. (Princeton: Princeton University Press, 1974), p. 595.
20. Josefa Heifetz Byrne, *Mrs. Byrne's Dictionary of Unusual, Obscure, and Preposterous Words* (1974; New York: Pocket Books, 1984).
21. Dagobert D. Runes, ed., *Dictionary of Philosophy*, rev. and enl. ed. (Totowa, N.J.: Rowman and Allanheld, 1983).
22. Stein, *Dictionary*.
23. Peter Nicholls, ed., *The Science Fiction Encyclopedia* (Garden City, N.Y.: Doubleday, 1979).
24. Preminger et al., *Encyclopedia*, p. 596.
25. See, for example, Sam J. Lundwall, *Science Fiction: What It's All About* (New York: Ace Books, 1971), p. 24.
26. Greg Bear, *Blood Music* (New York: Ace Books, 1985), p. 217.
27. Harlan Ellison, "I Have No Mouth and I Must Scream," in *Science Fiction: A Historical Anthology*, ed. Eric S. Rabkin (New York: Oxford University Press, 1983), pp. 467–83.
28. Bruce Sterling, *Schismatrix* (New York: Ace Books, 1985), p. 256.
29. See, for example, the article "War" in John L. McKenzie, *Dictionary of the Bible* (New York: Macmillan, 1965); or C. W. C. Oman, *The Art of War in the Middle Ages* (1885; Ithaca: Cornell University Press, 1953), especially pp. 62–63.
30. I treat this subject at length in "Reimagining War," in *Fights of Fancy*, ed. George Slusser and Eric S. Rabkin (Athens: University of Georgia Press, forthcoming).
31. Konrad Lorenz, *On Aggression* (1963; New York: Bantam Books, 1971), p. 32.
32. Stein, *Dictionary*.
33. Eugene Zamiatin, *We*, trans. Gregory Zilboorg (1920; New York: Dutton, 1924), p. 3.
34. Ralph Ellison, *Invisible Man*, Thirtieth Anniversary edition (1952; New York: Vintage, 1972), p. 496.
35. Ayn Rand, *Anthem* (New York: Signet, 1946 [fifteenth printing]), p. 123.
36. Margaret Atwood, *The Handmaid's Tale* (New York: Fawcett, 1985), p. 151.
37. Zamiatin, *We*, p. 22.
38. Ibid., p. 171.

39. Frederik Pohl, *Man Plus* (New York: Bantam Books, 1976), p. 121.

40. Lawless, *Technology*, p. 147.

41. John Varley, "Good-bye, Robinson Crusoe" (1977), in *The Barbie Murders* (New York: Berkley, 1980), p. 183.

42. Brian Stableford, in *The Anatomy of Wonder*, 3d ed., ed. Neil Barron (New York: Bowker, 1987), p. 327.

43. Gibson, *Neuromancer*, p. 3.

44. Sterling, *Schismatrix*, p. 253.

45. Robert A. Heinlein, *The Puppet Masters* (New York: Signet, 1951), p. 53.

46. Karl Kroeber, *Romantic Fantasy and Science Fiction* (New Haven: Yale University Press, 1988), p. 22.

47. Frederic Brown, "Arena," in *Science Fiction Hall of Fame*, vol. 1, ed. Robert Silverberg (New York: Avon, 1970), pp. 281–309.

"We're on

the Eve of

2000": Writers

and Critics

Speak Out on

Cyberpunk,

HyperCard,

and the

(New?)

Nature of

Narrative

. . . .

Terri Frongia and
Alida Allison

Fiction 2000" was an international symposium on the nature of fiction at the end of the twentieth century. Cosponsored by the University of Leeds and the new Eaton Program for Science Fiction and Fantasy Studies (part of the Center for Bibliographic Research of the University of California at Riverside), the "Fiction 2000" conference held in Leeds, England, gathered together noted scholars and writers from the United States and the United Kingdom between June 28 and July 1, 1989. Focusing specifically on the form of science fiction called cyberpunk, participants were invited to speculate on the ways and means by which traditional fictional narrative is undergoing transformation as we approach the millennium.

As the conference progressed, three major areas of speculation emerged and came to dominate the post-conference discussion between writers and critics. Permeating everything, of course, were reflections on the nature of cyberpunk itself, including its relationship to traditional narrative in general, and to science fiction in particular. Mimicking science fiction's own forward-looking gaze, cyberpunk's distinctive high-tech world naturally entered the scene through lively speculation on the second topic, the impact contemporary technology might have on fiction specifically, and on creativity in general. Speculation here focused on recent advances in computer technology, with HyperCard—an authoring tool and information-organizing system created by Bill Atkinson for application on Macintosh hardware—evoking especially strong reaction. HyperCard, with its variety of applications as hypertext (permitting the easy access of other texts from a central text or "script") or hypermedia (allowing the integration of visual—graphics, texts, images, and video—and audio data), offers authors a powerful new tool for creation. Its ability to work in a nonlinear representational mode that permits, through association, the free connection of ideas, words, and images, however, poses a new problem. Combined with the program's user friendliness, this feature gives all users of the program—whether author or reader—the possibility of accessing and manipulating the "script" material in their own ways. The exploratory and creative capabilities inherent in HyperCard thus naturally provoke the question "To whom does the text belong?" All of these concerns—especially over the reader's ability to freely explore and possibly alter the author's text through HyperCard—ultimately made significant contributions to the third, and broadest, of topics of postconference speculation: the shape and essence of fiction itself as it approaches the year 2000.

Present at the informal interview conducted by Alida Allison and Terri Frongia were American science fiction authors Greg Bear (*Eon*, *Blood Music*, *Queen of Angels*) and Lewis Shiner (*Frontera*, *Deserted Cities of the Heart*), and Anglo-Canadian fantasy writer Geoff Ryman (*The Warrior Who Carried Life*, *The Unconquered Country*, *The Child Garden*). American literary critics George Slusser and Istvan Csicsery-Ronay, along with British critic Paul Brazier, also took part. What follows is an often provocative discussion assessing the conference—its overall shape, nature, and success in dealing with critical questions posed by the cyberpunk phenomenon—and contemporary writing in general.

Allison: We'd like to start off with a quick retrospective view of the conference. Do you think any underlying structure could be discerned in the conference as a whole?

Frongia: I thought it began in a deceptively traditional, academic manner, because the opening session attempted to decide just what the cyberpunk "canon" might be, and how these texts might fit into literary tradition. Perhaps because of the emphasis on Gibson's *Neuromancer* this kind of endeavor produced, many people ended up with the perception that basically only this one book had been talked about extensively.

Csicsery-Ronay: I think *Neuromancer* was indeed talked about a lot, but only because many things seemed to converge on it—it was often used as a departure point or as common ground. For instance, I know in my own talk I did mention that novel, but I also discussed many texts—works by the Strugatsky brothers, by Stanislaw Lem, and even the film *Videodrome*, which is a work I keep going back to for some reason. Many others in science fiction were also talked about, like Alfred Bester, for example. I think the impression that much of the conference centered on *Neuromancer* may actually just be an effect of the convergence in time of certain of the talks. I don't perceive this as having been a "*Neuromancer* conference" at all.

Allison: I noticed that while a lot of discussion seemed to revolve around *Neuromancer*, it also focused on what I guess you could call narrative technique. It came to me that there seem to be two central aspects in contemporary science fiction: the almost-random expansion represented by new technologies like hypertext, on the one hand, and the controlled linearity of traditional literature, on the other. Could we perhaps characterize the conference by these two categories?

Shiner: I think those were indeed the poles where the center of the conference could be found. What amazed me about this conference was the way that the papers built on each other. Some of that may have been illusory, but most of it certainly wasn't. To me, a pattern started to take shape when George Slusser started us off with his discussion of the Frankenstein barrier. That was kind of the beginning of things, with the pattern continuing until Eric Rabkin finally broke through this barrier in his own talk. I thought that was a tremendous movement, which continued building right up to the point where David [Porush] came in and attempted to tie the whole thing together. And he left me behind, unfortunately.

Slusser: The truly remarkable thing is that none of this was even consciously concerted by us organizers, because none of us really talked to each other beforehand. I mean, it was like throwing things up into the air, and they just fell into a coherent configuration. We just took this stuff, and thought about it.

Shiner: Yes, I think the conference did have a very serious shape. For me, the central question of the conference became "How do you describe the indescribable? How do you know the unknowable?" And the answer became the oxymoron; SF is in itself a literature that relies heavily on the oxymoron, because it strongly achieves its effect. This is how you describe the indescribable—by the combination of opposites.

Slusser: The oxymoron also becomes a symbol of complementarity: you take both poles and you accept them, and they exist, even though they contradict each other. There they are. And finally you reach a point where you can build on that and move beyond.

Bear: It seems to me also that the best talks here weren't even really connected with cyberpunk per se, although they circled around it. They were more connected with trying to "eff" the ineffable.

Slusser: Well, but doesn't cyberpunk do the same thing? It's part of that movement, I feel.

Bear: Yes; it's part of science fiction.

Slusser: But it's not something that's pushed off on the side. I think a lot of people felt that, well, cyberpunk may be something that's a mainstream phenomenon, not a SF one. That's the way McCaffery did it in his *Mississippi Review* piece. I think he misunderstood the question entirely by saying that at last science fiction has become sophisticated, that it has finally come of age.

Shiner: There was no question in my mind even before I got here that this conference would end with no definition of cyberpunk, no agreement on what it would stand for, and nothing resolved whatsoever in that area. Because it can't. This conference doesn't have that power—only the verdict of history has that power. And we're seeing that verdict being made all the time, like when the *New York Times* calls a hacker "cyberpunk," or when *Keyboard Magazine* has a cyberpunk issue. This is defining cyberpunk, and it's our culture, not us, that will define it. All we can do is kind of react to what we see there, and let that stimulate us to other conclusions.

Bear: I've been thinking that maybe in some respects it was a mistake to have me here, because it was a mistake for Bruce [Sterling, in his *Mirrorshades* anthology] to bring me into the so-called cyberpunk fold. Although it was fun.

Shiner: It was a mistake for him to bring me in too, but that doesn't matter.

Slusser: Well, what you have in common is that you are contemporary writers, and that's really what we wanted for this conference.

Bear: Actually, I'm thinking more in terms of my own writing of science fiction. The way I see it, cyberpunk is an interesting social phenomenon, it's great conversation, and maybe something profound can be made out of it.

Slusser: You have to admit that it does have some strange and attractive force. Just before I left to come here I got an interesting letter from an undergraduate student who wrote: "I know nothing about science fiction. I don't like science fiction. But I read Gibson, and it was like somebody shot 300 volts through my body. I think this is something great. I feel illuminated by this." And this is not a science fiction reader!

I mean, this person said, "I don't like SF." There it was, right there, a testimonial to the power of this form of fiction.

Bear: But that's also some of the old bullshit that has always infuriated a science fiction writer: suddenly to have something new come along that readers attach to, but instead of their reacting with, "Gee, maybe I better look deeper into this," they say, "I want you to do that to me again the exact same way. Give it to me again. I really dug that. I hate everything else you've ever done, but give that to me again." And Gibson hates that too.

Slusser: But that's how audiences are, though—they may react in a way writers never intended. There's something strange and weird out there, a loose and independent force attached to the text. You know the old saying, "Go, little book." It goes, and, you know, you can't control it. You write it, it takes on its own life, and then somebody else messes with it. And in the case of cyberpunk, society seems to have found it to be a massive jolt.

Shiner: I think that's true. I think this thing has become something that was never intended, even by Sterling in his wildest dreams. I think what Sterling would have liked to have happen was just the critical recognition that cyberpunk was the most important thing in SF, the movement of the future, and that was that. And, possibly, he even wanted some recognition from others outside the field who might say, "Well, science fiction is finally getting relevant," or something else like that.

Bear: Judging from the text alone, Sterling indeed said that. But he also said something like, "Let's cut out all the rest of science fiction. We are not going to talk about these other writers, we are going to shove them aside. They're useless, they're dead, you might as well bury them."

Slusser: But in *Mirrorshades* he said that we're all steeped in the tradition of science fiction.

Bear: Yes, and then two years later he went back and said, "I deeply admire the career of Arthur C. Clarke. If I were to emulate any man and the way he lived his life, it would be Arthur C. Clarke." Not William Burroughs.

Shiner: Yeah, right. Was he supposed to say, "I want to be like Burroughs, a wasted junky in Kansas"?

Bear: Anyway, I think Bruce did have a contradiction within himself there.

Slusser: Well, it's tempting to want to get your piece of the action, and science fiction *has* been waiting a long time. You guys have always seemed to be working on the margins, and now, all of a sudden, you've "arrived"—you're being called mainstream.

Bear: But *have* we been working on the margins?

Slusser: I've never thought so, but many people do. I think you've been working in the mainstream, and I keep arguing this point: if any literature is mainstream in the twentieth century, it's science fiction. But you try and tell that to our academic colleagues—to many of them modern literature is still T. S. Eliot!

Bear: I guess the right question then is, "Who cares?" Of what importance are such people, academics or not?

Slusser: You don't care, except when you stop and think that there are some ten thousand universities in the country forming our youth, and that many are presenting this kind of outdated thinking.

Bear: Well, they may be forming our youth, but meanwhile we're subverting them! And you know, based on the mail I've been receiving, I've noticed a real increase in the age of our readership, which means we're probably attracting more mature, thoughtful readers.

Slusser: That may be. I mean, look at the difference between a Heinlein juvenile novel and what's being written today. Just the intellectual necessity of following along is important. I mean, you can read *Have Spacesuit Will Travel* and dig it when you're an adolescent, but it's pretty hard to read something like Shiner's *Deserted Cities of the Heart* and get everything you should out of it. You have to be at a certain level.

Bear: Certainly; that stuff is adult.

Slusser: My point is that science fiction is growing toward a different audience now.

Frongia: So you're saying that as the audience changes, so does the fiction. Are the academics, the critics, part of this changing scene as well?

Slusser: Recently, critics have claimed that they are the mediators between the different elements in literature. In other words, some of them think that the whole literary system can't function without a critic who can go from point A to point B—and the writers are, you know, the flies in the web, shall we say.

Bear: Well, I could really despise that. I hope there are none of those people here at this conference.

Slusser: Whether we agree with that attitude or not, we have to deal with it anyway, because in a very real sense we're caught between two worlds—

Bear: Yes, that's true, you are!

Slusser: We deal with that kind of thing in the institution, especially now with the tyranny of French criticism. For example, Roland Barthes critiques Robbe-Grillet and comes to feel that he should be writing a certain way: he tells the writer what to write, and the writer writes to his, the critic's, specifications.

Bear: It's never going to happen here.

Slusser: Well, you mentioned the HyperCard business yesterday. You know, if you train students on HyperCard, soon they start accessing your text, and soon they start playing their own fantasy with your words, your ideas, moving from this to that point, and pretty soon the only person who could control the act of reading is the critic who sets up the computer program!

Bear: No, you don't understand HyperCard, because HyperCard accesses the entire text; there are no pathways established at the beginning.

Slusser: All right, but what, then, is your text? Your text is the whole textual culture, that's what you're saying.

Bear: No, your text is the subject under discussion at that moment.

Slusser: OK, let's set up a more concrete example. Say that you're reading novels, that you're going to apply this program to the novels of Jane Austen.

Bear: If you're reading Jane Austen, then on HyperCard you would have access to any single aspect of her collected works. It's really the critic's dream more than the reader's dream. That's because the reader has to start at the beginning of the book and read it through in the sequence the author established.

Slusser: But that's exactly the point I'm trying to make. Reading is the experience of a linear thing, with you, the reader, filling in the gaps as you go, because the writer writes just so much description, and not more. She gives you just so many details, and that's it—the reader is supposed to use their imagination to fill that in, as they're moving linearly from point A to point B. But in this nonlinear process of HyperCard, they might never get to point B because they get sidetracked, for they're constantly going off on tangents, trying to find out this or that by using the program. And that kind of reader is going to develop a different kind of writing.

Allison: And that would be the death of the novel as we know it. Wouldn't this hypertext kind of thing also be the death of imagination?

Bear: Oh no, not at all. I see it rather as a radical expansion of the imagination. Sometimes when new trends begin, old guards such as you and I react with: "Jesus Christ, this is the end of civilization as we know it!" While there might in fact be a period of absolute barbarism, just like Europe after Rome, later you would have a Renaissance. And in today's fast-paced world, that kind of change would probably happen in fifteen years, not hundreds—and then suddenly, wham, you'll have this whole new thing there to use and to study. The only thing is that revolutions nowadays last only a short time, for we have two or even three of them in a lifetime. And adapting to them is pretty hard. In fact, I know a lot of writers who are terrified of this thought. And it will probably have a financial effect on nearly everyone.

Frongia: As you were speaking during the conference about the multimedia implications of HyperCard, you made a memorable, if somewhat inflammatory, comment. Do you care to repeat it?

Bear: Well, I was being a little more provocative than realistic at that time, when I said that HyperCard will be the death of individual artistry. What it no doubt *will* be is the beginning of a new form of literary artist—someone who will seem almost superhuman to us. Alexandre Dumas is an example from the past of what I have in mind, for he could illustrate his books as well as write them. That kind of talent would be a basic requirement for someone wishing to be an individual artist using this kind of system.

Allison: So what do you think the writer of 2000 will be like?

Bear: They would be a bitalented, or tri-, or even multitalented individual. Just try to imagine the kind of person who could compose their own music, illustrate their own highly sophisticated computer graphics by using all kinds of aids and advancements, write their text, and so on. The entire artwork would be like a multimedia, multisensory collage work.

Frongia: So you're expecting the artistic version of Renaissance Man to be generated out of this state-of-the-art system?

Bear: Yes, for I think the technology will power the shape of the individual. Of course, there could also be teams of artists creating a multifaceted, multisensory, multimedia experience, spreading out and eventually becoming something like real life, so that perhaps eventually you would actually be experiencing the novel as if you were one or two of the characters within it. In fact, it could even get to the point where you could actually read one of these works over an entire lifetime and never repeat the same passage twice; that's how complex they could get.

You could also have works that are never finished—imagine going into a fantasy world in which you never get to the end of the experience!

Frongia: But then you're kind of stuck in a maze or twilight zone, aren't you? The text would then become like Penelope's tapestry, which never gets finished, never finds its final form, because with all of the reader-manipulated permutations it is never completed, the reading is never consummated. Lew, you're a writer also. What do you think about an almost infinitely expandable text?

Shiner: Well, while listening to your discussion about HyperCard and the potential it offers for future narrative, I discovered something I've never consciously articulated before—not even to myself. I found that I strongly believe that there's a perfect and final form for every piece of fiction I do. I'm not interested in having alternative versions or expansions or contractions available. If I make a change in my fiction, I'm making it for a reason.

Frongia: So what are your thoughts about HyperCard then?

Shiner: To start with, I can't even visualize fiction in hypertext. If, say, the reader has a two-line paragraph of my work on the screen and decides to "click" on it to enter into an expanded description of something there, I'd have a problem with that. If I'd wanted the longer description in that paragraph, then I would've put the longer description there in the first place! I believe a work of fiction should contain exactly those things that it absolutely needs to accomplish its purpose, and nothing else.

Bear: Yes, but what if this new kind of work of fiction is ten thousand times more complex than what we can make now? It can still, perhaps, be considered "completed" in your sense. But it will be like a cyclical experience—it will end up being a whole new art form. Any given piece of it will have a proportion and a perspective that the whole will either enhance or expand upon.

Shiner: I would have to actually see something like that in order to visualize that kind of art form. I guess I'm just not that imaginative.

Bear: The closest thing we've got to a completed artwork like that would be something like Proust's Remembrance of Things Past.

Slusser: Which is still only words in print.

Shiner: With one important qualification—those words are presented with tremendous skill and care, in a very definite order.

Slusser: Indeed, and it's very linear, for the characters are presented as walking along, seeing here a cathedral, there a something else. Of course, these things trigger nonlinear associations and thoughts, but it's still a novel, and a linear one at that.

Shiner: In fact, the central metaphor of the damn novel is walking along a *specific* path, and seeing *specific* things, all of which are dictated by the author. In that sense, it remains very linear, and very different from hypertext.

Bear: But you also have to remember that it's based upon musical form, which is nonlinear, for you have a prelude, the development, a second part of the development; then you have a minor key, the restatement. And there's literally a minor key, because there's the character who falls in love with the daughter of the characters we've been following up to that point—and these two reenact the mistakes of the parents.

Shiner: Are you going to say then that music isn't linear? I think that's dangerous to say.

Bear: No, no, no. I'm saying that the novel's not linear, although the structure is.

Shiner: But you were just saying that its structure is based on musical forms, and music is in itself linear.

Bear: Well, a linear novel as I visualize it would have the young kid growing up and getting old.

Shiner: No, that's just a chronological structure.

Slusser: That's the problem with a lot of our terminology—it often confuses the issue. The structure of the novel is still linear, because the author is using only words to convey his story, and words are time marks.

Shiner: Yes. He's choosing certain words to present a specific path for the reader to follow. With hypertext all of that would just be thrown out the window. I mean, if you're just going to trick someone into thinking that they have freedom, but they are in fact following a predetermined path, then you're not really taking advantage of hypertext. With that system you must in fact allow multiple paths and readings.

Bear: Perhaps I need to express it in different terms. Here's how I think of it—and this might be liberating or it might be terrifying: if you think of a text as linear, yes, that's very desirable, because the author controls it. But what if you join that with the thought of a two-dimensional work of art? It spreads out on a different path, takes a different form—and all of a sudden I have a three-dimensional work of art.

Slusser: And that's where the pressure from critics would come in, perhaps changing the shape of the work. They seem to take over from the writer because they control one of the dimensions, the "verticality" of the text. By saying that the text is linear, by talking about its length and depth, they start interpreting, thus layering their own texts over that of the author.

Bear: Yes, but with hypertext what we've got is the author taking over the role of the critic, for he's putting his own layers in there first. I guess what it all comes down to is this: if you don't like what hypermedia promises to bring to the future of narrative, then make something up that you like. Everything is so fluid right now.

Shiner: Make your own art form. I just can't visualize a work that would be appropriate to a new form at this stage in my career.

Bear: Well, you've only been thinking about it for two days! I've been thinking about it for two years, and I can't imagine one—I still haven't broken out of the form of the novel either.

Slusser: But this is the beauty of our field: science fiction writers *are* thinking about these things, and that makes a big difference.

Bear: Yes, and I know about ten or fifteen of them personally who are writing interactive novels with HyperCard-type programs and gaming systems. They are not looking at this kind of thing as just a game, because they are beginning to say that they are actually writing a kind of novel, a novel in which the reader participates to a certain extent. But it's a whole new art form—even they themselves can't define it, although they're already *doing* it.

Shiner: I just can't see a "choose your own adventure" game ever becoming serious literature.

Bear: Well, I think at this point it's only like, say, prehistoric man's first grunt compared to the later oral tradition.

Slusser: There are also certain role-playing games, like *Dungeons and Dragons*, where people actually feel like they're improvising literature: they're playing roles, "writing" their own scripts, and so on.

Shiner: As a participant in a "shared world" project, I can see many advantages to that kind of collaborative, interactive experience. In fact, I've learned things from that project which have enhanced my own independent writing. The intriguing thing is to have different people writing the characters, because it gives you other views of their thoughts and actions. This is hyperrealism in a way, for you can experience the way that, say, six other people perceive and react to the same thing, and each of them has a different view of it. This is close to the way reality itself is experienced.

Slusser: That's right, and I think that's what makes it all so exciting.

Bear: Well, then, I guess you could think of hypermedia as being an enormous, three-dimensional, multimedia, shared-world experience.

Frongia: Whoa! Can we get back for a moment to some more familiar ground? What happens then to the writer's usual medium, to the supposed "supremacy of the word" in literature? What happens to the metaphor and the oxymoron, to the actual language the artist uses in order to create his or her own unique work? Isn't this key aspect going to be lost in this kind of new system?

Bear: Well, remember that there are visual metaphors as well as verbal ones. For instance, motion pictures can be extraordinarily powerful by the way they construct time and use two or three dimensions.

Shiner: I don't believe in the supremacy of the word, anyway; I believe in the supremacy of the image. In the first place, words to me are merely a means to establishing that image. I'm probably lying here, but I keep saying this.

Allison: And how do you see these beliefs fitting in with contemporary fiction, and with cyberpunk in particular?

Shiner: For me, what *Neuromancer* does brilliantly is to create images —I think it's a very visual book. Virtually everything Gibson says creates a picture in your head; it can talk directly to your right brain. And I admire that.

Bear: Yes, even his choice of names creates an image. For example, the name Wintermute creates a definite image in one's head, even giving it a character, even though you don't know what it [the entity] actually is.

Slusser: But that's one of the simplest techniques, and an old one too. In the nineteenth century writers tried to take a word and just let it shine, let its essence come forth to create its own world. Just a single word—you just touch something. That's what the romantics believed, with their whole sense of poetic language. All you have to do is name the thing, but name it in the right way. It's like magic, so writing itself is an act of magic. And that's the way I read *Neuromancer.*

Shiner: I agree that's operating to an extent there, but, on the other hand, many words and images have become dead—and so the writer has to find ways to bypass the reader's left brain. That is, you have to find a way to define something that's startling and original, something that will create pictures, and those pictures can talk to your right brain and communicate the thing. Images do this more directly than names or words.

Frongia: The interrelationship of words and images has been a long-standing fascination for many of us. But what about something newer, like cyberpunk's apparent fascination with violence? Violence is an aspect intimately associated with cyberpunk, and with the punk scene in general. I'd really like to know more about our new arrivals' perceptions of this dimension of contemporary fiction.

Ryman: Basically, violence is what really bugs me about cyberpunk. And I have to admit that it bugs me about my own writing too, sometimes.

Brazier: I think a joke Lew Shiner related yesterday is very telling. It goes: "How many cyberpunks does it take to change a light bulb? One, but he thinks he's an army." It's just this kind of thinking which encapsulates all that's nasty about cyberpunk. I'm not interested in cyborgs being killing machines and police and all of that rubbish. There are more important things to write about in fiction than a new and living kind of tank.

Frongia: I think a lot of people share that opinion.

Bear: Your comments bring to mind my own situation. I've got a book coming out that may be partially responsible for my discomfort at being here. I could not read *Neuromancer* after I finished my novel, *Queen of Angels*, because I just know some [people] are going to want to label it cyberpunk. It's a near-future novel with all the appropriate extrapolations from modern technology. About 150,000 words long, it's extremely dense in language and plot and everything else. It's not at all glitzy, and, although a lot of surface texture may exist, it's so far removed from anything cyberpunk does that I don't want its other qualities to be overlooked. I'm afraid that simply because its high-tech surface has been subsumed by cyberpunk they're going to label it that, or say that it's just an imitation of other such stuff. That's not what I want to happen at all.

Allison: Actually, I think it's pretty clear that cyberpunk, although apparently already here and gone, made its substantial impact despite, or perhaps because of, its flattened characters and emotions and its vision of dehumanized humanity. Cyberpunk seems to have contributed mostly a style, a surface texture.

Frongia: I agree. For me, what's really missing is the complexity of human experience, especially the interior or nonphysical aspect.

Shiner's *Deserted Cities of the Heart* and Sterling's *Islands in the Net* seem much more involved in these areas, although they still retain many qualities of the so-called cyberpunk phenomenon. Even Gibson's own "sequels" to *Neuromancer* [*Count Zero* and *Mona Lisa Overdrive*] are, comparatively speaking, much more human-oriented, more psychologically motivated.

Allison: Perhaps there's some potential, then.

Frongia: It seems to me that's exactly what cyberpunk, HyperCard, and contemporary fiction all have in common: their emphasis on multiplicity, on potentiality. Perhaps the shape of fiction beyond 2000 will be closer to this newly emerging modern sensibility, which seems to me the logical offspring of the marriage of cyberpunk—with its breathlessly paced, high-tech, brilliantly contemporary texture and style—to the traditional novelistic form. With or without the creative wonders advanced technology like HyperCard may introduce, it seems we have much to look forward to in fiction.

Contributors

Paul Alkon is Leo S. Bing Professor of English at the University of Southern California. His most recent book is *Origins of Futuristic Fiction*.

Alida Allison teaches English and childrens' literature at San Diego State University.

Gregory Benford is professor of physics at the University of California, Irvine, and a noted writer. His most recent novel, written with Arthur C. Clarke, is *Beyond the Fall of Night*.

Frances Bonner teaches in the English department at the University of Queensland.

John Christie teaches in the department of philosophy at the University of Leeds.

Istvan Csicsery-Ronay, Jr., teaches English and world literature at DePauw University, and is coeditor of *Science Fiction Studies*.

Ruth Curl is assistant to the Eaton curator at the University of California, Riverside, and currently teaches at the University of Redlands.

Robert Donahoo teaches at Texas Christian University, and has written on Flannery O'Connor and Tolstoy, as well as on cyberpunk.

Chuck Etheridge teaches at McMurry College and has published on American literature.

Terri Frongia holds a Ph.D. in comparative literature from the University of California, Riverside, and writes on Italo Calvino and the aesthetics of the marvelous.

John Huntington is professor of English at the University of Illinois at Chicago. His most recent book is *Rationalizing Genius*.

Brooks Landon is professor of English at the University of Iowa. His most recent work is *Aesthetics of Ambivalence: Rethinking SF Film in the Age of Electronic (Re)Production*.

Carol McGuirk teaches eighteenth-century literature at Florida Atlantic University. She wrote an SF column for the *New York Daily News* from 1980 to 1987.

Lance Olsen teaches American literature at the University of Idaho. His most recent book is *Circus of the Mind: Postmodernism and the Comic Vision*.

David Porush teaches in the department of literature and communication at Rensselaer Polytechnic Institute. He is the author of *The Soft Machine: Cybernetic Fiction*.

Eric S. Rabkin is professor of English at the University of Michigan, and has written widely on fantasy and science fiction.

Lewis Shiner is a noted writer. His most recent novel is *Glimpses*.

Tom Shippey is professor of medieval literature at the University of Leeds, and has written widely on J. R. R. Tolkien and science fiction.

Contributors

George Slusser is professor of comparative literature at the University of California, Riverside, and director of the Eaton program.

Gary Westfahl teaches English and writing at the University of California, Riverside, and has published numerous essays on Hugo Gernsback and science fiction.

Index

Index

Index